Visions of World Community

Throughout the history of Western political thought, the creation of a world community has been seen as a way of overcoming discord between political communities without imposing sovereign authority from above. Jens Bartelson argues that a paradox lies at the centre of discussions of world community. The very same division of mankind into distinct peoples living in different places that makes the idea of a world community morally compelling has also been the main obstacle to its successful realization. His book offers a philosophical and historical analysis of the idea of world community by exploring the relationship between theories of world community and changing cosmological beliefs from the late Middle Ages to the present.

JENS BARTELSON is Professor of Political Science in the Department of Political Science at Lund University. He is the author of *The Critique of the State* (Cambridge, 2001) and *A Genealogy of Sovereignty* (Cambridge, 1995).

Visions of World Community

JENS BARTELSON

CAMBRIDGE
UNIVERSITY PRESS

CAMBRIDGE UNIVERSITY PRESS
Cambridge, New York, Melbourne, Madrid, Cape Town, Singapore,
São Paulo, Delhi

Cambridge University Press
The Edinburgh Building, Cambridge CB2 8RU, UK

Published in the United States of America by Cambridge University Press, New York

www.cambridge.org
Information on this title: www.cambridge.org/9780521756679

© Jens Bartelson 2009

This publication is in copyright. Subject to statutory exception
and to the provisions of relevant collective licensing agreements,
no reproduction of any part may take place without
the written permission of Cambridge University Press.

First published 2009

Printed in the United Kingdom at the University Press, Cambridge

A catalogue record for this publication is available from the British Library

ISBN 978-0-521-76009-6 hardback
ISBN 978-0-521-75667-9 paperback

Cambridge University Press has no responsibility for the persistence or
accuracy of URLs for external or third-party internet websites referred to
in this publication, and does not guarantee that any content on such
websites is, or will remain, accurate or appropriate.

To Nicholas Greenwood Onuf

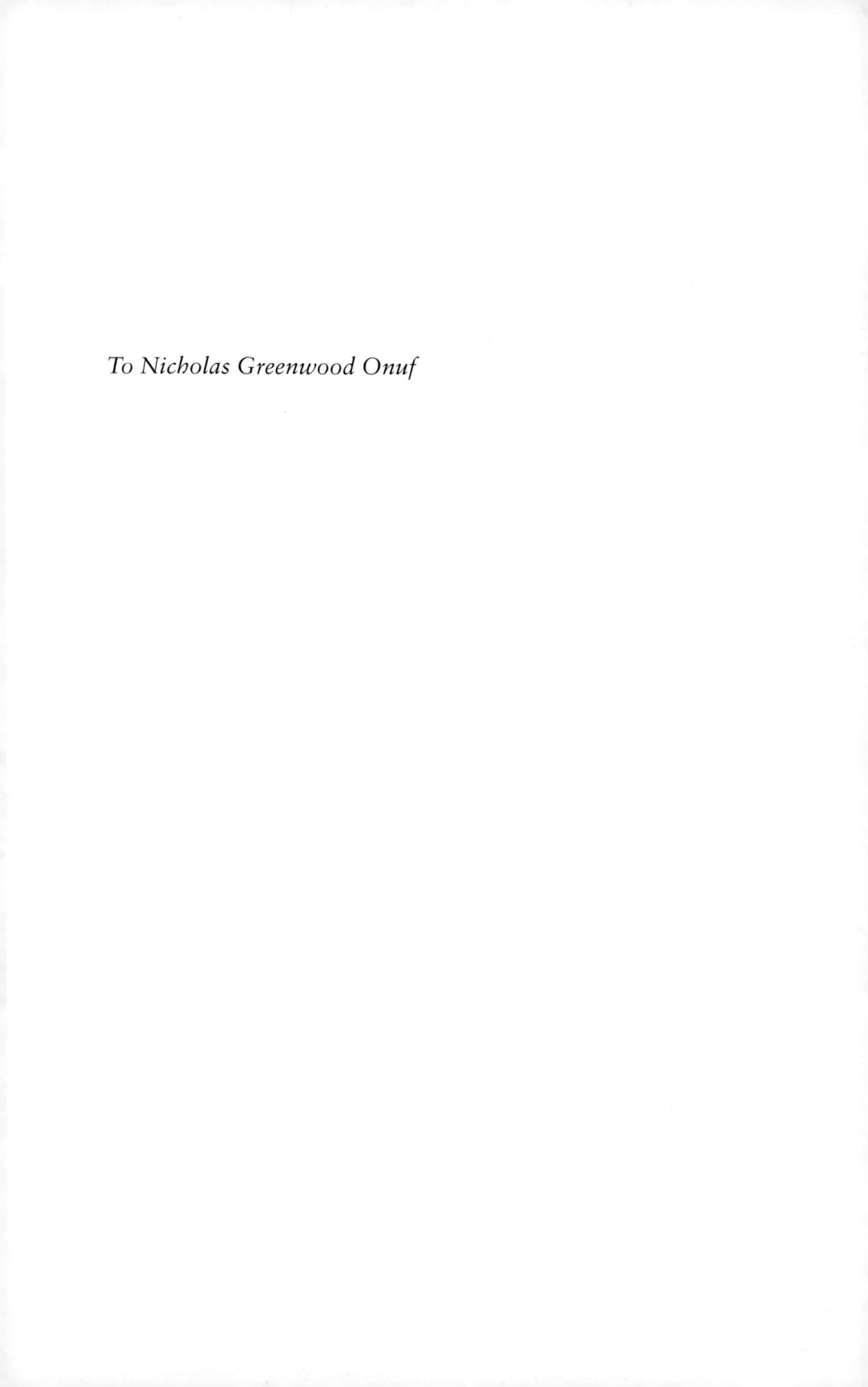

Of exactitude in science

In that Empire, the craft of Cartography attained such Perfection that the Map of a Single Province covered the space of an entire City, and the Map of the Empire itself an entire Province. In the course of Time, these extensive maps were found somehow wanting, and so the College of Cartographers evolved a Map of the Empire that was of the same Scale as the Empire and that coincided with it point for point. Less attentive to the Study of Cartography, succeeding Generations came to judge a map of such Magnitude cumbersome, and, not without Irreverence, they abandoned it to the Rigours of sun and Rain. In the western Deserts, tattered Fragments of the Map are still to be found, Sheltering an occasional Beast or beggar; in the whole Nation, no other relic is left of the Discipline of Geography.

From J. A. Suarez, 'Miranda Travels of Praiseworthy Men' (1658), in Jorge Luis Borges and Adolfo Bioy Casares, *Los Anales de Buenos Aires*, March 1946. Translated and reprinted in *A Universal History of Infamy* (Harmondsworth: Penguin, 1975), p. 131.

Contents

Preface		*page* ix
1	A conceptual history of world community	1
2	Paradoxes of world community	19
3	In the beginning was the world	46
4	Nationalizing community	86
5	Reinventing mankind	115
6	Globalizing community	141
7	Community unbound?	171
Bibliography		183
Index		211

Preface

One of the greatest challenges faced today by the social sciences is how to understand the world as essentially one single community. But despite all recent efforts in this direction, why has this proved so hard to achieve? This book responds to this question by offering a meditation on the many difficulties involved in articulating a coherent conception of a world community, trying to explain how these problems have emerged and why they seem so unsurmountable. By situating different historical conceptions of world community in the context of changing cosmological beliefs, I hope to show that the idea of world community once constituted the default setting of political thought and action, and thus not only antedated but also effectively conditioned the emergence of our modern and bounded forms of community. By making the latter look like a historical parenthesis, I hope to restore some sense of familiarity to a time when these modern sources of human belonging and fulfilment have been lost.

So, by its very nature, this book is based on intuition rather than on conviction. As such, it has grown out of random encounters with many sources which have traditionally attracted little or no interest from students of international political thought. Yet the very same reason why these sources have frequently been overlooked is precisely what makes them crucial to my present endeavour: they do not assume that communities have to be bounded or that authority has to be centralized for political order to be possible and viable. Instead, they point to those characteristics that draw human beings together in the hope of making both these requirements forever redundant. They contain visions, and as such they reflect those precious moments in the history of political thought when the contours of another world were revealed to those struggling to find a higher meaning in the often messy political realities of their day.

Many people have provided invaluable inspiration and support in the process of writing this book. As always, conversations with my old friend Nick Aronowitsch provided much of the initial inspiration. In a similar vein, discussions with Richard Little, Nick Onuf and Rob Walker have kept me on track over the years. Perhaps more unwittingly, Álvaro Dias Mendes provided me with a sanctuary in the Algarve for many summers, the tranquillity of which made the master plan for this book come easily after an ocean swim. I am also grateful to Chris Hill and Duncan Bell at Cambridge University for giving me the opportunity to discuss my early ideas about community in a very stimulating environment. Other colleagues put in lots of hard work. Olaf Corry, Martin Hall, Peter Haldén, Fritz Kratochwil, Henrik Larsen, Ulf Mörkenstam, Noel Parker, Casper Sylvest, Vibeke Schou Tjalve, Anders Wivel and Ole Waever all kindly commented upon individual chapters with great care, and eventually Mikkel Vedby Rasmussen and Anders Berg-Sørensen took upon themselves to read the entire manuscript and provided constructive suggestions for revision. Once submitted, it goes without saying that credits for the happy fate of the manuscript should go to John Haslam at Cambridge University Press. Finally, I am immensely grateful to Paulo Esteves, Mônica Herz, Nizar Messari, Eduardo Neves, and João Pontes Nogueira for inviting me to Pontifícia Universidade Católica do Rio de Janeiro and to Pontifícia Universidade Católica de Minas Gerais to present my work to receptive and challenging audiences.

J. B.
Lund, November 2008

1 | A conceptual history of world community

THIS is a book about the idea of a *world community* and its history. In the history of international thought, the creation of a world community has been seen as a way of overcoming discord between political communities without having to impose sovereign authority from above. Yet the very same division of mankind into distinct communities that makes the idea of a world community morally compelling has also been the main obstacle to its successful realization, since differences between peoples have made such a community hard to attain in practice. Consequently, many of those who have defended the idea of world community have done so by arguing that the world of sovereign states first has to be transcended in order to make way for a coming community of all mankind. As Hedley Bull described what he thought was the Kantian view of international morality, 'The community of mankind ... is not only the central reality in international politics, in the sense that the forces able to bring it into being are present; it is also the end or object of the highest moral endeavour.'[1]

But at this point we encounter a familiar paradox, since Bull was quick to add to this characterization that 'The rules that sustain coexistence and intercourse should be ignored if the imperatives of this higher morality require it.'[2] To him, such universalistic claims were nothing but barely concealed claims to imperial power, since precisely because of the pluralistic makeup of international society, every set of values can always be recast as an expression of some particular identity or interest.[3] As Anthony Pagden has recently formulated this dilemma,

---

[1] Hedley Bull, *The Anarchical Society. A Study of Order in World Politics* (London: Macmillan, 1977), p. 25.
[2] Bull, *Anarchical Society*, p. 25.
[3] See, for example, Thomas McCarthy, 'On Reconciling Cosmopolitan Unity and National Diversity', *Public Culture*, vol. 11, no. 1, 1999,

[it] may serve to remind us that if we wish to assert any belief in the universal we have to begin by declaring our willingness to assume, and to defend, at least some of the values of a highly specific way of life. For the reluctance to accept that, for many uncomfortable fact [sic], must weaken the argument against those for whom the values proclaimed by the modern liberal tradition, let alone anything resembling a categorical imperative, are simply meaningless.[4]

Hence every effort to impose a given set of values on the existing plurality of communities in the name of a common humanity is likely to be met with resistance on the grounds of its own very particularity. From this point of view, a real and genuinely inclusive world community is a dream incapable of realization, since every attempt to transcend the existing plurality in the name of some set of universal values is likely to create conflict rather than harmony.[5] It follows that theories of world community are nothing but ideologies of empire, cunningly crafted to justify the global spread and dominance of Western values.[6] This is where we still seem to

pp. 175–208; Tzvetan Todorov, *On Human Diversity: Nationalism, Racism, and Exoticism in French Thought* (Cambridge, MA: Harvard University Press, 1993), pp. 1–89.

[4] Anthony Pagden, 'Human Rights, Natural Rights, and Europe's Imperial Legacy', *Political Theory*, vol. 31, no. 2, 2003, pp. 171–99 at p. 173. See also Anthony Pagden, 'Stoicism, Cosmopolitanism, and the Legacy of European Imperialism', *Constellations*, vol. 7, no. 1, 2000, pp. 3–22.

[5] For different formulations of this problem, see Adda Bozeman, 'The International Order in a Multicultural World', in Hedley Bull and Adam Watson, eds., *The Expansion of International Society* (Oxford: Clarendon Press, 1984), pp. 387–406; Jens Bartelson, 'The Trial of Judgment: A Note on Kant and the Paradoxes of Internationalism', *International Studies Quarterly*, vol. 39, no. 2, 1995, pp. 255–72; Chris Brown, 'Cultural Diversity and International Political Theory: From the *Requirement* to "Mutual Respect"', *Review of International Studies*, vol. 26, no. 2, 2000, pp. 199–213; Naeem Inayatullah and David L. Blaney, *International Relations and the Problem of Difference* (New York: Routledge, 2004); Beate Jahn, 'Kant, Mill and Illiberal Legacies in International Affairs', *International Organization*, vol. 59, no. 1, 2005, pp. 177–207; Jeanne Morefield, *Covenants Without Swords: Idealist Liberalism and the Spirit of Empire* (Princeton, NJ: Princeton University Press, 2005).

[6] See R. B. J. Walker, *Inside/Outside. International Relations as Political Theory* (Cambridge: Cambridge University Press, 1993); Anthony

be stuck today, torn between what appear to be the conflicting demands of cosmopolitan and communitarian moral vocabularies.[7] As Seyla Benhabib has recently remarked, 'Our fate, as late-modern individuals, is to live caught in the permanent tug of war between the vision of the universal and the attachments of the particular.'[8] If true, this would imply that any successful attempt to defend the idea of world community must find a way to reconcile some set of universal values with the actual plurality of values currently embodied in international society.

I

But how did we get here? While many people today would like to find a way out of the above dilemma, most of them do not know where to look for inspiration. Therefore, in this book, I shall try to explain how and why we ended up with this way of formulating the problem of world community, and why we appear to be stuck with an inescapable tension between particularistic and universalistic accounts of human association. This amounts to undertaking a critical reconstruction of how world community has been constituted as a problem within international relations and political theory. This in turn forces us to engage what has been labelled the Kantian tradition within

---

D. Smith, 'Towards a Global Culture?' in Mike Featherstone, ed., *Global Culture. Nationalism, Globalization, and Modernity* (London: Sage, 1991), pp. 171–91; Craig Calhoun, 'The Class Consciousness of Frequent Travelers: Toward a Critique of Actually Existing Cosmopolitanism', *South Atlantic Quarterly*, vol. 101, no. 4, 2002, pp. 869–97; Timothy Brennan, *At Home in the World. Cosmopolitanism Now* (Cambridge, MA: Harvard University Press, 1997), pp. 1–118.

[7] See, for example, Molly Cochran, *Normative Theory in International Relations. A Pragmatic Approach* (Cambridge: Cambridge University Press, 1999); Richard Shapcott, *Justice, Community and Dialogue in International Relations* (Cambridge: Cambridge University Press, 2001), pp. 30–52. For a recent overview of this debate, see Robert Fine, 'Taking the "Ism" out of Cosmopolitanism. An Essay in Reconstruction', *European Journal of Social Theory*, vol. 6, no. 4, 2003, pp. 451–70.

[8] Seyla Benhabib, *The Rights of Others. Aliens, Residents, and Citizens* (Cambridge: Cambridge University Press, 2004), p. 16; Seyla Benhabib, *The Claims of Culture. Equality and Diversity in a Global Era* (Princeton, NJ: Princeton University Press, 2002), pp. 24–48.

international thought.[9] Yet in contrast to most existing accounts, I will suggest that the works of Immanuel Kant mark in important ways the end rather than the beginning of that tradition. After him, the basic ontological commitments underpinning the concept of world community became increasingly hard to sustain, and it became equally difficult to make coherent sense of that concept in a world of sovereign and secular nation-states. Hence, as I shall argue, our present inability to make coherent sense of the idea of world community is the outcome of a successful *nationalization* of the concept of community itself, a process through which the nation became the paradigmatic form of human association in theory and practice alike.[10] As I would like to suggest, this tragic outcome has been reinforced by a distinct logic of identity which is based on the notion that all sameness presupposes prior difference. This peculiar logic implies that the identity of a given political community derives from its differences from other communities. Famously associated with theorists like

---

[9] The Kantian tradition and the corresponding idea of world community have frequently been constructed as objects of suspicion within international relations theory. See, for example, Hedley Bull, 'Society and Anarchy in International Relations', in Martin Wight and Herbert Butterfield, eds., *Diplomatic Investigations* (London: Allen and Unwin, 1966), pp. 35–50; Martin Wight, *International Theory. The Three Traditions* (Leicester: Leicester University Press, 1991), pp. 30–50. For more recent discussions on the concepts of world society and world community within international relations theory, see Barry Buzan, *From International to World Society? English School Theory and the Structure of Globalization* (Cambridge: Cambridge University Press, 2004), pp. 27–45; Andrew Linklater and Hidemi Suganami, *The English School of International Relations: A Contemporary Reassessment* (Cambridge: Cambridge University Press, 2006), pp. 117–54. For a discussion of the relationship between international society and the traditions thought to constitute it, see Jens Bartelson, 'Short Circuits: Society and Tradition in International Relations Theory', *Review of International Studies*, vol. 22, no. 3, 1996, pp. 239–60.

[10] For a discussion, see Jonathan Ree, 'Cosmopolitanism and the Experience of Nationality', in Pheng Chea and Bruce Robbins, eds., *Cosmopolitics. Thinking and Feeling Beyond the Nation* (Minneapolis: University of Minnesota Press, 1998), pp. 77–90. Interestingly, a similar point was made a century ago by Friedrich Meinecke, *Cosmopolitanism and the National State* [1907] (Princeton, NJ: Princeton University Press, 1970), pp. 1–22.

Hegel and Carl Schmitt, the logic of Same and Other makes it hard to conceive of any identity – individual or collective – without inscribing this identity within a series of constitutive differences. Consequently, since all forms of human association are necessarily particularistic in character, a universal community of all mankind is impossible to attain unless a credible threat to all human existence can be constructed. Yet to the extent that such a threat would be posed by beings that would be other than human, this would automatically also call into question the anthropomorphic foundations of human community.[11] One remaining way to handle this predicament is through *mutual recognition* between communities. Not only are the mechanisms of mutual recognition believed to be responsible for the historical constitution of international society, but they are sometimes also regarded as a way of escaping the more undesirable consequences of international anarchy in the present.[12] But, as I would like to argue in this book, this logic of Same and Other is what makes the tension between particularistic and universalistic conceptions of human community look inescapable. Therefore, what is needed in order to overcome this tension is a theory of political identity that permits us to account for the sameness of political communities without appealing to their differences. As I would like to suggest in the historical parts of this book, not only is such an alternative account of political identity readily available when we know where to look, but also that such an account helps us to make new (or old) sense of the world of sovereign states by emphasizing that this world is fundamentally embedded within a larger social whole.

That the process of nationalization has been successful should be evident from the enduring nature and salience of nationalist assumptions in modern political thought. Modern nationalism is kept alive by the belief that national communities provide people with a sense of belonging that cannot be obtained elsewhere, and that such belonging

---

[11] See Alexander Wendt and Raymond Duvall, 'Sovereignty and the UFO', *Political Theory*, vol. 36, no. 4, 2008, pp. 607–33; Majid Yar, 'From Nature to History, and Back Again: Blumenberg, Strauss and the Hobbesian Community', *History of the Human Sciences*, vol. 15, no. 3, 2002, pp. 53–73.

[12] See Alexander Wendt, *Social Theory of International Politics* (Cambridge: Cambridge University Press, 1999), pp. 313–69.

is necessary to human fulfilment: these assumptions elevate the secular community into 'a sacred communion of the people'.[13] When such notions of human association emerged within modern social theory, they invoked a past characterized by a real sense of belonging, and contrasted it with the contractual modes of intercourse thought to be characteristic of political modernity. As Tönnies famously argued, 'there is a contrast between a social order which – being based upon consensus of wills – rests on harmony and is developed and ennobled by folkways, mores, and religion, and an order which – being based upon a union of rational wills – rests on convention and agreement, is safeguarded by political legislation, and finds its ideological justification in public opinion'.[14] In the context of modern social theory, the concept of community takes on meaning only by virtue of being distinct from that of society, and is distinct from the concept of society by its reference to a common identity rather than to the notion of a common interest.[15] At the core of these conceptions of community we find the idea that a community is an integrated whole, ultimately something more than the sum of its individual parts. Not only are such communities distinct from each other, but they are also categorically distinct from the international realm, precisely because the latter lacks the characteristics of communal life.[16]

[13] Anthony D. Smith, *Chosen Peoples. Sacred Sources of National Identity* (Oxford: Oxford University Press, 2003), pp. 13–32. Compare Bernard Yack, 'Popular Sovereignty and Nationalism', *Political Theory*, vol. 29, no. 4, 2001, pp. 517–36.
[14] Ferdinand Tönnies, *Community and Society: Gemeinschaft und Gesellschaft* (Minneapolis: Michigan State University Press, 1957), p. 223. For a justification of this assumption, see Norbert Elias, *The Society of Individuals* [1939] (New York: Continuum, 1991), pp. 1–67. For the spatial requirements of belonging, see Gaston Bachelard, *The Poetics of Space* [1958] (Boston: Beacon Press, 1994).
[15] For the distinction between identity and interest as the basis for different theories of social order, see Alessandro Pizzorno, 'On the Individualistic Theory of Social Order', in Pierre Bourdieu and James S. Coleman, eds., *Social Theory for a Changing Society* (Boulder, CO: Westview, 1991), pp. 209–31. For their congruence in modern notions of the nation, see Bernard Yack, 'The Myth of the Civic Nation', in Ron Beiner, ed., *Theorizing Nationalism* (Albany: State University of New York Press, 1998), pp. 103–18.
[16] See Émile Durkheim, *The Division of Labor in Society* (London: Macmillan, 1964), pp. 405–6; Andrew Vincent, *Nationalism and*

More surprisingly, similar beliefs concerning the necessity and desirability of bounded communities are shared even by those who are suspicious of modern nationalism in its cruder forms. As Charles Taylor has argued, 'The rather different understandings of the good we see in different cultures are the correlative of the different languages which have evolved in those cultures.'[17] To Rogers Smith, while 'the organization of humanity into particular political peoples' is certainly based on the crafting of narratives and therefore not set in stone, 'this crafting may be unavoidable if we are to sustain vital and deeply cherished political, historical, and cultural traditions and to organize human beings for the productive pursuit of their happiness and welfare'.[18] Even advocates of multiculturalism remain fond of the nation, since 'Most people would rather be free and equal within their own nation ... than be free and equal citizens of the world, if this means that they are less likely to live and work in their own language and culture.'[19] Hence, if we are to believe these authors, there can be no morality outside the boundaries of particular communities, since morality is nothing but 'the voice of ourselves as members of a community'.[20] Thus, given these basic ideas about the nature of human communities, and given these basic assumptions about the way their political identities are formed, we cannot but perceive the universal and particular as fundamentally opposed, and as long as these categories are stuck in opposition, the emergence of a world community will be but a distant dream.[21]

Particularity (Cambridge: Cambridge University Press, 2002), pp. 36–62.
[17] Charles Taylor, *Sources of the Self. The Making of Modern Identity* (Cambridge, MA: Harvard University Press, 1989), p. 91.
[18] Rogers M. Smith, *Stories of Peoplehood. The Politics and Morals of Political Membership* (Cambridge: Cambridge University Press, 2003), p. 9. For a critique, see Bonnie Honig, *Democracy and the Foreigner* (Princeton, NJ: Princeton University Press, 2001), pp. 73–106.
[19] Will Kymlicka, *Multicultural Citizenship* (Oxford: Clarendon Press, 1995), p. 76.
[20] Richard Rorty, *Contingency, Irony, and Solidarity* (Cambridge: Cambridge University Press, 1989), p. 59.
[21] For a similar argument, see Jonathan Seglow, 'Universals and Particulars: The Case of Liberal Cultural Nationalism', *Political Studies*, vol. 64, 1998, pp. 963–77.

But these particularistic conceptions of community have become a source of trouble today. In an age when it is widely believed that global flows of people and information have made political communities less homogeneous than they once were, traditional notions of political identity have become increasingly difficult to sustain.[22] Provided that the concept of community has been understood as more or less coextensive with that of the nation, a loss of national identity equals a loss of community, which now allegedly 'remains stubbornly missing, eludes our grasp and keeps falling apart, because the way in which this world prompts us to go about fulfilling our dreams of secure life does not bring us closer to their fulfilment'.[23] Such a loss of community is widely believed to pose a threat to modern democracy, since it seems to presuppose the prior existence of a people or a bounded community.[24] Simultaneously, many of the problems that modern societies have to confront are boundless in character. Problems of sustainability and justice transcend national boundaries, yet there is no political authority at the global level that could enforce efficient solutions.[25] And in those issue areas in which supranational institutions have proved efficient, they have suffered from a lack of legitimacy that can no longer be solved by an appeal to traditional conceptions of people or nation, but must be addressed with reference to wider conceptions of community.[26] In sum, and as Agamben remarked over a decade ago, 'The novelty of the coming politics is

---

[22] See, for example, John Urry, *Sociology Beyond Societies. Mobilities for the Twenty-First Century* (London: Routledge, 2000); Zygmunt Bauman, *Globalization. The Human Consequences* (Cambridge: Polity Press, 1998).

[23] Zygmunt Bauman, *Community* (Cambridge: Polity Press, 2001), p. 144.

[24] For this theme, see Pierre Rosanvallon, *Democracy Past and Future* (New York: Columbia University Press, 2006), pp. 189–217; James Tully, 'The Unfreedom of the Moderns in Comparison to their Ideals of Constitutional Democracy', *Modern Law Review*, vol. 65, no. 2, 2002, pp. 204–28.

[25] See, for example, Thomas Nagel, 'The Problem of Global Justice', *Philosophy and Public Affairs*, vol. 33, no. 2, 2005, pp. 113–47; Thomas Dietz, Elinor Ostrom and Paul C. Stern, 'The Struggle to Govern the Commons', *Science*, vol. 302, 2003, pp. 1907–12.

[26] See, for example, Bert Van Roermund, 'Sovereignty: Unpopular and Popular', in Neil Walker, ed., *Sovereignty in Transition* (Oxford: Hart,

that it will no longer be a struggle for the conquest and control of the state, but a struggle between the State and the non-State (humanity), and insurmountable disjunction between whatever singularity and the State organization.'[27]

Given the problems faced by modern societies, the idea of a world community seems morally attractive, yet profoundly problematic. With few exceptions, accounts of the normative foundations of global authority have been silent about the possibility of a world community as the ultimate source of political legitimacy.[28] This silence is strange, especially in the light of the fact that one of the characteristic assumptions of modern political theory is that *all* political authority ultimately ought to derive its legitimacy from the consent of the people or community brought under its sway.[29] It is therefore hard to see how it would be possible to justify *any* global political authority without at least implicitly invoking the possibility of a world community, either as its normative foundation or as its empirical outcome. Yet, as I shall argue in this book, redefining the concept of community so that it becomes possible to make coherent sense of the idea of world community necessitates a wholesale change in the way we understand political identity. We need a theory of identity that makes it possible to regard the universal and the particular as mutually implicating rather than as fundamentally opposed – a theory of identity that also makes it possible to regard human beings and the communities that they inhabit as embedded in a more comprehensive human community than that commonly exemplified by the nation. As I would like to suggest in the next section, imagining these things becomes much easier once we start to situate visions of world community in the context of cosmological belief within which they have traditionally been articulated.

2003), pp. 33–54; Hans Lindahl, 'Sovereignty and Representation in the European Union', in Walker, *Sovereignty in Transition*, pp. 87–114.

[27] Giorgio Agamben, *The Coming Community* (Minneapolis: University of Minnesota Press, 1993), p. 85.

[28] For an overview, see Jens Bartelson, 'The Concept of Sovereignty Revisited', *European Journal of International Law*, vol. 17, no. 2, 2006, pp. 463–74.

[29] See Jens Bartelson, *The Critique of the State* (Cambridge: Cambridge University Press, 2001), pp. 6–8.

II

Like most other socio-political concepts, the concept of community is ambiguous as a result of having been constantly contested and repeatedly recycled within political thought during past centuries. Since one of the primary tasks of this book is to explore some of the changes the concept has undergone as a result of all this contestation and recycling, any initial effort to define the concept of community would be to close the field of inquiry prematurely. At this stage of the inquiry we need to remain as open as possible to what the concept of community means or ought to mean in the present, in order to be able to better understand what it has meant in the past. However, once such a historical analysis has been accomplished, we might be able to recover meanings that do indeed transcend the particular contexts in which this concept has been used. Such continuity would in turn allow us to speak of a distinct tradition of thought, and from such a tradition we might be able to infer some more general theoretical observations about the concept of world community and the conditions of its meaningful usage. Yet the historical ambition of this book puts restrictions on what can be meaningfully accomplished in philosophical terms. While my aim is to provide a general sketch of what the concept of world community might mean and entail, I cannot provide any account of the principles according to which such a community ought to be governed in order to be legitimate and viable. The central concern of this book is instead to analyse the conditions of possibility of such a community. I will refer to the sum total of these conditions as the *social ontology* of world community.

Yet a few preliminary words need to be said about the object of our inquiry. Before the concept of community was nationalized, community was believed to be universal in scope and boundless in character. These conceptions of a universal and boundless community were essentially conceptions of *human* community, insofar as they were based on the assumption that human beings are distinct from members of other species, rather than on assumptions about what makes this or that group of people unique, and thus distinct from other groups of people. Far from being unproblematic, this distinction was drawn with reference to capacities believed to be uniquely human, such as the faculties of language and reason. Not only were human beings believed to share these capacities in common, but these capacities were also believed to make it possible for human beings to share other things in common as well. Human beings were thus believed to share a set of capacities which make it possible to enter into meaningful intercourse with one another, and to establish communities on the basis of the shared symbols and values such exchanges might give rise to.

Hence visions of world community assume that community is always potentially present whenever human beings are present. Such a universal community exists by virtue of those uniquely human capacities being used by human beings. It is not meaningful to distinguish *categorically* between communities of different scope, since all human communities derive from the same underlying and species-wide capacities. While all human beings are members of this universal community simply by virtue of sharing in common the essential capacities for intercourse, they are also members of particular communities by virtue of the fact that the use of these capacities results in different symbols and values being shared by different peoples in different places. But since all communities formed by distinct peoples are made up of individual human beings, they stand in essentially the same relationship to the wider community of all mankind as does the individual human being. Furthermore, since they derive their existence from common human capacities, all communities are formed through processes of *co-constitution*, which involve a constant exchange of symbols and values resulting from intercourse between communities of different size and scope. As a consequence, human communities are *interpenetrating*, since they are likely to share at least some significant symbols and values in common. Such interpenetration also implies that their institutions and practices will display some family resemblance and a degree of *isomorphism*. Human beings, as well as the communities to which they happen to belong, are therefore *essentially embedded* within a wider community of all mankind within which the totality of human relations unfolds across time and space.

The logic of identity implied in accounts of world community is very different from the logic of identity we normally encounter in accounts of state formation and international relations. In the absence of any compelling evidence of extraterrestrial life, conceptions of world community have not been based on any differentiation between 'us' and 'them', but rather on the idea that mankind constitutes one single community by virtue of its members sharing the capacities for forming social bonds. Consequently, if belonging to a community is indeed an integral part of what it means to be a human being, there is no need to transcend the existing order of states in order to bring a world community into being. Such a world community is already immanent by virtue of the shared capacities for intercourse.

As I will argue in this book, important signs of the social ontology of world community can be found in the cosmological contexts within which visions of world community have been articulated since the Middle Ages. Many of these visions assume a very intimate relationship between cosmology and the nature of human community, sometimes to the point of regarding them as inseparable. In the present book, however, I shall assume that the relationship between cosmological beliefs and conceptions of human community is contextual in character, insofar as knowledge of the former helps us make sense of the latter, and vice versa. The cosmological context deserves attention, partly because such beliefs were of crucial importance to many of those who articulated conceptions of community, partly because without prior knowledge of the cosmological context in which these conceptions were articulated, they would simply fail to make sense other than as mere curiosities of a distant past. Attention to cosmological change might help us to understand how and why conceptions of community have changed, while attention to changing conceptions of community might help us to understand how and why cosmological beliefs have changed.[30] By implication, one of the challenges posed by the idea of world community is that of constructing a cosmology common to all mankind, so that all human beings will eventually come to inhabit the same conceptual world.[31]

As I will try to show, some cosmological beliefs clearly matter more than others when making sense of ideas of world community.

---

[30] See Clarence J. Glacken, *Traces on the Rhodian Shore. Nature and Culture in Western Thought from Ancient Times to the End of the Eighteenth Century* (Berkeley: University of California Press, 1967). For a different attempt to make sense of this connection, see Stephen Toulmin, *Cosmopolis. The Hidden Agenda of Modernity* (Chicago: University of Chicago Press, 1990), pp. 67–9.

[31] For this suggestion, see Bruno Latour, 'Whose Cosmos, Which Cosmopolitics: Comments on the Peace Terms of Ulrich Beck', *Common Knowledge*, vol. 10, no. 3, 2004, pp. 450–62.

Those cosmological beliefs that concern the geographical makeup of the planetary surface are of particular relevance, since they have very direct implications for the possibilities of human intercourse. Most visions of world community assume that mankind forms one single community partly by virtue of inhabiting the same planetary space. Consequently, visions of world community tend to regard the actual division and dispersion of mankind as accidental, and try to explain how and why the division and dispersion have taken place with reference to cosmological beliefs about the makeup of the planetary surface. As we shall see, the facts of division and dispersion have been explained in a variety of ways, each of them reflecting underlying assumptions about the planet and its place in a larger cosmos. Finally, since visions of world community take the unity of mankind as their starting point, they are likely to locate the sources of human fulfilment within a larger cosmological framework rather than within particular communities. This fact makes it difficult to separate such visions from the theological contexts within which they were originally articulated, but also goes some way to explain why such visions have largely been lost to modern and secular political thought. In secular terms, a belief in the idea of a world community entails the assumption that human fulfilment is best achieved through the *emancipation* of human beings from belonging to individual communities, and that this can best be achieved through intercourse with human beings from other communities. Hence visions of world community typically provide justifications for resistance against all those forms of political authority that are premised on the necessary compartmentalization of mankind into distinct communities.

This book tries to tell a story sympathetic to such visions, while trying to remain as open as possible to their changing content across time. This task is strategically limited to *Western* visions of world community, since these are the ones most frequently suspected of being imperial ideologies rather than anything else. Since their universalistic aspirations have become difficult to take seriously, they therefore deserve renewed consideration. But although these visions are based on notions of a common human identity, their accounts of that identity vary to the point of being incommensurable. The resulting tension between the universality of their claims and the undeniable particularity of their origin animates much of the argument of this book. One way to proceed, then, would be to historicize this tension by showing how it has come into being in order to make its contingency apparent – and hopefully its eventual passing away more likely.

This analytical strategy forces us to confront this tension in its different historical guises without enjoying the privilege of having any clean methodological slate from which to proceed. Rather, the topic at hand should make us acutely aware that the historicist ambition to contextualize conceptual meaning pushes our interpretations in a particularistic direction, while the philosophical ambition to analyse specific conceptions of community independently of their historical context forces our hand in a more universalistic direction.

Furthermore, and to some extent, this tension between historical and philosophical perspectives results from the different views of language that also sustain different conceptions of community. On the one hand, the very concept of a bounded community has been historically associated with theories that take natural languages to be expressive or constitutive of the particular community in which they are used. Interpretations that are indebted to this view of language contain a discernible particularistic bias, insofar as they locate the sources of conceptual meaning in the specific historical context in which the concept in question is used.[32] On the other hand, there is a similar affinity between universalistic conceptions of community and dreams of a language common to all mankind, and some visions of world community have indeed been based on the idea of a universal language that would transcend the linguistic divisions of the human species.[33]

Therefore, it is difficult to conduct our inquiry without running the risk of unduly privileging either particularistic or universalistic conceptions of community through our choice of methods. If we based our analysis on a nominalist view of concepts and their meaning, we would be tempted to conclude that the only kind of community that

---

[32] Charles Taylor, *Human Agency and Language. Philosophical Papers 1* (Cambridge: Cambridge University Press, 1985), pp. 215–47. See also Taylor, *Sources of the Self*, pp. 91, 368–76.

[33] Hans Aarsleff, *From Locke to Saussure: Essays on the Study of Language and Intellectual History* (Minneapolis: University of Minnesota Press, 1982); Sheldon Pollock, 'Cosmopolitan and Vernacular in History', in Carol A. Breckenridge, Sheldon Pollock, Homi K. Bhabha and Dipesh Chakrabarty, eds., *Cosmopolitanism* (Durham, NC: Duke University Press, 2002), pp. 15–53.

A conceptual history of world community

exists consists of particular and bounded groups of people with moral languages of their own creation. Yet, should we subscribe to a realist view of concepts, we would then easily be led to assume that human community is always already universal and given, and that actually existing particular communities are but instantiations of this primordial community. Thoughtlessly taking any of these routes would not only replay Locke's quarrel with the scholastics, but would also merely transpose the problem inherent in our topic to another level, but without helping us reformulate it in a way that is congenial to a coherent solution.[34]

Later in this book, we shall see how similar dilemmas were handled during periods when ontology and politics were less easily separable than they are today. But in order to get there, we need to find a way out of philosophical problems which would otherwise distract us from our path. In order to write the history of the concept of world community, we need a way to make philosophical sense of the idea of co-constitution that allows us to understand how conceptions of community with very different scope have conditioned each other within different cosmological contexts. And in order to make any moral sense of the idea of world community, we need a way of distinguishing between visions of world community and ideologies of empire.

I believe Ian Hacking has provided what we need for our purposes: a doctrine he has termed *dynamic nominalism*. This doctrine is helpful in three different ways. First, since it stipulates that concepts are but general names, it encourages us to analyse how universals are constructed by means of such general names, as well as how these are translated into particular instantiations. Second, as universals are being made by human beings through the creative use of the linguistic resources at their disposal, it is possible to conceive of the relationship between the universal and the particular as a two-way street, the universal being particular only to the same extent as the particular contains an element of universality.[35] This compels us to focus on the co-constitution of different conceptions of community, as well as on how this relationship has been conceived in the past. Third, this

---

[34] For a similar suggestion, see Vincent, *Nationalism and Particularity*, pp. 7–9.
[35] See Ian Hacking, *Historical Ontology* (Cambridge, MA: Harvard University Press, 2002), pp. 99–114.

doctrine might help us draw a crude distinction between visions of world community and ideologies of empire. In philosophical terms, visions of world community are theories of how human beings construct common beliefs and values on the basis of their meaningful experience of intercourse. By contrast, ideologies of empire typically take the universal validity of some such construct for granted, and then proceed by superimposing it upon other beliefs or values, regardless of *their* claims to validity.

But since the first Western visions of world community were forged by the Stoics, would it not be reasonable to start with them, especially since they have exercised an enormous influence on all subsequent thought on world community? 'Let us embrace with our minds', writes Seneca, 'two commonwealths: one great and truly common ... the other the one to which the particular circumstances of birth have assigned us ... which pertains not to all men but a particular group of them.'[36] Yet, arguably, the way the Stoics understood the relationship between these two commonwealths has little in common with the problems faced by modern theories of cosmopolitanism.[37] Since my historical account is intended to explain how world community became a problem in modern political thought, it would not make sense to write a history of this concept that aspires to be in any sense definitive. But even if my focus on early modern and modern conceptions of world community is motivated by the ambition to write a history of present problems, we will inevitably hear an echo of the Stoics throughout the pages to come, since most authors who have struggled to articulate visions of world community have felt compelled to engage the Stoics, albeit in very different ways.

Far from claiming to be an exhaustive account of theories of world community, the following account is based on a set of examples, selected with the exclusive aim of making sense of our present predicament. The result is a historical narrative of several overlapping

[36] Seneca, *De Otio* 4, quoted in Malcolm Schofield, *The Stoic Idea of the City* (Cambridge: Cambridge University Press, 1991), p. 93. See also H. C. Baldry, *The Unity of Mankind in Greek Thought* (Cambridge: Cambridge University Press, 1965).

[37] See Peter Euben, 'The Polis, Globalization, and the Politics of Place', in Aryeh Botwinick and William E. Connolly, eds., *Democracy and Vision: Sheldon Wolin and the Vicissitudes of the Political* (Princeton, NJ: Princeton University Press, 2001), pp. 256–89.

conceptual trajectories, each of which would make little sense in the absence of our problematic present. Yet once we start to regard universalistic and particularistic conceptions of community as mutually implicating rather than as fundamentally opposed, we will be struck by the apparent lack of novelty in our present debates, as well as by the wealth of philosophical options available in the past. Although solutions to our problems certainly cannot be distilled from that past, it implies that in order to be able to solve our own problems, we must understand how they became problems in the first place, and how the range of possible solutions to these problems have been handed down to us as part of the same package deal.[38]

In order to accomplish this task, the historical analysis is based on three main types of sources. First, I have consulted writings which have defined and defended different conceptions of world community. Here I am deliberately going for the big ones, focusing on those works which are regarded as canonical texts, the reason for this choice being precisely their canonical status. In recent years, many of these canonical texts have been subject to reinterpretations that have emphasized their role in justifying European domination. In this book, I would like to suggest that we should indeed take at least some of their claims about the nature of world community more seriously, even if it remains true that these visions often have been used to justify practices that go against their very spirit. As I have argued above, this does not imply that we should return to a less contextually sensitive reading of those texts, but rather that we should situate these works within a context that is different from that of European imperialism. As I would like to suggest, even if many works within the cosmopolitan canon have sometimes been used in order to legitimize imperialism and colonialism, many of them were also written in response to changes in the framework of cosmological beliefs, and the perceived implications of these changes for mankind as a whole. Also, since an important part of my story concerns the nationalization of the concept of community, this forces me to pay attention to how such visions of world community were actually twisted into defences

---

[38] For a discussion of the relationship between past and present in the study of political thought, see Jens Bartelson, 'Philosophy and History in the Study of Political Thought', *Journal of the Philosophy of History*, vol. 1, no. 1, 2007, pp. 101–24.

of early modern imperial projects. Yet, as I hope to make clear, there is an inherent limit to this nationalization of conceptions of community that makes a return to the universalistic default setting easier than normally suspected by the critics of empire. Second, in order to make sense of the cosmological contexts within which these visions evolved, I have mainly relied on existing scholarship on the history of physics, geography, cartography, and natural history. Third, in order to convey an understanding of how these conceptions of community and cosmology might have been connected in actual practice, I have drawn on travelogues from different periods, as well as on existing scholarship on the history of travel.

The rest of this book is organized as follows. In the next chapter, I shall analyse some contemporary theories of world community, arguing that they fail to make coherent sense of this concept simply because they assume that communities have to be bounded in order to qualify as communities in the first place. In Chapter 3, I shall describe how universalistic conceptions of human community were assembled during the late Middle Ages, and how these were later transformed in response to changes in cosmological belief during the Renaissance. In Chapter 4, I shall focus on the emergence of particularistic conceptions of community from the seventeenth century onwards, and how these were sustained by forging a link between memory and political identity. In Chapters 5 and 6, I analyse some critical responses to these tendencies during the eighteenth century, and how this criticism culminated in efforts to integrate different conceptions of community into a more encompassing framework in Enlightenment political thought. Chapter 7 discusses the social ontology and normative import of the concept of world community in the light of the historical argument of this book.

2 | Paradoxes of world community

IN the previous chapter, I said that bounded conceptions of community have become a major source of trouble, since many of the political problems we have to confront today are boundless in character. In this chapter, I shall try to substantiate this claim through a critical overview of contemporary cosmopolitan theory. My argument is very simple. While many political theorists would like to expand the scope of political community beyond the world of states, the conceptual means at their disposal carry significant semantic baggage from that very world. Consequently, their proposals are prone to project vaguely nationalistic assumptions onto the new forms of political life they struggle to flesh out and justify, yet most of this 'nationalism' is but a corollary of the underlying assumption that communities have to be bounded in order to qualify as communities in the first place.[1]

But as long as we believe that communities need to be bounded, we will find it difficult to make coherent sense of the concept of world community, since a community cannot be fully inclusive and still have boundaries. Although this chapter cannot claim to provide any exhaustive analysis of contemporary theories of world community, the intention is to show that their underlying social ontology gives rise to a set of paradoxes that are impossible to solve within the same

---

[1] For discussions of methodological nationalism within the social sciences, see Ulrich Beck, 'The Cosmopolitan Perspective: Sociology in the Second Age of Modernity', in Steven Vertovec and Robin Cohen, eds., *Conceiving Cosmopolitanism. Theory, Context, and Practice* (Oxford: Oxford University Press, 2002), pp. 61–85; Bruce Robbins, 'Actually Existing Cosmopolitanism', in Pheng Chea and Bruce Robbins, eds., *Cosmopolitics. Thinking and Feeling Beyond the Nation* (Minneapolis: University of Minnesota Press, 1998), pp. 1–19. For a critique, see Catherine Lu, 'The One and Many Faces of Cosmopolitanism', *Journal of Political Philosophy*, vol. 8, no. 2, 2000, pp. 244–67.

conceptual framework within which they have been formulated. As I will try to show in this chapter, contemporary theories of world community either fail to fully articulate the universalistic assumptions upon which they are based, or they unwittingly reproduce a logic of identity according to which communities are identical to themselves only by virtue of being different from each other. Thus, if we want to find a way out of the resulting problems, we must first find a way out of that particularistic social ontology and that conceptual framework. As I shall argue, this is possible only by positing a larger social whole within which all human communities are embedded, as well as a vantage point over and above the plurality of individual communities from which this larger social whole can be understood.

I shall start this overview by describing what has become the standard argument in favour of world community in the literature – that of cosmopolitan democracy. I shall then briefly discuss theories of global justice and their ambiguous relationship to the concept of world community. Since both cosmopolitan democracy and global justice presuppose the possibility of a global culture, I shall discuss this problem in terms of the prospects of a common identity. Finally, I shall suggest that the best way to handle the resulting paradoxes of world community is by telling a story that makes it plain that they are the outcome of historical contingencies rather than of logical necessities.

I

To the extent that visions of world community were discussed during the last century, they were seen as remedies for international anarchy. For many years, different versions of internationalism focused on how the undesirable effects of international anarchy could be moderated or overcome by reinforcing institutions such as international law and diplomacy. Although these proposals diverged widely in terms of their philosophical assumptions and political implications, the possibility of a world government or any other form of supranational authority was normally ruled out on the grounds of its undesirability or impracticality.[2] By contrast, more recent arguments in favour of

---

[2] See, for example, Sylvester J. Hemleben, *Plans for Peace Through Six Centuries* (Chicago: University of Chicago Press, 1943); Francis H. Hinsley, *Power and the Pursuit of Peace* (Cambridge: Cambridge

a world community assume that some form of society already exists at the global level, and that some forms of political authority exist independently of sovereign states. As Martin Shaw has argued, a global realm has emerged through the 'development of a common consciousness of human society on a world scale'.[3] But although many authors agree that social relations now take place on a global scale, the fact that the concept of society largely remains understood in territorial terms has made it hard to account for the *sui generis* character of such a global society, as well as its principles of differentiation.[4] This apparent lack of agreement about the structure and composition of global society has not kept theorists from discussing what it *ought* to look like, however. When debating the normative principles according to which this global society ought to be governed, many authors imply that it can be turned into a *community* by institutionalizing

---

University Press, 1963); Stanley Hoffmann, *The State of War. Essays on the Theory and Practice of International Relations* (New York: Praeger, 1965). More recent scholarship includes Kjell Goldmann, *The Logic of Internationalism. Coercion and Accommodation* (London: Routledge, 1994); Andreas Osiander, 'Rereading Early Twentieth-Century IR Theory: Idealism Revisited', *International Studies Quarterly*, vol. 42, no. 3, 1998, pp. 409–32; Casper Sylvest, 'Interwar Internationalism, the British Labour Party, and the Historiography of International Relations', *International Studies Quarterly*, vol. 48, no. 2, 2004, pp. 409–32; Casper Sylvest, 'Continuity and Change in British Liberal Internationalism, c. 1900–1930', *Review of International Studies*, vol. 31, no. 2, 2005, pp. 263–83. On the question of world government, see Yael Tamir, 'Who is Afraid of a Global State?', in Kjell Goldmann, Ulf Hannerz and Charles Westin, eds., *Nationalism and Internationalism in the Post-Cold War Era* (London: Routledge, 2000), pp. 244–67.

[3] Martin Shaw, *Theory of the Global State. Globality as an Unfinished Revolution* (Cambridge: Cambridge University Press, 2000), p. 13.

[4] For this difficulty and some ways of overcoming it, see John Urry, *Sociology Beyond Societies. Mobilities for the Twenty-First Century* (London: Routledge, 2000); John W. Meyer, John Boli, George M. Thomas and Francisco O. Ramirez, 'World Society and the Nation-State', *American Journal of Sociology*, vol. 103, no. 1, 1997, pp. 144–81; Niklas Luhmann, 'World Society as a Social System', in Niklas Luhmann, *Essays on Self-Reference* (New York: Columbia University Press, 1990), pp. 175–90; Mathias Albert, '"Globalization Theory": Yesterday's Fad or More Lively than Ever?' *International Political Sociology*, vol. 1, no. 2, 2007, pp 165–82.

these normative principles, and by giving global authorities enough clout to enforce them. Assumptions like these have begged questions about the legitimacy of global forms of authority in the absence of anything resembling a global *demos*, and this has in turn compelled scholars to rethink the concept of community *tout court*. This kind of argument comes in two different but mutually reinforcing versions, as follows.

First, if we take globalization to bring – among other things – a virtually unrestricted flow of capital and the unbridled reign of market forces at the global level, it becomes tempting to focus on its corrosive effects on state autonomy. As Held states, 'Modern democratic theory and practice was constructed upon Westphalian foundations. National communities, and theories of national communities, were based on the presupposition that political communities could, in principle, control their destinies.'[5] When domestic politicians seek to regain control over national economies, they do so by ceding at least some autonomy to supranational institutions unless they want to lose out completely to the corporate world. Yet such ceding of autonomy comes at a price, since formal authority and control over outcomes is then moved outside the scope of domestic democratic institutions. What once was within the purview of due democratic deliberation is now increasingly a matter of multilateral agreements between government officials at different levels.[6] Deprived of any real power, domestic democratic institutions become increasingly hollow. From this follows two main strategic options for the democratically minded: either to argue in favour of increased independence from *both* global market forces and supranational institutions, or to opt for a *democratization* of those supranational institutions in order to tame them and restore some consensual legitimacy to their decisions. Otherwise

---

[5] David Held, 'The Transformation of Political Community: Rethinking Democracy in the Context of Globalization', in Ian Shapiro and Casiano Hacker-Cordón, eds., *Democracy's Edges* (Cambridge: Cambridge University Press, 1999), pp. 84–111, at p. 90.

[6] Held, 'Transformation of Political Community', pp. 96–7. See also Jan Aart Scholte, *Globalization. A Critical Introduction* (London: Macmillan, 2000), pp. 132–58; Kjell Goldmann, *Transforming the European Nation-State* (London: Sage, 2001), pp. 74–106; Saskia Sassen, *Losing Control? Sovereignty in an Age of Globalization* (New York: Columbia University Press, 1996), pp. 51–8.

nobody is in charge and no one is accountable, and we have no way left to influence our destiny as citizens.[7]

Second, if we take globalization to bring – again among other things – a virtually unrestricted flow of information and people, it becomes tempting to focus on the corrosive effects of this on the *identity* of national political communities. Transnational flows of people and information might compromise the socio-cultural homogeneity of a people, and since it takes a people to constitute the *demos* necessary for democratic institutions to be legitimate, those transnational flows might subvert the foundations of modern democracy by pushing cultural plurality to an intolerable limit. In order for a people to be able to govern themselves, they need to know who they are: a people and not a multitude of strangers. In the absence of such a political community, democracy as such becomes unthinkable – and global forces are sometimes believed to challenge this foundational identity.[8]

Theories of cosmopolitan democracy usually buy into some version of the above scenario, and then proceed by rethinking the foundations of political community in light of the challenges posed by globalization, however defined.[9] To achieve this, cosmopolitan

---

[7] For the former proposition, see Leo Panitch, 'Globalization and the State', *Socialist Register*, 1994, pp. 60–91; for the latter proposition, see, for example, Daniele Archibugi, 'Demos and Cosmopolis', *New Left Review*, vol. 13, January/February 2002, pp. 24–38; David Held, 'Democracy and Globalization', in Daniele Archibugi, David Held and Martin Köhler, eds., *Re-imagining Political Community. Studies in Cosmopolitan Democracy* (Cambridge: Polity Press, 1998), pp. 11–27.

[8] Held, 'Transformation of Political Community', pp. 98–9. See also Scholte, *Globalization*, pp. 159–83; Goldmann, *Transforming the European Nation-State*, pp. 107–25; Zygmunt Bauman, *Globalization. The Human Consequences* (Cambridge: Polity Press, 1998), pp. 55–76; Urry, *Sociology Beyond Societies*.

[9] See, for example, Andrew Linklater, *The Transformation of Political Community. Ethical Foundations of the Post-Westphalian Era* (Cambridge: Polity Press, 1998); Rainer Bauböck, 'Political Community Beyond the Sovereign State, Supranational Federalism, and Transnational Minorities', in Vertovec and Cohen, *Conceiving Cosmopolitanism*, pp. 110–38; Richard Bellamy and Dario Castiglione, 'Between Cosmopolis and Community: Three Models of Rights and Democracy within the European Union', in Archibugi *et al.*, *Re-Imagining Political Community*, pp. 152–78; Daniele Archibugi, 'Cosmopolitan Democracy

theorists are compelled to explain how political community beyond the nation-state is possible, and how democratic governance can be justified within such a community. Cosmopolitan theorists frequently start their argument by pointing out that democracy – at least in the shape we know it – has historically and conceptually been associated with the nation-state. They then proceed by arguing that if the nation-state is indeed challenged by global forces and consequently is about to lose its status as a predominant locus of authority and source of community, then the only way to save democracy is by redefining political community so that it can include people irrespective of their citizenship in existing states. Instead of several exclusive *demoi*, we need but one all-inclusive *demos* in order to realize the virtues of popular sovereignty in an increasingly globalized world.[10] As Held has recently argued, 'the implementation of what I call a cosmopolitan democratic law and the establishment of a community of all democratic communities – a cosmopolitan community – must become an obligation for democrats'.[11] Consequently, the creation of a world community would require that 'Rightful authority or sovereignty can be stripped away from the idea of fixed borders and territories and thought of as, in principle, an attribute of basic cosmopolitan democratic law which can be drawn upon and enacted in diverse realms.'[12]

But how is this *demos* to be defined and legitimized? Two main ways of solving this problem compete in the literature. First, we find the idea that a global *demos* ought to include *all* human beings in order to handle the prevailing mismatch between territorially bounded democratic communities and territorially unbounded authority. Each citizen of the world should have an equal voice, since each serious political concern is likely to be of global scope.[13]

---

and its Critics: A Review', *European Journal of International Relations*, vol. 10, no. 3, 2004, pp. 437–73; David Held, 'Principles of Cosmopolitan Order', in Gillian Brock and Harry Brighouse, eds., *The Political Philosophy of Cosmopolitanism* (Cambridge: Cambridge University Press, 2005), pp. 10–38.

[10] David Held, *Cosmopolitan Democracy and the Global Order* (Cambridge: Polity Press, 1995), pp. 221–86.
[11] Held, 'Transformation of Political Community', p. 106.
[12] Held, 'Principles of Cosmopolitan Order', p. 26.
[13] Linklater, *Transformation of Political Community*, pp. 193–212.

Second, we find the idea that those who are affected by a particular decision should be included in the *demos*, so that what constitutes the scope of the *demos* in question will vary with the nature of the issue at hand. Each issue should therefore be settled by those affected by the outcome in each particular case, not by mankind as a whole.[14] As Held has recently formulated this principle, 'it connotes that those significantly affected by public decisions, issues, or processes, should, *ceteris paribus*, have an equal opportunity, directly or indirectly through elected representatives, to influence and shape them'.[15]

But as both Näsström and Wendt have shown, justifying these solutions is very difficult, since the transition from our present situation, in which political communities are bounded, to an unbounded global community of all mankind has to take the present situation into consideration: in order for this new community to enjoy democratic legitimacy, it has to be considered legitimate by its prospective citizens.[16] That is, it must be democratically constituted, rather than forced upon them by some global political authority. But this merely begs the question who these citizens are, a decision that itself cannot be settled by any democratic process, since that process then would presuppose exactly what it is supposed to yield.

The second solution is equally problematic, since we then have to face the question of how to determine who is and is not affected by a particular decision, and this might of course lead to divergent interpretations in each individual case. But if democratic legitimacy is wanted, who is affected and who is not should be settled in ways that are themselves democratic: that is, by those affected. Ergo: who

---

[14] Daniele Archibugi, 'Principles of Cosmopolitan Democracy', in Archibugi et al., *Re-Imagining Political Community*, pp. 198–228; David Held, 'Cosmopolitanism: Globalisation Tamed?', *Review of International Studies*, vol. 29, no. 4, 2003, pp. 465–80.
[15] Held, 'Principles of Cosmopolitan Order', p. 14.
[16] Sofia Näsström, 'What Globalization Overshadows', *Political Theory*, vol. 31, no. 6, 2003, pp. 808–34; Alexander Wendt, 'A Comment on Held's Cosmopolitanism', in Shapiro and Hacker-Cordón, *Democracy's Edges*, pp. 127–33, at p. 131. For a comment on these paradoxes, see also Marc G. Doucet, 'The Democratic Paradox and Cosmopolitan Democracy', *Millennium: Journal of International Studies*, vol. 34, no. 1, 2005, pp. 137–55.

is affected should be decided by those affected. Thus, both ways of justifying a global democratic community in terms that are themselves democratic presuppose the prior existence of that community, trapping these attempts to construct a global *demos* into a vicious circularity. We are therefore forced to conclude that a world community cannot be justified with recourse to principles of democratic theory, since these principles presuppose that the political unit in question is already legitimate.[17]

This kind of criticism has forced cosmopolitan democrats to look for other ways of justifying the existence of a global community with recourse to principles *other* than those derived from democratic theory. One way out of the above paradox would then be to argue that every community has ultimately to be premised on the principles of equal worth and dignity of individuals, their capacity for autonomous agency, and on notions of responsibility and accountability. A future world community would ideally be an expression of these fundamental principles of cosmopolitan order, based on 'the universal or regulative principles which delimit and govern the range of diversity and difference that ought to be found in public life'.[18] These assumptions can then be freely combined with an impartiality requirement, thus 'focusing our thoughts and testing the intersubjective validity of our conceptions of the good'.[19] Several other authors have responded to this challenge as well. To Cochran, justifying a world community is primarily a matter of restating the conditions of individual autonomy and agency in pragmatist terms, and displaying 'a commitment to democratic institutions which allow for the possibility of communities of practical deliberation among persons'.[20] In practice, this becomes a matter of reconciling democratic institutional approaches to the problem of community, with practices that may help institutionalize

---

[17] For a similar argument, see Robert Dahl, 'Federalism and the Democratic Process', in J. R. Pennock and John W. Chapman, eds., *Liberal Democracy* (New York: New York University Press, 1983), pp. 95–108. Also Robert Dahl, 'Can International Organizations be Democratic?', in Shapiro and Hacker-Cordón, *Democracy's Edges*, pp. 19–36.

[18] Held, 'Principles of Cosmopolitan Order', pp. 18, 12–13.

[19] Held, 'Cosmopolitanism', pp. 471–2.

[20] Molly Cochran, *Normative Theory in International Relations. A Pragmatic Approach* (Cambridge: Cambridge University Press, 1999), p. 277.

a pragmatist ethic from the bottom up.[21] To Dryzek, a similar result could be accomplished by 'establishing deliberative democratic control over the terms of political discourse and so the operation of governance in the international system'.[22] But advocates of transnational democracy seem unbothered by the fact that attempts to universalize these liberal democratic institutions presuppose exactly what they are supposed to yield, namely a global community. This difficulty has led others to suggest that even if one single global *demos* is an idea incapable of realization, we might well conceive of a transnational and potentially global polity in terms of the aggregate relations between multiple and interdependent communities. In the absence of a genuine cosmopolitan community, such a transnational polity could become a source of democratic political authority.[23] While each individual community ideally ought to be governed according to democratic principles internally, the relations between them should also be democratized, both in order to solve conflicts of competence between them and to secure freedom from domination within that transnational polity.[24] Yet, in a sense, this argument brings us back to square one, since it begs the question how such a transnational polity could provide an independent source of legitimate authority at the global level without being categorically distinct from individual communities, and hence inviting problems similar to those of a global *demos*.

These attempts to define and defend different conceptions of cosmopolitan democracy all face the same underlying difficulty: namely, that of specifying the scope of the relevant political community in terms that do not give rise to pragmatic paradoxes. This difficulty does not derive from the normative principles drawn upon when justifying the *ideal* of cosmopolitan democracy. Rather, it derives from the

---

[21] Molly Cochran, 'A Democratic Critique of Cosmopolitan Democracy: Pragmatism from the Bottom-Up', *European Journal of International Relations*, vol. 8, no. 4, 2002, pp. 517–48.

[22] John Dryzek, 'Transnational Democracy', *Journal of Political Philosophy*, vol. 7, no. 1, 1999, pp. 30–51, at p. 48.

[23] James Bohman, 'Republican Cosmopolitanism', *Journal of Political Philosophy*, vol. 12, no. 3, 2004, pp. 336–52.

[24] James Bohman, 'From *Demos* to *Demoi*: Democracy across Borders', *Ratio Juris*, vol. 18, no. 3, 2005, pp. 293–314. See also James Bohman, 'The Democratic Minimum: Is Democracy a Means to Global Justice?', *Ethics and International Affairs*, vol. 19, no. 1, 2005, pp. 101–16.

particularistic social ontology that restricts the *applicability* of these principles to bounded and homogeneous communities. Although cosmopolitan and transnational democrats have struggled to formulate principles that could provide a world community with independent normative foundations, they have failed to grasp that the underlying problem is an ontological one. There is simply no corresponding conception of world community to match the universalistic aspirations of cosmopolitan democrats – just an ontological void in between communities. In the absence of a coherent account of a larger social whole of which particular peoples form part, universalistic normative principles will be very difficult to apply other than by means of a series of domestic analogies, thereby inviting the above paradoxes.

II

According to the cosmopolitan vision of global democracy described above, a world community of some kind is necessary in order to legitimize political institutions of global governance. The creation of such a world community is thus regarded as instrumental in relation to a set of political institutions rather than an end in itself. But to what extent is the idea of a world community capable of standing on its own feet, without being just an extension of the institutional requirements of a given form of governance? Answering this question compels us to inquire into the moral foundations of the concept of world community, and with reference to moral principles *independently* of its role in legitimizing different forms of global political authority. From this point of view, theories of world community have to be built on sound normative foundations, since such foundations are indispensable to *any* community irrespective of its scope and size.[25]

In this section and the next, I shall analyse some attempts to provide the normative foundations of a world community, along with some of the standard objections raised against them. Again, the purpose of the analysis is to demonstrate how their common understanding of human community keeps them from resolving the tension between universalistic and particularistic accounts of political identity and values.

---

[25] For the distinction between political and moral visions of world community, see Fred Dallmayr, 'Cosmopolitanism. Moral and Political', *Political Theory*, vol. 31, no. 3, 2003, pp. 421–42.

The most widespread way of addressing problems of world community in contemporary political theory and academic international relations is in terms of *rights* and *justice*. These problems have traditionally been formulated against the backdrop of international anarchy. From this point of view, rights and justice face dim prospects in the absence of any global political authority that could enforce them, and the best we can hope for is positive agreements among sovereign states that secure a minimum of respect for basic human rights, and perhaps the alleviation of extreme poverty.[26] Those who want to make a stronger case in favour of global rights and justice have typically been compelled to dispute the ethical foundations of state sovereignty, by arguing that the sovereign state should not be regarded as the exclusive source of moral obligation.[27]

Today most of these problems have been reformulated, since many now believe that at least some measure of global authority is exercised independently of state sovereignty, and that the legitimacy of that authority ought to depend on its ability to safeguard basic human rights at the global level. Yet the relationship between theories of global justice and the idea of world community remains highly ambiguous. Although few theorists of global justice assume that the prior existence of a world community is necessary for global justice to be possible, many hold that the institutionalization of rights at the global level is necessary to realize a world community. It is common to argue that the possibility of a world community hinges on the ability to extend some of the rights and obligations already enjoyed by most citizens of liberal democratic states beyond the territorial boundaries of these states into the global realm.[28] The main sticking point in this

---

[26] For an account of this tension, see Jack Donnelly, 'Twentieth-Century Realism', in Terry Nardin and David R. Mapel, *Traditions of International Ethics* (Cambridge: Cambridge University Press, 1992), pp. 82–111. See also Allen Buchanan, 'In the National Interest', in Gillian Brock and Harry Brighouse, eds., *The Political Philosophy of Cosmopolitanism* (Cambridge: Cambridge University Press, 2005), pp. 110–26.

[27] See R. J. Vincent, 'The Idea of Rights in International Ethics', in Nardin and Mapel, *Traditions of International Ethics*, pp. 250–69.

[28] For pioneering versions of this argument, see Charles R. Beitz, *Political Theory and International Relations* (Princeton, NJ: Princeton University Press, 1979); Stanley Hoffmann, *Duties Beyond Borders: On the Limits and Possibilities of Ethical International Politics* (Syracuse, NJ: Syracuse

debate has concerned whether individuals or communities should be considered the ultimate locus of rights, and hence also the ultimate subject of justice. On the one hand, if the individual is conceived as the most basic bearer of rights, the corresponding principles of justice ought to be applicable irrespective of any boundaries, and should apply equally to all human beings regardless of their nationality or citizenship. On the other hand, if the rights of individuals are thought to derive from their membership of particular communities, then the applicability of the corresponding principles of justice is restricted by the existence of boundaries between these communities, and the different national allegiances of individuals.

Let us start with this latter kind of theory. Such theories accept the division of humanity into distinct peoples, and then proceed to redress the more undesirable consequences of this division, but without advocating a wholesale transformation of the present order. Here John Rawls provides us with a well-known textbook example. To him, communities simply have to be bounded, since the existence of boundaries is a condition of possible justice: each particular community is 'a closed system isolated from other societies'.[29] Even though he draws a crucial distinction between states and peoples in order to endow the latter with moral qualities that cannot be easily attributed to the former, peoples are peoples precisely by virtue of their allegiance to common political institutions. While these peoples cannot lay claim to sovereignty in the same way as states can, the requirement that they share common institutions – 'a reasonably just constitutional democratic government' – nevertheless implies a weak form of internal sovereignty.[30] Furthermore, as Rawls makes clear, 'in the absence of a world-state, there *must* be boundaries of some kind, which when viewed in isolation will seem arbitrary, and ultimately depend on historical circumstances'.[31] Thus, 'the Law of Peoples is an extension of a liberal conception of justice for a domestic regime to a

University Press, 1981). For an overview of their implications, see Chris Brown, *International Relations Theory. New Normative Approaches* (Hemel Hempstead: Harvester, 1992).

[29] John Rawls, *A Theory of Justice* (Cambridge, MA: Harvard University Press, 1971), p. 8.

[30] John Rawls, *The Law of Peoples* (Cambridge, MA: Harvard University Press, 1999), pp. 23–7.

[31] Rawls, *Law of Peoples*, p. 39.

Society of Peoples'.[32] As has been pointed out by some of his critics, such uncritical acceptance of the division of mankind into distinct peoples, however limited their sovereignty, nevertheless amounts to a kind of thinly disguised nationalism. As Kuper has argued, 'It is true that many people have cultural allegiances, but persons have many other allegiances too, and the idealisation of a homogeneous nation removes the possibility of any basic political consideration of how those claims ought to be prioritized.'[33] Thus, toleration ends at state boundaries, since 'it respects groups rather than persons ... allowing their entitlements to be dictated by the dominant group in their vicinity, whether they like that group or not'.[34]

This brings us over to the second kind of theory. In response to this restriction, other scholars have tried to globalize the Rawlsian theory by starting out from a *single* global original position in which individual human beings, and not societies, partake. These scholars thus dispute the moral legitimacy of the existing division of mankind into distinct peoples. To Pogge, the 'ultimate unit of concern are human beings, or persons – rather than, say, family lines, tribes, ethnic, cultural, or religious communities, nations, or states'.[35] Similarly, to Jones, 'nation-state borders lack any fundamental ethical standing and ... the demands of global justice include various positive actions aimed at protecting the vital interests of everyone, regardless of their location, nationality, or citizenship'.[36] These theories then go on to justify the idea that each person has certain inalienable and inviolable rights, and that these rights transcend all boundaries and trump all obligations that derive from belonging to particular communities. Yet

---

[32] Rawls, *Law of Peoples*, p. 55.
[33] Andrew Kuper, 'Rawlsian Global Justice Beyond *The Law of Peoples* to a Cosmopolitan Law of Persons', *Political Theory*, vol. 28, no. 5, 2000, pp. 640–74, at p. 655.
[34] Martha Nussbaum, 'Beyond the Social Contract: Capabilities and Global Justice', in Brock and Brighouse, *The Political Philosophy of Cosmopolitanism*, pp. 196–218.
[35] Thomas W. Pogge, 'Cosmopolitanism and Sovereignty', *Ethics*, vol. 103, 1992, pp. 48–75, at p. 48; Thomas Pogge, 'Cosmopolitanism: A Defence', *Critical Review of International Social and Political Philosophy*, vol. 5, no. 3, 2002, pp. 86–91.
[36] Charles Jones, *Global Justice. Defending Cosmopolitanism* (Oxford: Oxford University Press, 1999), p. 2.

the fact that such principles of justice are universally valid does not preclude the possibility that they may 'nevertheless be best instituted through a plurality of bounded republican states, linked by commitments to international justice and cosmopolitan right'.[37]

Now arguments like the above are frequently met with the objection that states and nations, or any other particularistic forms of community, nevertheless still remain inescapable features of global political life. Since the existence of bounded communities poses a very real constraint on the universal acceptance of rights and principles of justice, they cannot and should not be wished away. Instead, these features ought to be taken seriously by theories of cosmopolitan justice, which otherwise assume that the bearers of rights are relatively unaffected by their belonging to concrete communities.[38] All rights and principles of justice presuppose the existence of some kind of political community in order to be meaningful, since they are ultimately based on obligations between fellow members of human communities, rather than on any abstract principles. But since such obligations are currently weak or lacking in the global realm, the only source from which they can be derived is the very particular communities within which they have emerged and taken hold.[39] This kind of criticism has left theories of global justice open to the same kind of objections that have been directed against other universalistic theories of justice, since they allegedly assume that individuals are devoid of those characteristics that would make them fit members of concrete communities of other human beings of flesh and blood, and hence also unable to enter into the necessary obligations.[40]

But what if we reformulate this problem in terms of personal morality? This could be done by asking how the prospective members of a world community should ideally perceive themselves and the moral

---

[37] Onora O'Neill, 'Bounded and Cosmopolitan Justice', *Review of International Studies*, vol. 26, no. 1, 2000, pp. 45–60, at p. 59.
[38] Cf. Jones, *Global Justice*, pp. 227–33.
[39] Thomas Nagel, 'The Problem of Global Justice', *Philosophy and Public Affairs*, vol. 33, no. 2, 2005, pp. 113–47, at p. 146.
[40] For well-known formulations of this objection, see Michael Sandel, *Liberalism and the Limits of Justice* (Cambridge: Cambridge University Press, 1982); Michael Walzer, *Thick and Thin: Moral Argument at Home and Abroad* (Notre Dame, IN: University of Notre Dame Press, 1994), pp. 63–83.

choices they have to face. In order to handle the tradeoff described above, some authors have tried to resolve the underlying tension between universalistic and particularistic conceptions of morality by turning it into a problem of existential choices. As real people of flesh and blood inhabit both spheres simultaneously, the challenge consists in reconciling the loyalty felt to one's own community with the loyalty that ought to be felt towards mankind as a whole. As the hero of *The Home and the World* (1915) proclaims, 'I am willing ... to serve my country; but my worship I reserve for Right which is far greater than my country. To worship my country as a god is to bring a curse upon it.'[41] Or, as Nussbaum has formulated the corresponding duty, 'we should give our first allegiance to no mere form of government, no temporal power, but to the moral community made up by the humanity of all human beings'.[42] Yet the tension between different and conflicting loyalties that each human has to confront pushes this philosophical duality into the core of the self and its quest for integrity in the face of conflicting moral pressures. As Appiah has argued, this conflict can be resolved if 'The cosmopolitan patriot can entertain the possibility of a world in which everyone is a rooted cosmopolitan ... with their own cultural particularities.'[43] So even if there is no longer any sharp disagreement about the ultimate locus of moral obligation – mankind as a whole – resolving the moral dilemma now becomes a matter of making individual choices between conflicting allegiances.[44]

Now this move merely transposes the basic moral dilemma to a new level. We would still have to choose between understanding ourselves as members of a distinct community or as members of mankind as a whole, which is exactly the kind of tragedy which Tagore so vividly described in his novel. Either we enjoy our fully fledged humanity

---

[41] Rabindranath Tagore, *The Home and the World* (Harmondsworth: Penguin, 1985), p. 29.

[42] Martha Nussbaum, 'Patriotism and Cosmopolitanism', in Joshua Cohen, ed., *For Love of Country. Debating the Limits of Patriotism* (Boston: Beacon Press, 1994), pp. 3–17, at p. 7.

[43] Kwame Anthony Appiah, 'Cosmopolitan Patriots', in Cohen, *For Love of Country*, pp. 21–9, at p. 22.

[44] For a discussion, see Richard Rorty, 'Justice as a Larger Loyalty', in Pheng and Robbins, *Cosmopolitics,* pp. 45–58; Michael Walzer, 'Spheres of Affection', in Cohen, *For Love of Country*, pp. 125–7.

within particular communities, while grudgingly acknowledging that the rights we happen to have derive from our membership in those communities rather than from our belonging to mankind as a whole; or, we enjoy a set of basic rights simply by virtue of being distinct from members of other species, while reluctantly conceding that that part of our humanity which might derive from our belonging to a particular community is an ethically irrelevant part of our personality. Again we seem faced with another version of the choice between a position that insists on the embedded nature of both rights and their bearers, and a thin cosmopolitanism that remains premised on the universality of rights and the unencumbered character of their individual loci.[45]

But, in my reading, the point conveyed by Tagore is that this dilemma is a false one, since in his narrative it has been brutally *imposed* by fervent nationalists upon human beings who otherwise would live in blissful ignorance of its tragic implications. Yet arguably, in order to be sustainable in the present world, theories of rights and justice must find a way to split the difference between universal principles and particularistic commitments such as those springing precisely from patriotism and nationalism.[46] These theories would have to explain how the constraints posed by these forces can be overcome, so that rights and principles of justice can be implemented within or outside the existing framework of nation-states.[47] Paradoxically, then, 'the most likely path toward some version of global justice is through the creation of patently unjust and illegitimate global structures of power that are tolerable to the interests of the most powerful current nation-states'.[48]

---

[45] For an analysis of this tension, see Cochran, *Normative Theory*, pp. 1–76.

[46] For a sophisticated attempt in this direction, see Kok-Chor Tan, *Justice without Borders. Cosmopolitanism, Nationalism and Patriotism* (Cambridge: Cambridge University Press, 2004), pp. 85–197. See also Kok-Chor Tan, 'The Demands of Justice and National Allegiances', in Brock and Brighouse, *The Political Philosophy of Cosmopolitanism*, pp. 164–79.

[47] See, for example, Thomas Risse, Stephen C. Ropp and Kathryn Sikkink, *The Power of Human Rights: International Norms and Domestic Change* (Cambridge: Cambridge University Press, 1999).

[48] Nagel, 'The Problem of Global Justice', p. 146.

Although the above theories imply that a world community might result from successful efforts to institutionalize principles of rights and justice on a global scale, the debate between different positions is based on the assumption that the global realm is composed of either particular and distinct communities or individual human beings, but never both simultaneously. These assumptions help to convey the impression that a tension between universalistic and particularistic moral standards is an inescapable part of the human condition, rather than a contingent outcome of a series of accidental conceptual changes. By the same token, while the above theories tend to rule out the existence of a more encompassing social whole, of which both communities and individual human beings could form part, they nevertheless assume that some kind of world community would ensue, could the tension between the universal and the particular be successfully overcome. But *whose* rights and *which* justice are we talking about?

III

Addressing this question brings us over to the possibility of creating a world community on the basis of a *common identity*. As we saw above, theories of global justice invariably make tacit assumptions about the bearers of rights and their identity. We have also seen how these assumptions constituted a blind spot of these theories, and how they therefore were unable to envisage any human community over and above particular ones. Against this backdrop, some scholars have tried to reformulate the problem of world community in terms of identity. To them, creating such a community is primarily a question of reconciling different and conflicting political identities, rather than a matter of institutionalizing any given set of political or moral principles on a global scale. To reformulate the problem of world community in terms of identity is to pose the question of under what conditions human beings are able to understand other human beings in other communities, to the point that they actually begin to share important values in common that transcend their differences. Formulated in this way, the problem of world community concerns the extent to which relations between communities with different values are conducive to such a fusion of horizons. From this point of view, a world community can only be constituted through a broad intercultural agreement about basic norms and values, and such an agreement presupposes that the underlying moral frameworks are both commensurable and compatible.

Unsurprisingly, authors who agree that the creation of a more inclusive community beyond the nation-state is highly desirable have sharply divergent views when it comes to the ontological and ethical foundations of such a community. Although most of them are very suspicious of the principled versions of universalism discussed above, they are nevertheless compelled to identify some basic unity behind the global diversity of values in order to be able to make any coherent sense of the idea of a world community at all. Hence, in their attempts to come to terms with global diversity, they are faced with the problem of explaining how the basic values necessary to constitute a world community can indeed be shared and upheld without recourse to any ready-made universals. In the rest of this section, I shall discuss three main solutions to this problem, derived from discourse ethics, hermeneutics, and pluralism respectively.

Let us start with the attempts to globalize discourse ethics. In the absence of any thick moral universals, writes Linklater, we can at least hope for 'a thin conception of universality which defends the ideal that every human being has an equal right to participate in dialogue to determine the principles of inclusion and exclusion which govern global politics'.[49] To Linklater, the way to world community goes through an extension of the moral point of view provided by discourse ethics. Such discourse ethics are based on the idea that 'all human beings have an equal right to belong to communication communities where they can protest against actions which may harm them', and that they 'enter dialogue with the conviction that no-one knows who will learn from whom, and that all should strive to reach agreements which rely as far as possible on the force of the better argument'.[50] From this point of view, 'norms cannot be valid unless they can command the consent of everyone whose interests stand to be affected by them'.[51] This requires that no person or position is excluded from the dialogue

---

[49] Linklater, *Transformation of Political Community*, p. 107. See also Robert Fine and Will Smith, 'Jürgen Habermas's Theory of Cosmopolitanism', *Constellations*, vol. 10, no. 4, 2003, pp. 469–87.

[50] Andrew Linklater, 'Dialogic Politics and the Civilising Process', *Review of International Studies*, vol. 31, no. 1, 2005, pp. 141–54, at p. 147.

[51] Linklater, *Transformation of Political Community*, p. 91.

in advance, and that the interlocutors possess enough moral maturity to engage in dialogue rather than letting the exchange degenerate into verbal warfare. Similarly, to Benhabib, 'only those norms and normative institutional arrangements are valid which can be agreed to by all concerned under special argumentation situations called discourses'. This theory 'cannot limit the scope of *moral conversation* only to those who reside within nationally recognized boundaries; it must view the moral conversation as potentially extending to all of *humanity*'.[52] Only by making distinctions between existing political communities more fluid and negotiable can we hope to move towards 'a postmetaphysical and postnational conception of cosmopolitan solidarity which increasingly brings all human beings, by virtue of their humanity alone, under the net of universal rights'.[53] Even within a society of states, discourse ethics might provide a welcome antidote to the crude exercise of power, thereby strengthening the communal dimension of this society.[54] Although 'egalitarian reciprocity will probably never be realized in a world community where states and peoples are at different levels ... norms of universal respect and egalitarian reciprocity ... are guideposts for our intuitions'.[55]

From a hermeneutic position, the stronger the sense of cultural relativism, the harder it becomes to defend even a thin universalism, however. As Mehta describes the possibility of world community, it would require 'more than simply the willingness or ability to adopt a reflective standpoint that allows distance from one's own presuppositions. It may also require a prior ethic grounded in the supposition that in dealing with important matters like the meaning of life and the practices that express those meanings, the conclusion of reflection will be necessarily varied.'[56] Or, in the words of Taylor, it is 'reasonable to suppose ... that cultures have provided the

---

[52] Seyla Benhabib, *The Rights of Others. Aliens, Residents, and Citizens* (Cambridge: Cambridge University Press, 2004), pp. 13–14. Italics in original.
[53] Benhabib, *Rights of Others*, p. 21.
[54] Thomas Risse, '"Let's Argue": Communicative Action in World Politics', *International Organization*, vol. 54, no. 1, 2000, pp. 1–39.
[55] Seyla Benhabib, *The Claims of Culture. Equality and Diversity in a Global Era* (Princeton, NJ: Princeton University Press, 2002), p. 37.
[56] Pratap Bhanu Mehta, 'Cosmopolitanism and the Circle of Reason', *Political Theory*, vol. 28, no. 5, 2000, pp. 619–39, at pp. 627–8.

horizon of meaning for large numbers of human beings, of diverse characters and temperaments, over a long period of time'.[57] From this point of view, different people from different communities not only have different moral standards, but might entertain radically different understandings of the world as well. So even if some moral codes transcend existing cultural differences, the ability of members of different communities to understand each other is limited due to profound differences in worldview. Consequently, the creation of a world community becomes a matter of achieving mutual understanding through dialogue. Thus, according to Dallmayr, 'a thick conversation may well be the most urgent need in our world today. The point is not to dominate, manipulate, or lecture others "from on high", but to take them seriously in their lifeworlds as members of the global community.'[58]

Some of those who accept this diagnosis believe that the hermeneutic predicament itself is sufficiently universal to both necessitate and facilitate dialogue, and that the shared meanings that hopefully emerge from such a dialogue can then constitute the communicative foundation of a universal community of mankind. The dialogical situation itself possesses certain traits that make a universal community possible, and irrespective of whether interlocutors fulfil the requirements of discursive decency listed by authors like Linklater and Benhabib. As Shapcott has argued, 'The term community itself implies a collectivity exhibiting a high degree of homogeneity of identity and consensus among its members and, therefore, a lack of "difference" between them. A universal community, one that in principle includes all members of the species, must by virtue of being a community, exclude or deny important differences amongst its members.'[59] Even if an imagined community like this is tailored to include as many

---

[57] Charles Taylor, 'The Politics of Recognition', in *Philosophical Arguments* (Cambridge, MA: Harvard University Press, 1995), pp. 225–56, at p. 256.

[58] Fred Dallmayr, 'Conversations across Boundaries: Political Theory and Global Diversity', *Millennium*, vol. 30, no. 2, 2001, 331–47, at p. 346.

[59] Richard Shapcott, *Justice, Community, and Dialogue in International Relations* (Cambridge: Cambridge University Press, 2001), p. 2. See also Richard Shapcott, 'Cosmopolitan Conversations: Justice Dialogue and the Cosmopolitan Project', *Global Society*, vol. 16, no. 3, 2002, pp. 221–43.

human beings as possible, it nevertheless has to be bounded, since in the absence of a common and clearly demarcated identity it would cease to be a community. There is thus a tension between the concept of community and the idea of human diversity: Shapcott suggests that this tension can be resolved through acts of communication and understanding, since 'recognition of the shared quality of identity in turn rests on, and is mediated through, the shared quality of language'.[60] Finally, this argument can be brought full circle by arguing that the way to a world community would require a new definition of selfhood that liberates the self from the ethical restraints of particular communities through his or her encounter with the other, through a mutual awareness of the embedded character of *any* ethics.[61]

When given a global twist, both discourse ethics and hermeneutics face similar problems, albeit of different severity. These theories formulate the question of world community as a quest for a common identity and common values. Starting from the assumption that human beings are already situated within particular communities, they ask how the epistemic and moral differences between these communities can be mediated. In the absence of any pre-constituted universals, the possibility of construing a world community hinges on the possibility of recognition and understanding between both communities and their members, which is to be achieved through dialogue. Yet this ambition to reconcile particular moral standards within a larger framework leaves these theories open to the objection that however thin their universalism, the foundations of any such intercultural understanding will necessarily reflect the concerns or predispositions of some particular identity, and thus ultimately be expressions of the very predicament they seek to escape.[62] To Benhabib, for example, 'it is inconceivable that democratic legitimacy can be sustained without some clear demarcation of those in the name of whom the laws have been enacted from

---

[60] Shapcott, *Justice, Community, and Dialogue in International Relations*, pp. 12–13.
[61] Louiza Odysseos, 'On the Way to Global Ethics?', *European Journal of Political Theory*, vol. 2, no. 2, 2003, pp. 183–208.
[62] See, for example, William E. Connolly, 'Cross-State Citizen Networks: A Response to Dallmayr', *Millennium*, vol. 30, no. 2, 2001, pp. 349–55; Thomas Diez and Jill Steans, 'A Useful Dialogue? Habermas and International Relations', *Review of International Studies*, vol. 31, no. 2, 2005, pp. 127–40, esp. pp. 136–40.

those upon whom the laws are not binding'.[63] Therefore, being based on the idea of mutual recognition, these theories cannot but affirm the very particularity they struggle to overcome, since they seem to presuppose that the master distinction between Same and Other is always already present as a condition of possible identity.[64]

Finally, to pluralists, all of the above proposals reflect far too much faith in rationalism and universalism. Their solution is to accept and celebrate the actual plurality of identities as an expression of human diversity, while trying to identify practices that can mediate those differences that threaten this diversity. These critics are acutely aware that the present division of mankind into territorially bounded communities poses a severe constraint on any attempt to transpose the ideals of democracy and justice into the global sphere, but nevertheless believe attempts in this direction to be necessary in order to counteract the dark forces reigning in the global realm.[65] To Connolly, therefore, the task at hand is to find a way through which 'some elements of a democratic ethos can extend beyond the walls of the state'.[66] By the same token, to Kristeva, the challenge posed by alien cultures is less a question of integration and assimilation under any given universal, than a question of realizing that we are *all* strangers to a certain extent, irrespective of where we happen to be and where we happen to belong.[67] Similarly, to Honig, any hopes for a world community reside in our encounters with the Other, encounters which may serve to disrupt illusions of sameness and which thereby ultimately create openness.[68] When properly understood and carefully handled,

---

[63] Benhabib, *The Rights of Others*, p. 220.
[64] For a critical analysis of the idea of recognition as a source of identity and morality, see Patchen Markell, *Bound by Recognition* (Princeton, NJ: Princeton University Press, 2003).
[65] See, for example, David Campbell, 'The Deterritorialization of Responsibility: Levinas, Derrida, and Ethics after the End of Philosophy', in David Campbell and Michael J. Shapiro, eds., *Moral Spaces. Rethinking Ethics and World Politics* (Minneapolis: University of Minnesota Press, 1999), pp. 29–56.
[66] William E. Connolly, *The Ethos of Pluralization* (Minneapolis: University of Minnesota Press, 1995), p. 155.
[67] Julia Kristeva, *Étrangers à nous-mêmes* (Paris: Gallimard, 1988), pp. 249–90.
[68] Bonnie Honig, 'Ruth, the Model Émigré: Mourning and the Symbolic Politics of Immigration', in Pheng and Robbins, *Cosmopolitics*, pp. 192–215.

such encounters can be a means of '(re)founding, inaugurating and animating a democratic politics ... within and across borders without presupposing a unified *demos* stabilized by the metaphorics of national kinship'.[69] Or, as Connolly has argued, 'By affirming without existential resentment the element of contestability in regulative ideas that move us, we contribute to a plural matrix appropriate to the late-modern world. The possible consolidation of such a matrix involves cultivation of agonistic respect between parties who proceed from diverse, overlapping sources.'[70] In more practical terms, the values of a democratic global community would be best served by an 'energetic politics of citizen pressure within and above traditional state politics, pressure designed to move states and corporations in directions resisted by the inertia of Empire'.[71]

For all their suspicions of the nation-state, these authors have obvious difficulties articulating alternative visions of community that extend beyond their boundaries. Even if they would like to move beyond the current international system, and replace it with political practices and institutions that would better reflect the demands of human diversity and cultural plurality in a globalized world, these authors are hesitant to specify the organizing principles of any global forms of community. According to the logic of their own argument, any such attempt would be a step in a universalistic direction, and hence also necessarily an expression of some particular identity or interest. These authors tend to regard the preservation of human diversity within as well as outside communities as a virtue, but have very little to say about how these communities and their members might be able to relate beyond the point of mere coexistence. As a consequence, they also find it difficult to explain what would possibly keep a world characterized by such an agonistic plurality of values and identities from degenerating into pure antagonism and collapsing into realist tragedy. This difficulty is aggravated by the fact that they rarely make any clear assumptions about the kind of political authority that could possibly and legitimately prevent that outcome. Again,

---

[69] Bonnie Honig, *Democracy and the Foreigner* (Princeton, NJ: Princeton University Press, 2001), p. 40.
[70] William E. Connolly, 'Speed, Concentric Culture, and Cosmopolitanism', *Political Theory*, vol. 28, no. 5, 2000, pp. 596–618.
[71] William E. Connolly, *Pluralism* (Durham, NC: Duke University Press, 2005), p. 158.

the particularistic social ontology to which these authors subscribe makes it difficult to understand the global realm as little more than a moral void, populated by a multitude of particular communities. From this point of view, the concept of world community also becomes little more than a rhetorical device that can be freely used in order to criticize the institutions and practices of modern statehood in the name of a mankind which in fact never has been and never will be united anyway. If this is true, the idea of world community would be 'in danger of remaining a pious and irresponsible desire, without form and without potency, and of even being perverted at any moment '.[72]

IV

In this chapter, we have seen how theories of cosmopolitan democracy and global justice presuppose the possibility of a world community, but fail to account for its composition other than by means of domestic analogies. This failure has led other scholars to discuss the prospect of a world community in terms of its underlying identity and the values that such a community ideally ought to be based on, in the hope that such a community could be realized through dialogue and mutual understanding. But apart from their obvious differences, the theories discussed in this chapter assume that the world ultimately consists of a plurality of distinct and bounded communities populated by individual human beings. Beyond the boundaries of those particular communities there is no human community worthy of the name. The absence of a global culture and the lack of a common historical memory makes a world community hard to achieve, but nevertheless a worthy aspiration given the dark forces of globalization conspiring against human fulfilment. To my mind, the main reason why these authors have found it difficult to make coherent sense of the concept of world community is the particularistic ontology that is foundational to most modern theories of community. As long as we remain committed to this particularistic ontology, we will have a hard time making theoretical sense of any kind of human community over and above the plurality of particular communities presently embodied in the states system. One reason why people remain committed to this

---

[72] Jacques Derrida, *On Cosmopolitanism and Forgiveness* (London: Routledge, 2001), pp. 22–3.

kind of ontology is semantic, since the concept of community is most frequently taken to refer to bounded forms of human association, thereby disqualifying unbounded forms of association by definition. Another reason has to do with the logic of identity frequently employed when accounting for the formation of particular communities and their identities. According to what has become a widespread assumption within the social sciences, the identity of a given political community requires it to be different from other communities of the same kind. Sameness presupposes otherness, and identity presupposes difference.[73] Consequently, particular communities derive their identity from a game of recognition that takes place between them during their formative phases, in which case their 'identities and their corresponding interests are learned and then reinforced in response to how actors are treated by significant Others'.[74] But as long as we regard this logic of identity as a predominant source of human belonging and identification, the formation of a community of all mankind will look highly unlikely simply because there are no human Others left that could provide it with a sense of sameness.

Theories of world community are based on a different logic of identity and locate the sources of human belonging and fulfilment at a different level of human existence. If we want to make sense of the concept of world community, it must be understood as being something more than the sum total of its parts. Theories of world community typically posit such a larger whole by understanding human community as a universal and boundless phenomenon. Such a

---

[73] See, for example, William E. Connolly, *Identity\Difference: Democratic Negotiations of Political Paradox* (Ithaca, NY: Cornell University Press, 1991). For a critique of this assumption within international relations theory, see Richard Ned Lebow, 'Homer, Vergil and Identity in International Relations', in Gideon Baker and Jens Bartelson, eds., *The Future of Political Community* (London: Routledge, 2009), pp. 144–74.

[74] Alexander Wendt, *Social Theory of International Politics* (Cambridge: Cambridge University Press, 1999), p. 327. See also Erik Ringmar, *Identity, Interest and Action. A Cultural Explanation of Sweden's Intervention in the Thirty Years War* (Cambridge: Cambridge University Press, 1996); Axel Honneth, *The Struggle for Recognition. The Moral Grammar of Social Conflicts* (Cambridge: Polity Press, 1995), pp. 71–91, 160–70.

community exists by virtue of human beings sharing certain capacities in common that make it possible for them to share other things in common as well. Since the experience of community is an integral part of what it means to be a human being, all restrictions on the membership of any community are accidental and morally arbitrary. All communities and their members ought to be viewed as fundamentally embedded within this larger whole, and the fact of overlapping membership between communities of different scope makes it meaningless to uphold any categorical distinction between them. Instead, they are mutually implicating: while particular communities are instantiations of a universal community of all mankind, a universal community exists only by virtue of being thus instantiated.

In order to be able to view all human communities as parts of such a larger social whole, visions of world community are typically constructed with reference to imagined vantage points above the sociopolitical realm. Such vantage points have traditionally been provided by cosmological beliefs about the planet and its surface. Not only do these beliefs help to account for the unity of mankind and the causes of its division and dispersion, they also include assumptions about how the makeup of the planet has conditioned the intercourse between different peoples from different places. From here it has been a short step to argue that such intercourse will help to create and sustain social bonds between different peoples from different places, and that any obstacles to such intercourse ought to be overcome through human ingenuity for the purpose of bringing members of the human species closer together within this universal community.[75]

As I shall try to show in subsequent chapters, articulating visions of world community has largely been a matter of constructing such overarching vantage points, and then turning them into starting points for political and legal theory. Once this cosmological dimension is taken into consideration, it should become obvious that visions of world community cannot be reduced to mere expressions of particular interests and identities, but that they ought to be seen in the larger context

---

[75] For a discussion of such assumptions, see Walter D. Mignolo, 'The Many Faces of Cosmo-Polis: Border Thinking and Critical Cosmopolitanism', in Carol A. Breckenridge, Sheldon Pollock, Homi K. Bhabha and Dipesh Chakrabarty, eds., *Cosmopolitanism* (Durham, NC: Duke University Press, 2002), pp. 157–88.

of the evolution and gradual spread of a scientific worldview. Doing this amounts to writing a history of the concept of world community: while such a history cannot tell us what a world community ought to look like, it might provide important insights into its social ontology by outlining the basic requirements of its existence. In the next chapter, I shall describe how the concept of a universal and boundless community of all mankind was articulated and used in the context of late medieval and Renaissance cosmology. In order to understand why such visions of world community were later marginalized within modern political thought, we need to understand how they were replaced by particularistic ones. Thus, in Chapter 4 I shall describe how the concept of community was nationalized, and how this nationalization was to a large extent carried out by drawing on those very universalistic conceptions that were subsequently marginalized and eventually forgotten. In Chapter 5, I shall describe how the concept of world community was recovered in response to the practices of the early modern states, and how this concept was turned into a powerful tool of moral critique. In Chapter 6, I shall describe how these critical visions were translated into a comprehensive political and legal doctrine, and how our present predicament has resulted from a selective and distorted uptake of this doctrine. In Chapter 7, I shall return to some of the philosophical problems discussed in this chapter.

3 | *In the beginning was the world*

SUMMARIZING the main trends in medieval philosophy, Maurice De Wulf once argued that medieval philosophers were driven by a 'wish to correct the defects arising from the plurality of the states, by a unifying theory, the universal community of men'. Yet he was quick to caution the modern reader that 'it seems superfluous to point out that the *humanitas universitas* of the thirteenth century did not constitute a society of nations in the modern sense of the term'.[1] But what kind of entity was envisaged by medieval writers? In this chapter, I shall try to provide a partial answer to this question, as well as describe how such an imagined community of all mankind was replaced by early modern notions of a world composed of different peoples. In order to account for this transition, I shall try to situate these conceptions of community in the cosmological contexts within which they were articulated.[2] As I would like to suggest in this chapter, the medieval cosmology that had confined a united mankind to an *orbis terrarum* was replaced by a new worldview according to which a divided mankind was dispersed onto the dry surface of a *rotunditate absoluta*. In the next chapter, I shall try to show how this latter conception became crucial to subsequent attempts to explain and justify the existence of particular communities within a wider political and legal framework of nations and empires.

While some existing accounts have emphasized the importance of changing cosmological beliefs when explaining the emergence of sovereign states, none of them have bothered to systematically relate the contemporary conceptions of community to the cosmological

---

[1] Maurice De Wulf, *Philosophy and Civilization in the Middle Ages* (Princeton, NJ: Princeton University Press, 1922), pp. 116, 125.
[2] Here I am following a suggestion by Peter Harrison, *The Bible, Protestantism, and the Rise of Natural Science* (Cambridge: Cambridge University Press, 1998), pp. 266–73.

context within which they were articulated.[3] One possible reason for this neglect is the fact that these stateless parts of our past are intrinsically hard to subject to historical analysis: most historiography still takes the existence of bounded political communities for granted. Thus, as Fasolt has noted, 'the mere existence of that past threatens historical self-consciousness with dissolution'.[4] What makes these parts of the past so difficult to understand is the fact that the meta-historical coordinates necessary to historical writing themselves are contested during this period. If no clear and agreed senses of before and after and up and down can be read from the sources themselves, the historian's task becomes difficult if not impossible. The most common solution to this problem has been to project modern understandings of time and space back onto the past; yet those parts of the past risk becoming incomprehensible if we take the modern meanings of the concepts of space and time to be given starting points of historiography.[5] Hence, if we want to gain a more precise understanding of the stateless parts of our past, we must attend to the history of these concepts as well, and explore the connections between *their* historical trajectories and that of our main topic, the concept of community. The corollary is that if we want to gain knowledge of this world as it looked to its inhabitants *before* they were divided into different peoples, we cannot take the facts of division and dispersion for granted. For in order for these facts to make any sense at all, there has to be another space where division and dispersion can be said to take place. And in order for the human species to be divided and dispersed, there has to be something there to divide and disperse in the first place.

---

[3] John Gerard Ruggie, 'Territoriality and Beyond: Problematizing Modernity in International Relations', *International Organization*, vol. 47, no. 1, 1993, pp. 139–74; Hendrik Spruyt, *The Sovereign State and its Competitors. An Analysis of Systems Change* (Princeton, NJ: Princeton University Press, 1994), pp. 59–77.

[4] Constantin Fasolt, *The Limits of History* (Chicago: University of Chicago Press, 2003), pp. 27–8.

[5] See Reinhart Koselleck, 'Transformations of Experience and Methodological Change: A Historical-Anthropological Essay', in Reinhart Koselleck, *The Practice of Conceptual History. Timing History, Spacing Concepts* (Stanford, CA: Stanford University Press, 2002), pp. 45–83.

I

As Reynolds has noted, during the Middle Ages 'the word community and its derivatives were used very widely, with a range of meanings which apparently needed little or no definition, so the values they embodied were too fundamental to need much spelling out'.[6] But while these values found expression in villages, cities and kingdoms, it was also widely assumed that beyond this multitude of communities Christian society also constituted one single universal community to which all human beings ultimately belonged.[7] As Gierke once pointed out, in medieval political thought 'Mankind is one Partial Whole with a final cause of its own, which is distinct from the final causes of Individuals and from those of other Communities.'[8]

This notion that mankind constitutes one single community could be justified in at least two different ways in medieval theology. First, and according to scriptural authority, every human being is a member of the same universal community by virtue of sharing a common descent, that of being sons and daughters of Adam. Second, the church defined *itself* as a community of believers, held together by their sacred communion with Christ. While the precise nature of this liturgical bond was subject to much debate, its universal character remained largely undisputed. This fact made every human being at least potentially a Christian, and thus also potentially a member of a universal community by virtue of his or her faith alone.[9] The belief that medieval Christendom constituted one single community was further reinforced by the legacy of the Roman Empire, whose possible restoration remained a crucial premise of political thought

---

[6] Susan Reynolds, *Kingdoms and Communities in Western Europe 900–1300* (Oxford: Clarendon Press, 1997), p. 3.

[7] For a classic study, see Otto Gierke, *Community in Historical Perspective* [1868–1913] (Cambridge: Cambridge University Press, 1990).

[8] Otto von Gierke, *Political Theories of the Middle Age* (Cambridge: Cambridge University Press, 1900), p. 10.

[9] See, for example, Walter Ullmann, *Principles of Government and Politics in the Middle Ages* (London: Methuen, 1974), pp. 33ff, 97ff; Walter Ullmann, *A History of Political Thought: The Middle Ages* (Harmondsworth: Penguin, 1965); Walter Ullmann, *Medieval Foundations of Renaissance Humanism* (London: Paul Elek, 1977); Janet Coleman, *A History of Political Thought. From the Middle Ages to the Renaissance* (Oxford: Blackwell, 2000).

and action well into the early modern period.[10] Yet the importance of these conceptions of human community to the coherence of medieval political thought has frequently been downplayed. Many scholars have projected the concerns of modern political theory back onto the Middle Ages, and have thereby focused more on the problems of authority and sovereignty than on questions of community and society.[11] But since there was nothing like modern sovereignty to be found during the Middle Ages, I shall suggest that we ought to pay renewed attention to the question of community if we want a fuller understanding of what distinguishes medieval from early modern political thought.[12]

In this section, I shall focus on one exemplary vision of universal community, that of Dante Alighieri. One reason for this choice is the persistent tendency to interpret his work as little more than a justification of imperial authority, while his underlying conception of community has mostly been neglected by students of political thought.[13] While Dante certainly did defend imperial authority, he did so in a way which had profound and lasting implications for subsequent attempts to conceptualize a community of all mankind

---

[10] See Andreas Osiander, 'Before Sovereignty: Society and Politics in *Ancien Régime* Europe', *Review of International Studies*, vol. 27, special issue, 2001, pp. 119–45; Frances A. Yates, *Astraea. The Imperial Theme in the Sixteenth Century* (London: Routledge, 1975).

[11] One of the best examples of this practice remains Michael Wilks, *The Problem of Sovereignty in the Later Middle Ages: The Papal Monarchy with Augustinus Triumphus and the Publicists* (Cambridge: Cambridge University Press, 1963).

[12] See Osiander, 'Before Sovereignty', p. 144. For a different formulation of this problem, see Cary J. Nederman, 'Empire and the Historiography of European Political Thought: Marsiglio of Padua, Nicholas of Cusa, and the Medieval/Modern Divide', *Journal of the History of Ideas*, vol. 66, no. 1, 2005, pp. 1–15.

[13] See, for example, Marjorie Reeves, 'Marsiglio of Padua and Dante Alighieri', in Beryl Smalley, ed., *Trends in Medieval Political Thought* (Oxford: Basil Blackwell, 1965), pp. 86–104; Quentin Skinner, *Foundations of Modern Political Thought*, vol. I (Cambridge: Cambridge University Press, 1978), pp. 16–18; Anthony Pagden, *Lords of all the World. Ideologies of Empire in Spain, Britain and France c. 1500–c. 1850* (New Haven, CT: Yale University Press, 1995), pp. 29–31. An exception in this regard is A. P. D'Entrèves, *Dante as a Political Thinker* (Oxford: Clarendon Press, 1952), pp. 47–51.

independently of the theological justifications mentioned earlier. In order to overcome the limitations of existing Christian and imperial ideas of community, Dante tried to reconceptualize human community by positing the existence of a collective mind common to all members of the human species.[14]

In order to substantiate this view, I shall focus on the *Monarchia* (*c*. 1314). When read as a treatise in political philosophy, *Monarchia* invites a focus on the question of political authority, since it sets out to discuss the legitimacy of temporal monarchy, understood as 'a single sovereign authority set over all others in time'.[15] In the context in which Dante was writing, his arguments are only fully intelligible against the backdrop of the conflict between spiritual and temporal claims to authority that animated medieval political theology. While most medieval authors agreed that some temporal authority had become indispensable, given the discord into which the human race had lapsed after the Fall, the proper locus of such authority was constantly contested during the Middle Ages.

As we might recall from Augustine, human discord flows from two different sources. The first source is our inescapable sinfulness as human beings; the second is a consequence of what happened at Babel. The loss of a common language brought upon humanity a loss of community, and thus the sacred bond constituted by common descent was also weakened by this most unfortunate event. As we learn from the *City of God*, the world is beset by discord, since 'if two men, each ignorant of the other's language, meet, and are compelled by some necessity not to pass on but to remain with one another, it is easier for dumb animals … to associate together than these men, even though both are human beings'.[16] Yet while human sinfulness was beyond remedy in the terrestrial condition in which men were now found, the broken communicative bond between them could perhaps be restored. Even if what happened at Babel could not be

---

[14] For the difficulties of the ancients in applying the concept of community beyond the *polis*, see Thomas Pangle, 'Justice Among Nations in Platonic and Aristotelian Political Philosophy', *American Journal of Political Science*, vol. 42, no. 2, 1998, pp. 377–97.

[15] Dante Alighieri, *Monarchy* (Cambridge: Cambridge University Press, 1996), I.ii, p. 4.

[16] Augustine, *The City of God Against the Pagans* (Cambridge: Cambridge University Press, 1998), XIX, 7.

undone, it might perhaps be possible to reverse some of its unwanted consequences, or so it was believed.[17]

From this diagnosis an important hypothesis followed which was crucial to the way the problem of political order was understood before claims to territorial sovereignty had begun to pose serious challenges to both imperial and papal authority. As Ullmann has remarked, 'It was the threat of fragmentation inherent in the thesis of national sovereignty [sic] which prompted him to use the Thomist framework constructively to prevent a disintegration otherwise unavoidable and to indicate how unity embracing all men can be achieved, and not merely the unity of Christians.'[18] So rather than simply assuming that authority in some form – whether spiritual or temporal – was a necessary condition of political order, some authors held that the existence of community was a *sufficient* condition of concord. While our sinful nature cannot be redeemed in this world, discord might be overcome by identifying what men share in common beyond the obvious diversity of languages and customs. Much attention was devoted to the search for the sources of such concord and the civic virtues necessary to collective salvation.[19]

To Dante, reason and logic seemed to provide precisely what was needed to restore this communicative bond. Following Aristotle, Dante establishes the truth of his propositions by recourse to first principles, 'since every truth which is not itself a first principle must be demonstrated with reference to the truth of some first principle'.[20] Thus, the legitimacy of any temporal authority must be measured against the purpose of man, and in relation to human society as a whole. The purpose of that human society is defined with reference to the potential of the whole of mankind, its intellectual potentiality,

---

[17] See Umberto Eco, *The Search for the Perfect Language* (Oxford: Blackwell, 1995), pp. 7–24.
[18] Walter Ullmann, 'Dante's "*Monarchia*" as an Illustration of a Politico-Religious "*Renovatio*"', in Walter Ullmann, *Scholarship and Politics in the Middle Ages* (London: Variorum, 1978), pp. 101–13, at p. 105.
[19] For an account, see Ernst Kantorowicz, 'Pro Patria Mori in Medieval Political Thought', *American Historical Review*, vol. 56, no. 3, 1951, pp. 472–92. See also Teresa Rupp, 'Damnation, Individual and Community in Remigio dei Girolami's *De Bono Communi*', *History of Political Thought*, vol. 21, no. 2, 2000, pp. 217–25.
[20] Dante, *Monarchy*, I.i, p. 4.

and 'since that potentiality cannot be fully actualized all at once in any one individual ... there must needs be a vast number of individual people in the human race, through whom the whole of this potentiality can be actualized'.[21] According to Dante, 'the activity proper to mankind considered as a whole is constantly to actualize the full intellectual potential of humanity, primarily through thought and secondarily through action'.[22]

In order to attain this end, universal peace is necessary, and in order to attain such peace, a universal monarchy – or empire – is necessary. Since we find but one ruler in most human communities, the same rule ought to apply to the universal community of all mankind as well. As Dante argues, 'mankind is most a unity when it is drawn together to form a single entity, and this can only come about when it is ruled as one whole by one ruler'.[23] Mankind can only be genuinely free when it is under the rule of a monarch, for then 'it exists for its own sake and not for the sake of something else'.[24] Allowing for variations in customs and climate, mankind is to be ruled by the universal monarch 'in those matters which are common to all men and of relevance to all, and is to be guided towards peace by a common law'.[25] All lesser communities such as cities and kingdoms are not only part of the universal empire of all mankind, but do also ultimately owe their status as communities to this membership, much in the same way as the individual substance could be said to derive its existence from the universal category within which it is included.[26]

All of this took a little help from Virgil. At this point in time, memories of ancient Rome maintained a strong hold on political imagination, but so also did Augustine's refutation of the claim that the Roman Empire had been founded on justice rather than on force.[27] Thus, in the *Second*

---

[21] Dante, *Monarchy*, I.iii, p. 6–7. [22] Dante, *Monarchy*, I.iv, p. 8.
[23] Dante, *Monarchy*, I.viii, p. 13. [24] Dante, *Monarchy*, I.xii, p. 21.
[25] Dante, *Monarchy*, I.xiv, p. 25.
[26] Ullmann, 'Dante's "*Monarchia*"', p. 108.
[27] Nicolai Rubinstein, 'The Beginnings of Political Thought in Florence. A Study in Medieval Historiography', *Journal of the Warburg and Courtauld Institutes*, vol. 5, 1942, pp. 198–227, at pp. 217–18; see also D'Entrèves, *Dante as a Political Thinker*, pp. 28–30. For the refutation of Roman claims to legitimate empire, see Augustine, *City of God*, book XIX, ch. 21. For the context of this idea, see J. A. Watt, 'The Theory of Papal Monarchy in the Thirteenth Century: The Contribution of the Canonists', *Traditio*, vol. 20, 1964, pp. 179–318.

Book, Dante begins by justifying the view that the Roman people had indeed established their dominion over other peoples by right rather than might, and that their conquests were in accordance with divine will. These conquests also testify to the superior virtue of the Roman people, as they were ordained to rule over all other peoples by nature, while having the public good as their goal. Therefore 'the Roman people subjecting the world to its rule did so in accordance with right, and as a consequence took upon itself the dignity of empire by right'.[28] Dante thereby established the proposition that the legitimacy of imperial authority cannot derive from an empire being forcefully imposed upon foreign peoples, but rather from its inherently just character and its voluntary acceptance by those peoples.

Having demonstrated the legitimacy of the Roman Empire, Dante proceeds to discuss the possible sources of such legitimate authority in the present. Thus, in the *Third Book*, Dante proceeds to refute claims to the effect that temporal authority had been conferred on the emperor by the pope, or otherwise had been derived from that source. The claims based on the Donation of Constantine are invalid because 'Constantine was not in a position to give away the privileges of empire, nor was the church in a position to accept them.' This was so 'since to divide the empire would be to destroy it – for empire consists precisely in the unity of universal monarchy – it is clear that whoever embodies imperial authority is not allowed to divide the empire ... from this it is clear that the emperor ... cannot change it, because he derives from it the fact that he is what he is'.[29] So we must conclude that the church could not have accepted this donation as a possession; nor could Constantine have given it as an irrevocable gift.[30] Dante then goes on to demolish the claim that the authority of the emperor derives from that of the pope: since the 'pope must not be referred to any other man, it remains that the emperor along with all other men must be referred to him'.[31] But this is to conflate accident with substance, since what makes the pope a pope and the emperor an emperor is nothing but a set of social relationships:

If therefore papal and imperial office, being relationships of authority, are to be referred to the principle of authority, from which they derive their

---

[28] Dante, *Monarchy*, II.v, p. 44.   [29] Dante, *Monarchy*, III.x, pp. 81–2.
[30] Dante, *Monarchy*, III.x, p. 83.   [31] Dante, *Monarchy*, III.xii, p. 84.

differentiating characteristics, then pope and emperor will be referable to some entity in which it is possible to discern that principle of authority without the other differentiating characteristics. And this will either be God himself, in whom all principles form an absolute unity, or else some entity lower than God, in which the principle of authority, derived from the absolute principle and differentiating itself from it, becomes distinctive and individual.[32]

From this Dante concludes that imperial authority derives *directly* from God and from no other source. But in order to understand this, Dante writes, 'it must be borne in mind that man alone among created beings is the link between corruptible and incorruptible things … if he is considered in terms of each of his essential constituent parts, that is soul and body, man is corruptible; if he is considered only in terms of one, his soul, he is incorruptible'.[33] It is for this reason that man needs to be subject to two different kinds of authority, 'the supreme Pontiff, to lead mankind to eternal life in conformity with revealed truth, and the emperor, to guide mankind to temporal happiness with the teachings of philosophy'.[34] With those words we appear to have come full circle, since the authority of both pope and emperor cannot only be measured by the standards of heaven, but also by the earthly standards of man, since man himself is exactly that lower entity 'in which the principle of authority, derived from the absolute principle and differentiating itself from it, becomes distinctive and individual'.[35] So, in the final analysis, universal empire seems as necessary to the unity of humanity as the unity of humanity seems essential to the legitimacy of that empire.[36]

As Kantorowicz has remarked on this solution, 'Dante thus transferred the age-old struggle about the superiority of either pope or emperor to a plane differing from customary argumentations when

---

[32] Dante, *Monarchy*, III.xii, p. 86.   [33] Dante, *Monarchy*, III.xvi, p. 91.
[34] Dante, *Monarchy*, III.xvi, p. 92.
[35] Ernst Kantorowicz, *The King's Two Bodies. A Study in Medieval Political Theology* (Princeton, NJ: Princeton University Press, 1957), p. 458.
[36] For a different interpretation that locates Dante's vision within the conceptual boundaries of the *polis*, see Peter Armour, 'Dante and Popular Sovereignty', in John Woodhouse, ed., *Dante and Governance* (Oxford: Clarendon Press, 1997), pp. 27–45.

he referred both powers to their absolute standards, those of *deitas* and *humanitas*.'[37] And we might as well add that it was the latter concept that furnished the ground for judging the legitimacy of the temporal order in terms that are themselves temporal. If we focus exclusively on the implicit conception of authority, the idea of a universal empire looks very unrealistic when situated in the context of contemporary political theology. But if we focus on the conception of community it presupposes, the idea of a universal empire looks more like a regulative idea with which to judge the division of authority between the two swords.[38] Ultimately, the solution which Dante proposes does not rely on any divinely instituted authority – whether of pope or emperor – but rather on the potentiality of universal human community, which can sustain such authority only by realizing the true potentials of man. The underlying message is simple: man can only become lord over himself by coming into himself.

But how should we understand this appeal to potentiality? As Agamben has remarked, 'There is in effect something that humans are and have to be, but this something is not an essence nor properly a thing: It is the simple fact of one's own existence as possibility or potentiality.'[39] Following this suggestion makes it possible to uncover another layer of meaning in Dante's argument: since 'the highest potentiality of mankind is his intellectual potential or faculty', the ultimate foundation of the universal community of mankind is the intellectual oneness or unity of the human race.[40] This view of the human intellect deserves some elaboration, since it has been neglected by most students of Dante's political thought.[41] Indeed, much of what Dante

---

[37] Kantorowicz, *The King's Two Bodies*, p. 460.

[38] For this point, see E. L. Fortin, *Dissidence et philosophie au moyen âge. Dante et ses antécédents* (Paris: Vrin, 1981), pp. 126–7.

[39] Giorgio Agamben, *The Coming Community* (Minneapolis: University of Minnesota Press, 1993), p. 43. Dante, *Monarchy*, II.x, p. 59; III.ii, p. 64. See also Giorgio Agamben, 'Tradition of the Immemorial', in *Potentialities. Collected Essays in Philosophy* (Stanford, CA: Stanford University Press, 1999), pp. 104–15, at p. 109.

[40] Dante, *Monarchy*, I.iii, p. 7.

[41] Strangely so, since this conception was one reason why Pope John XXII had copies of the *Monarchia* burned in Bologna in 1329. See Larry Peterman, 'Introduction to Dante's *Monarchia*', *Interpretation*, vol. 3, 1973, pp. 174–5. A notable exception is Donna Mancusi-Ungaro, *Dante*

says about human community is evidence of the fact that political and ontological problems were inseparable in medieval theology.[42]

During the thirteenth century, the view that the human intellect constituted one separate substance common to all men was identified with Aristotelian philosophy.[43] Yet some of the implications of this view were very disturbing to the church. Insofar as we all participate in the unity of this common intellect, we also participate in its eternity. And if this is the case, it also implies that the human species as a whole enjoys immortality, rather than its individual members. The idea of one single intellect drawing humanity together into one single immaterial unity not only disregarded distinctions of faith, but also implied that it was hard to hold individuals responsible for their own salvation, and thus for the life of their own souls. If – thanks to such species-wide immortality – salvation is a collective enterprise, why should one bother to lead a virtuous life at all? The idea of the intellect as a separate substance common to all men offered an easy way to escape the pressures exerted by the ecclesiastical authorities upon the individual soul: thus William of Tocco could report on one very clever French soldier who was unwilling to atone for his sins, because 'if the soul of the blessed Peter is saved, I shall also be saved; for if we know by one intellect, we shall share the same destiny'.[44]

Hence, many scholastics had strong reasons to want to refute the idea that there is one and the same intellect for all human beings, an intellect in which individuals merely partake. Indeed, this idea had proved

    and the Empire (New York: Peter Lang, 1987), pp. 127–79. Other authors have denied that the idea of a separate intellect is of any importance – see Étienne Gilson, *Dante et la philosophie* (Paris: Vrin, 1953) – or neglected it – see Patrick Boyde, *Perception and Passion in Dante's Comedy* (Cambridge: Cambridge University Press, 1993), pp. 173–92.

[42] For the opinion that there were no such connections, see Charles Zuckerman, 'The Relationship Between Theories of Universals to Theories of Church Government in the Middle Ages: A Critique of Previous Views', *Journal of the History of Ideas*, vol. 36, no. 4, 1975, pp. 579–94.

[43] Beatrice H. Zedler, 'Introduction', in Thomas Aquinas, *On the Unity of the Intellect Against the Averroists*, ed. Beatrice H. Zedler (Milwaukee, WI: Marquette University Press, 1968), pp. 1–19.

[44] Quoted in Paul A. Canto, 'The Uncanonical Dante: The Divine Comedy and Islamic Philosophy', *Philosophy and Literature*, vol. 20, no. 1, 1996, pp. 138–53, at p. 146.

so challenging to medieval orthodoxy that Aquinas devoted an entire *opusculum* to its refutation. As he states, 'take away from men the diversity of intellect ... and it follows that nothing of the souls of men would remain after death except a unique intellectual substance, with the result that reward and punishment and their difference disappear'.[45] Consequently, on 10 December 1270, the bishop of Paris ordered the excommunication of those responsible for propagating this idea.[46]

But what, more exactly, were ecclesiastical authorities opposing? Originally, the doctrine of *monopsychism* had grown out of efforts to explain how different human beings could attain knowledge of the same universal truths independently of each other, a problem which had been a perennial source of controversy at least since Plato's *Meno*. When the doctrine of monopsychism now reappeared in medieval philosophy, it was largely thanks to Averroës, and his effort to make sense of some of the more obscure remarks on the nature of the human soul that we find in Book III of Aristotle's *De anima*. In his *Long Commentary on the De Anima of Aristotle*, Averroës sets out to account for the science of the soul, and tries to explain why this science must supply the key principles of all other sciences, including those of metaphysics.[47] By turning *De anima* into the centrepiece of Aristotelian philosophy, he also submitted himself to a peculiar logical constraint according to which everything pertaining to the human mind had to be defined as being completely free of matter. The human intellect must be thought of as pure and unpolluted by any material substance, and so every inferential connection with the concept of matter had to be severed conclusively. The science of the soul, writes Averroës, 'is generally helpful and enables the acquisition of confirmation regarding first principles, since from this science

---

[45] Thomas Aquinas, *On There Being Only One Intellect*, in Ralph McInerny, *Aquinas Against the Averroists* (West Lafayette, IN: Purdue University Press, 1993), pp. 17–145, at p. 19.

[46] Ralph McInerny, 'Introduction', in McInerny, *Aquinas Against the Averroists*, pp. 1–15.

[47] Similar views are also found in his comments on the *Metaphysics*. See Charles Genequand, *Ibn Rushd's Metaphysics. A Translation with Introduction of Ibn Rushd's Commentary on Aristotle's Metaphysics, Book Lam* (Leiden: E. J. Brill, 1986), pp. 49–53. For an overview, see Herbert A. Davidson, *Alfarabi, Avicenna, and Averroes on Intellect* (Oxford: Oxford University Press, 1992).

we acquire knowledge of the first causes of propositions'.[48] Among the ideas thought to be useful in this respect we find the notion of a separate *possible intellect*, since this idea provides a key to understanding certain powers and functions peculiar to the human condition. The possible intellect, writes Averroës, 'is defined as that which is in potency all the intentions of universal material forms and is not any of the beings in fact before it thinks any of them'.[49] That is to say, the existence of his separate intellect explains the relative uniformity in human cognition when it comes to certain kinds of truths, since 'the need for an immaterial reception of universal forms in knowing requires that what receives them be a separate intellect and yet be something which is capable of reception'.[50]

What Averroës seems to mean is that the existence of such a separate intellectual substance is necessary if we want to account for the fact that human beings tend to perceive similar things in similar ways and arrive at similar conclusions from similar premises, since 'These intelligibles in act in the separate Material Intellect are the referents for the notions expressed by us in universal propositions of science.'[51] If there were many intellects instead of just one, the propositions formed by science would lack a common referent, since to each individual intellect would be matched distinct objects of knowledge. So in order to grasp what is universal there must be a universal intellect which is ontologically separate from the individual members of the human species, and therefore also ultimately constitutive of the cognitive capacity of that species. The introduction of this concept not only furnished an explanation of the striking congruence of human reason, but also a way of making sense of the human species as being something categorically distinct from its individual parts, a *humana civilitas* in Dante's terminology.

---

[48] Averroës, *Long Commentary on the De Anima of Aristotle*, quoted in Richard C. Taylor, 'Averroes on Psychology and the Principles of Metaphysics', *Journal of the History of Philosophy*, vol. 36, no. 4, 1998, pp. 507–23, at p. 514.
[49] Taylor, 'Averroes on Psychology and the Principles of Metaphysics', p. 514.
[50] Taylor, 'Averroes on Psychology and the Principles of Metaphysics', p. 515.
[51] Taylor, 'Averroes on Psychology and the Principles of Metaphysics', p. 515.

According to Mancusi-Ungaro, 'the possible intellect is one for all men and … a multitude of generations of human beings will enable the whole of mankind to acquire universal knowledge'.[52] So if the possible intellect is understood as a wholly separate entity, then individual human beings are rational only by virtue of sharing in this separate substance, yet without ever becoming identical with it. Provided that we accept the idea of such a possible intellect, the unity of humanity ultimately resides in the necessity of knowing itself as such a unity in order to be able to know anything at all, since in order for an object to be intelligible, it must exist in an intellect. And in order for the intellect to exist, it has to be thought of as separate from those who plug into it. Yet due to the peculiar character of this possible intellect, there is a reflexive loop within which our knowledge is conditioned by our knowing ourselves as participants in a knowing substance: the intellect and the intelligible turn out to be identical within this scheme. According to Chak Tornay, the historical significance of this doctrine was that 'it elevated the human power of thought from its isolated state of particularity to the superindividual level, where the mind becomes an absolute unity, universal, impersonal and ontologically objective in character'.[53] Thus, the very *humanitas* envisaged by Dante is a condition of possible knowledge that we must accept on the same grounds as we accept the law of non-contradiction: without *humanitas*, there can be no *logos*, Dante seems to imply.[54]

Let us finally note how Dante makes use of the Aristotelian distinction between actuality and potentiality when justifying his claim that a universal monarchy is essential to the well-being of this *humanitas*. Quoting the *Metaphysics*, Dante holds that 'The movement from potentiality to actuality comes about by means of something which is already actual.'[55] As we have seen above, since singular authority is justified with reference to a singular humanity as well as conversely, the gradual attainment of reason by humanity will in the end make it identical with the universal monarch himself – its actuality. Hence, in the final analysis, the sovereignty of the emperor is but an allegorical

---

[52] Mancusi-Ungaro, *Dante and the Empire*, p. 150.
[53] Stephen Chak Tornay, 'Averroes' Doctrine of the Mind', *Philosophical Review*, vol. 52, no. 3, 1943, pp. 270–88, at p. 286.
[54] See Fortin, *Dissidence et philosophie*, pp. 33–49, 95–127.
[55] Dante, *Monarchy*, I:xiii, p. 22.

expression of the fundamental unity of humanity. We are again trapped in the mirrors of medieval reflexivity: humanity appears to be its own first principle, sovereign over itself only by virtue of first having become fully identical with itself.

As we have seen in this section, the way in which Dante understands universal community derives neither from the view that this community consists of fellow descendants of Adam, nor from the view that such a community is restricted to the faithful. In the context of late medieval theology, Dante was thus a dissident insofar as he opposed the dominant views of his age.[56] When situated in this context, the notion of a universal human community we encounter in *Monarchia* addresses not the irreversible outcome of the Fall – the corruption of human nature – but rather the lack of community resulting from the confusion of tongues. Dante's response to this problem is to turn humanity into a conveyor of a universal *logos*, and thus also into a condition of possible knowledge.[57] But while Dante could claim to have solved the problem of discord with reference to purely human standards, this solution also amounted to a *divinization* of humanity that was hard to reconcile with central tenets of medieval Christianity. Such reconciliation could only be achieved after the contestable origins of this doctrine had been forgotten, and the idea of humanity successfully merged with the image of Christ.[58] But how did this vision of world community fit with the basic assumptions of medieval cosmology?

II

The universal community envisaged by Dante is unlimited in its scope, insofar as it encompasses mankind as a whole irrespective of any social and religious differences between groups of men. But it is nevertheless subject to a certain geographical limitation, since the

---

[56] Fortin, *Dissidence et philosophie*, pp. 129–63.
[57] Eco, *Search for the Perfect Language*, pp. 25–52.
[58] Ernst Cassirer, *The Individual and the Cosmos in the Renaissance* (Philadelphia: University of Pennsylvania Press, 1972), pp. 38, 40, 90, 98, 101, 109; Erwin Panofsky, *Studies in Iconology. Humanistic Themes in the Art of the Renaissance* (New York: Harper and Row, 1962), pp. 129–69.

jurisdiction of the universal monarch is bounded by the ocean.[59] But why did Dante regard the ocean as a limit, and what was lurking beyond that limit?

In order to answer these questions, we must take a detour into late medieval cosmology and geography. Doing this, we are bound to discover that the world Dante inhabited was very different from ours, and that his vision of community was strongly conditioned by the cosmological assumptions of his time. Like most of his contemporaries, he accepted 'the divinely created organization of the Universe as a prototype of the first principles which govern the construction of human communities'.[60] Consequently, when these principles are questioned during the late fifteenth century, and then gradually replaced by a heliocentric worldview during the following century, Dante's vision of community becomes hard to sustain.

Medieval cosmology was based on a variety of sources, most of which distinguished between a celestial and a terrestrial region. While the former embraced everything from the moon to the limits of the universe, the latter included everything below the moon to the centre of the earth.[61] In this section and the next, I shall focus mainly on the latter, and only to the extent that it is relevant for understanding how the problem of world community changed in response to changing ideas about the structure of the terrestrial region.

Let us start with some of the main assumptions about the terrestrial region. According to Genesis 1:9, there was a division between the zones reserved for earth and water respectively. These zones were mutually exclusive, so where there was water, there could be no earth, and conversely. So certainly, from a biblical perspective, the ocean was indeed a limit, since its beginning literally marked the end of the known and inhabitable world. The Latin and Greek terms most frequently used to describe this world were *orbis terrarum* or *oikoumene*. The former referred to the three interconnected continents – Europe, Asia, and Africa – which were surrounded by an impenetrable ocean beyond which life was thought to be unlikely or

---

[59] Dante, *Monarchy*, I.xi, p. 18.
[60] Gierke, *Political Theories of the Middle Age*, p. 8.
[61] See Edward Grant, *Planets, Stars, and Orbs. The Medieval Cosmos, 1200–1687* (Cambridge: Cambridge University Press, 1994), pp. 11–45.

even impossible. At the centre of the *orbis terrarum* was Jerusalem, the Holy City. Ideally, the borders of the *orbis terrarum* ought to coincide with those of the *oikoumene*: even though primarily a geographical concept, the *oikoumene*, 'in its most essential meaning, can be defined as a region made coherent by the intercommunication of its inhabitants, such that ... no tribe or race is completely cut off from the people beyond it'.[62] But beyond the *oikoumene* no human life was to be found. As Cosgrove has noted, 'despite constituting different nations – some yet to be redeemed – the population of the *oikoumene* constituted *humanitas*'.[63] Both concepts thus restricted the habitat of humanity to the northern hemisphere, since the southern hemisphere consisted of a torrid zone, at the end of which the quasi-mythological Antipodes were to be found.[64] The question of whether the latter really existed and were inhabited, and if inhabited, whether by men or by monstrous races, was the subject of considerable debate during the Middle Ages.[65]

In this context it has been argued that the affirmation of a common human descent simply required that the existence of the Antipodes should be denied, or that the existence of monsters was required in order to distinguish humanity from its others.[66] This problem was further complicated by the fact that it was formulated with reference to pre-Newtonian notions of up and down. Given these notions, belief in life at the Antipodes was refutable with recourse

---

[62] James S. Romm, *The Edges of the Earth in Ancient Thought. Geography, Exploration, and Fiction* (Princeton, NJ: Princeton University Press, 1992), p. 37; Denis Cosgrove, *Apollo's Eye A Cartographic Genealogy of the Earth in the Western Imagination* (Baltimore, MD: Johns Hopkins University Press, 2001), pp. 41–53.

[63] Cosgrove, *Apollo's Eye*, pp. 24, 63.

[64] Thomas Goldstein, 'Geography in Fifteenth-Century Florence', in John Parker, ed., *Merchants and Scholars. Essays in the History of Exploration and Trade* (Minneapolis: University of Minnesota Press, 1965), pp. 11–32. See also E. H. Bunbury, *A History of Ancient Geography*, vol. II (New York: Dover, 1959), pp. 546ff.

[65] See, for example, Augustine, *City of God*, XVI: 8–9. For an account, see John Block Friedman, *The Monstrous Races in Medieval Art and Thought* (Cambridge, MA: Harvard University Press, 1981), pp. 37–58.

[66] Valerie I. J. Flint, 'Monsters and the Antipodes in the Early Middle Ages and Enlightenment', *Viator*, vol. 15, 1984, pp. 65–80.

to a simple *reductio*, since whether inhabited by men or monsters, this life must be hard indeed, and for physical reasons alone. Is there anyone silly enough, asked Lactantius, 'to believe that there are men whose feet are higher than their heads? Or that things which lie on earth with us hang downwards with them, and trees and fruits grow the wrong way up, and rain and snow and hail fall upwards onto the ground?'[67]

These and other scary geographical assumptions ensured that the medieval traveller stayed safely within the limits of the *orbis terrarum*. They were also widely represented or implied in medieval guidebooks and travelogues. Many of these dealt with specific places of great symbolic importance to the devout Christian, such as Jerusalem, Rome and Santiago de Compostela. They offered advice on how to get to those places, as well as what to see and do once there. Books like *Mirabilia urbis Romae* (c. 1143), *Libellelus de locis sanctis* (c. 1172) and, above all, *Codex Calixtinus* (1140/50), served as authoritative sources of information for many travellers during the Middle Ages.[68] These books reveal a way of travelling peculiar to this period which also reflects the geographical assumptions above, as well as the possibilities and limitations posed for human intercourse in general.

The paradigmatic way of travelling during this period is by way of *pilgrimage*. As we might recall from Augustine, pilgrimage contributes to the formation of the community of all mankind: 'The heavenly city, while on its earthly pilgrimage, calls forth its citizens from every nation and every tongue. It assembles a band of pilgrims, not caring about any diversity in customs, laws and institutions whereby they severally make provisions for the achievement and maintenance of earthly peace.'[69] But apart from being instrumental in the formation of a universal community, what distinguishes pilgrimage from other ways of travelling is the expected outcome of the travelling experience itself. Typically, the pilgrim sets out along a *known* route that will

---

[67] Lactantius, *Divine institutiones*, quoted in Flint, 'Monsters and the Antipodes', p. 68.
[68] Bendict of St Peters, *The Marvels of Rome* (New York: Italica Press, 1986); Theoderich of Würzburg, *Guide to the Holy Land* (New York, Italica Press, 1986); William Melczer, ed., *The Pilgrim's Guide to Santiago de Compostela* (New York: Italica Press, 1993).
[69] Augustine, *City of God*, XIX, 17.

take him from one place to another and back, the destination also being known in advance, and being chosen because of its symbolic significance and for the rewards thought to ensue from having been to such a place.[70] These expected rewards normally involved some kind of spiritual fulfilment: some pilgrims went to Santiago in order to pray; others went there in order to ask for forgiveness of their sins. Still others were sent there by different authorities for punishment and self-purification.[71] But for the majority of pilgrims to Santiago, 'those six to nine months spent on the road in strange lands and among strange people mean the only occasion to cast a glimpse upon broader existence, to measure for once the world and its wonders'.[72]

Medieval guidebooks also reflect the relationship between different peoples at this point in time. As Reynolds has observed, while medieval people thought of themselves as divided into distinct and aboriginal peoples, 'the belief in separate peoples was itself a shared belief, and not one which seems to have been induced by any obvious differences between the social and political arrangements of the various peoples'.[73] Hence the *Codex Calixtinus* starts by describing the different routes leading to Santiago and the towns encountered along these routes, along with observations concerning the kinds of people one is likely to encounter. For example, we learn that the Navarrese are 'debauched, perverse, perfidious, disloyal, and corrupt, libidinous, drunkard, given to all kinds of violence, ferocious and savage, impudent and false, impious and uncouth, cruel and quarrelsome', and that they, unsurprisingly, 'make use of animals for incestuous [*sic*!] fornication'.[74] After a happy escape out of their territory, the pilgrim's attention is now directed to the remains of St Giles, as well

---

[70] For an overview, see Norbert Ohler, *The Medieval Traveller* (Woodbridge: Boydell Press, 1989); also Lionel Casson, *Travel in the Ancient World* (Baltimore, MD: Johns Hopkins University Press, 1994). For a brilliant analysis of different paradigms of travelling, see Jas Elsner and Joan-Pau Rubiés, 'Introduction', in Jas Elsner and Joan-Pau Rubiés, eds., *Voyages and Visions. Towards a Cultural History of Travel* (London: Reaktion Books, 1999), pp. 1–56.
[71] Melczer, 'Introduction', in *The Pilgrim's Guide to Santiago de Compostela*, pp. 40–1.
[72] Melczer, 'Introduction', p. 42.
[73] Reynolds, *Kingdoms and Communities in Western Europe*, p. 8.
[74] Melczer, *The Pilgrim's Guide*, pp. 94–5.

as to the unsuccessful attempt to 'snatch away quite fraudulently the venerable arm of the blessed confessor … towards far-away shores'.[75] Safe in Santiago, we are given a detailed account of the churches and shrines to be found there, as well as practical information pertaining to the reception of pilgrims in the town.

But pilgrimage also offered a way of overcoming mutual prejudice in the name of a universal community. Among the attractions that made many pilgrims choose Santiago rather than Rome as their destination of choice were the many miracles associated with St James, the only apostle buried west of Rome. Not only did St James make a regular appearance in miraculous visions, but the town of Santiago de Compostela had the highest number of miracles reported during the Middle Ages. As most of these miracles involved pilgrims – as spectators as well as beneficiaries – St James became the pilgrim saint par excellence, and an entire cult evolved around his name and life. An interesting source in this respect is the sermon *Veneranda dies*, composed by Pope Calixtus in his honour. Written with the aim of overcoming discord between pilgrims from different parts of the *orbis terrarum*, we learn that 'Many belittle what they do not understand; the French belittle the Germans, and the Romans belittle the Greeks, because they do not understand the other's language.'[76] Consequently, by virtue of being open to anyone irrespective of their origin – including the 'impious Navarrese' – the cult of St James provided a symbolic community where these differences and prejudices could be downplayed, since 'All languages, tribes, and nations go to him in troops and phalanxes, fulfilling their vows to God with thanksgiving and bearing tributes of praise.'[77] While this cult was based on the miraculous powers associated with St James, the perception that this saint was able to perform miracles became, through its gradual dissemination throughout Europe, constitutive of an entire community of

---

[75] Melczer, *The Pilgrim's Guide*, p. 102.
[76] *Introductory Letter of Pope Calixtus*, in Thomas F. Coffey, Linda Kay Davidson and Maryjane Dunn, *The Miracles of Saint James. Translations from the Liber Sancti Jacobi* (New York: Italica Press, 1996), pp. 3–7, at p. 5.
[77] *The Sermon of the Blessed Pope Calixtus for the Solemn Feast of the Choosing and Translation of Saint James the Apostle, which is Celebrated on the Third Calends of January*, in Coffey et al., *The Miracles of Saint James*, pp. 8–56, at p. 18.

pilgrims. As such, it represented a way of overcoming human discord that was fully consonant with the Augustinian diagnosis of its linguistic causes. Thanks to the vast numbers of people involved, and to the boundless nature of the activity of pilgrimage itself, this and other cults melted together into a society of its own, with its own culture and its own legislation.[78]

An even more intriguing example of medieval pilgrimage is provided by a travelogue entitled *The Itinerary of Benjamin de Tudela* (1159). Since Jews were considered infidels and as such subjected to legal restrictions and discriminating practices during the Middle Ages, they often found reason to relocate in response to persecution or pressures to convert to Christianity.[79] But if we follow in Benjamin's footsteps, we are bound to discover that his itinerary closely matches the view of the world described by Christian geographers. As Benjamin wanders about, he stays safely within the limits of *orbis terrarum*, while bravely exploring its inhospitable and dangerous fringes. His journey is also one of pilgrimage, but rather than looking for places to pray, he is looking for places where his expatriated Jewish brethren can find refuge from persecution by Christians. Within this medieval world into which Benjamin brings us, there is no spatial congruence between political authorities and communities, a fact which greatly facilitates his endeavour: while Benjamin carefully attends to and discusses the different forms of political life he encounters in different places, he implies that the cultural and religious continuity of the Jewish people would be best served by maintaining as much geographical mobility as possible within the *orbis terrarum*.[80]

The world encountered in medieval travelogues and guidebooks is thus limited by the same geographical parameters which enable the experience of community within the *oikoumene* thus defined. But since there is literally nothing to be found outside the limits of

---

[78] Melczer, 'Introduction', pp. 35–63.
[79] See, for example, James Muldoon, *Popes, Lawyers, and Infidels. The Church and the Non-Christian World 1250–1550* (Liverpool: Liverpool University Press, 1979), pp. 23–7, 30–2, 50–2.
[80] *The Itinerary of Benjamin de Tudela. Travels in the Middle Ages* (Malibu, CA: Joseph Simon/Pangloss Press, 1983). For other sources on the concept of community within the Jewish tradition, see Michael Walzer, ed., *The Jewish Political Tradition*, vol. II: *Membership* (New Haven, CT: Yale University Press, 2003).

the known world, whatever is told that cannot be located within the *orbis terrarum* is either false, or simply too absurd to be taken seriously. Yet within these geographical limits, these books convey the impression of a boundless world that is traversed by all sorts of people for a variety of noble and not-so-noble purposes, travelling being a normal rather than an exceptional activity in medieval European society. And, interestingly, the kind of fulfilment thought to ensue from pilgrimage is not unlike that later promised to accrue from the membership of nations.

III

But this worldview was soon to be replaced, and so were the conception of community and the motives for travelling. As Headley has argued:

The awareness of the accumulated new lands and peoples on a transformed and enlarged terraqueous globe reinforces the cognitive impact of the accomplishment whereby the formerly preconceived yet formidable barriers preventing access to other continents and peoples have been dissolved by a rare combination of reason and experience. The machine of discovery … had not only produced an immense perceptual challenge and epistemological problem but also the realization of an almost totally accessible and inhabitable global arena in which to contend with this problem.[81]

But, as I intend to show in this section, the cosmological changes that effectively turned the world into *one* place conditioned the emergence of the new conceptions of mankind that emerged largely simultaneously. Gradually, the notion of a relatively uniform mankind is replaced by assumptions about human diversity, and is accompanied by attempts to understand this diversity as a consequence of the prior dispersion of the human species into different corners of the earth.[82]

---

[81] John M. Headley, 'The Sixteenth-Century Venetian Celebration of the Earth's Total Habitability: The Issue of the Fully Habitable World for Renaissance Europe', *Journal of World History*, vol. 8, no. 1, 1997, pp. 1–27, at p. 24.

[82] For a different version of this argument, see Cosgrove, *Apollo's Eye*, pp. 1–28.

The translation of Aristotle's *De caelo* stimulated new cosmological speculations among scholars. By the late thirteenth century, Aristotelian cosmology and its geographical implications had become integrated within Christian doctrine.[83] According to this theory, the earth was fixed at the centre of the sublunary sphere, and was composed of the four elements that made up all matter in this region of the universe. Reflecting their different densities, the four elements were thus neatly arranged in distinct and concentric spheres. In the absence of external disturbances, these elements could be expected to settle into four stable concentric spheres, with the element earth naturally at the geometric centre of the globe.[84] But this theory could not explain why not all land was covered with water, and thus turned any observation to the contrary into an anomaly. Provided that the Aristotelian laws of motion were correct, and the movements of the heavenly bodies sufficiently regular, the world should in fact be completely submerged in water. Even more puzzling was the question of why dry land was found where it was found, and what the existence of a continuous landmass in turn implied for the problems of habitability and navigation.[85] Curiously, Dante was among those who tried to solve this problem. In his *Divine Comedy*, he had described the earth and its lower regions largely in terms consonant with the Aristotelian worldview. But later, in his *Questio de aqua et terra* (1320), he proposed that the cause of the protrusion of land above water was the influence of the stars, which attracted land upwards, and by vapours being generated in the bowels of the earth.[86]

---

[83] Grant, *Planets, Stars, and Orbs*, pp. 50–6; Thomas S. Kuhn, *The Copernican Revolution: Planetary Astronomy in the Development of Western Thought* (Cambridge, MA: Harvard University Press, 1957), p. 108; Cosgrove, *Apollo's Eye*, pp. 36–8.

[84] Grant, *Planets, Stars, and Orbs*, pp. 630–5; Kuhn, *Copernican Revolution*, pp. 81–2; Cosgrove, *Apollo's Eye*, pp. 72–8.

[85] Thomas Goldstein, 'The Renaissance Concept of the Earth and its Influence upon Copernicus', *Terrae Incognitae*, vol. 4, 1972, pp. 19–51.

[86] Dante Alighieri, *A Question of the Water and of the Land*, trans. C. H. Bromby (London: David Nutt, 1897), p. 54. The authenticity of this manuscript has been disputed. See Bruno Nardi, *La caduta di lucifero e l'autenticità della 'Quaestio de aqua et terra'* (Turin: Società Editrice Internazionale, 1958); John Freccero, 'Satan's Fall and the *Quaestio de aqua et terra*', *Italica*, vol. 38, 1961, pp. 99–115.

But this problem could not be satisfactorily resolved within an Aristotelian framework, since the assumption that earth and water were divided into two distinct spheres was intimately connected to the idea that the centre of the terrestrial globe coincided with the centre of the universe. This implied that any revision of astronomical beliefs about the place of the earth within the universe would necessitate a revision of geographical assumptions about the composition of the planetary surface, as well as conversely.[87] And since assumptions about the planetary surface of the latter were intimately connected with assumptions about the essential unity of mankind and the biblical causes of its geographical dispersion, any revision of this framework of cosmological beliefs would also call for a corresponding redefinition of human community and its place within the cosmological framework.[88] Above all, changes in the cosmological outlook during the fifteenth century brought a renewed faith in the capacity of mankind to shape its own destiny independently of divine intervention.[89]

The works of Nicholas of Cusa provide us with a nice example of how intimate the connection between cosmology and community was during the Renaissance. Having eroded the basis of the distinction between the celestial and the terrestrial spheres, Nicholas first proposed a cosmology that recognized no given centre of the universe.[90] As we learn from his *De docta ignorantia* (c. 1440), 'there is only one indivisible humanity and specific essence of all human beings. Through *it* all individual human beings are numerically distinct human beings, so that Christ and all human beings have the same humanity, though the numerical distinctness of the individuals remains unconfused.'[91]

---

[87] Kuhn, *Copernican Revolution*, pp. 99–132.
[88] See Harrison, *The Bible, Protestantism, and the Rise of Natural Science*. See also Clarence J. Glacken, *Traces on the Rhodian Shore. Nature and Culture in Western Thought from Ancient Times to the End of the Eighteenth Century* (Berkeley: University of California Press, 1967), pp. 176–253.
[89] Cassirer, *Individual and Cosmos in the Renaissance*, pp. 101–19. For an example, see Giovanni Pico della Mirandola, 'Oration on the Dignity of Man', in Ernst Cassirer, Paul Oskar Kristeller and John H. Randall, eds., *The Renaissance Philosophy of Man* (Chicago: University of Chicago Press, 1948), pp. 223–54.
[90] Cassirer, *Individual and Cosmos in the Renaissance*, pp. 24–29.
[91] Nicholas of Cusa, *De docta ignorantia*, III.8, in *The Complete Philosophical and Theological Treatises of Nicholas of Cusa*, ed. Jasper

Consistent with this view, in *De coniecturis* (1442–3), he turns this humanity into a condition of all knowledge, 'For the power of its oneness encompasses all things, and it keeps them within the bounds of its own region to such an extent that none of them escape its power ... For humanity is the contracted beginning of the creating, governing, and conserving of its own order.'[92] He then goes on to investigate 'the variety of all the inhabitants of our world with respect to their temperament, shapes, vices and morals, subtlety and grossness', and is able to conclude that 'there is but a single nature of a single species – a nature partaken of in different ways by all men'.[93] These conclusions are further elaborated in *De pace fidei* (1453). In this short treatise, Nicholas poses the problem of peaceful coexistence between different religions. In order to overcome all strife inspired by differences in faith, he proposes that 'all the diverse religions be harmoniously reduced, by the common consent of all men, unto one inviolable religion'.[94] In order to achieve such concord, Nicholas suggests that beyond all religious differences there is a single source of wisdom that is not only common to all religions, but which is also prior to all of them and hence presupposed by each of their gods. 'For just as there are no white things if whiteness does not exist, so if the deity does not exist, there are no gods.'[95] To Nicholas, the existence of such a universal community beyond all differences of faith was a corollary of a cosmology that no longer recognized any natural hierarchy in the universe, and hence no superior authority above that of a naturally diversified mankind.[96]

But perhaps an even more important step towards expanding the scope of human community was taken when the assumption of two

---

Hopkins, vol. I (Minneapolis: Arthur J. Banning, 2001), pp. 111–59, at pp. 132–3.

[92] Nicholas of Cusa, *De coniecturis*, II.14, in *Nicholas of Cusa: Metaphysical Speculations*, ed. Jasper Hopkins (Minneapolis: Arthur J. Banning, 2000), pp. 163–297, at p. 236.

[93] Cusa, *De coniecturis*, II.14, p. 237.

[94] Nicholas of Cusa, *De pace fidei*, III, in *Nicholas of Cusa's De Pace Fidei and Cribratio Alkorani*, ed. Jasper Hopkins (Minneapolis: Arthur J. Banning, 1990), pp. 633–70, at p. 637.

[95] Cusa, *De pace fidei*, VI, p. 640.

[96] For an analysis, see Cary J. Nederman, *Worlds of Difference. European Discourses of Toleration c.1100–c.1550* (University Park: Pennsylvania State University Press, 2000), pp. 85–97.

distinct spheres of earth and water was abandoned in favour of the idea that these elements together form a single sphere with one common centre of gravity. Once this was done, there was no longer any reason to believe that the human race was confined to one single landmass, or that the ocean constituted an impenetrable limit beyond which no human life was to be found. Thus Chapter 3 of Copernicus's *De revolutionibus orbium coelestium* (1543) is entitled 'How Earth Together With Water Forms One Globe'. Here Copernicus sets forth some of the prerequisites for conceiving of the earth as one planet among others, being a solid sphere capable of both rotation and revolution. The assumption of an *orbis terrarum*, a single and continuous protrusion of land is incorrect, writes Copernicus:

This can be established by the fact that from the ocean inward the curvature of the land does not mount steadily in a continuous rise. If it did, it would keep the sea water out completely and in no way permit the inland seas and such vast gulfs to intrude. Furthermore, the depth of the abyss would never stop increasing from the shore of the ocean outward, so that no island or reef or any form of land would be encountered by sailors on the longer voyages.[97]

This argument led to the establishment of three related points. First, rather than being united into one landmass, there are numerous different land formations distributed relatively evenly across the spherical surface of the globe. Second, rather than existing in separate spheres and having different centres of gravity, the elements of earth and water share the same centre of gravity. Third, the planet as a whole is best represented as a solid geological mass whose chasms are filled with water, the totality being one perfectly shaped sphere, a *rotunditate absoluta*. Copernicus had thus managed to refute the view that the earth consisted of two spheres, located in a fixed position at the centre of the universe.[98] According to the view set forth in *De revolutionibus*, the ocean is no longer a limit, but rather a transcontinental waterway, connecting different and discontinuous land formations to each other.

[97] Nicolaus Copernicus, *On the Revolutions of the Heavenly Spheres*, trans. Edward Rosen (Baltimore, MD: Johns Hopkins University Press), ch. 3.
[98] Goldstein, 'Renaissance Concept of the Earth', p. 40.

The cosmological changes effected by Cusa and Copernicus brought a shift in the vantage point from which questions of humanity and community could be formulated and answered. When the earth no longer constituted the given centre of the universe, these questions could now be formulated with reference to an imagined point of view situated above the terraqueous globe, and answered with reference to the intercourse between different people from what were now interconnected continents. As Juan Vives noted in 1531, 'The whole globe is opened up to the human race, so that no one is so ignorant of events as to think that the wanderings of the ancients ... are to be compared with the journeys of these travellers.'[99]

But it is also possible to argue that the concept of an *orbis terrarum* had been abandoned in practice before it was formally refuted by Copernicus, the impetus coming from the cartographical research being conducted during the fifteenth century. While being greatly facilitated by the new conceptions of space that emerged at this point in time, cartographical research was to a large extent motivated by the search for safer and cheaper trade routes to the East Indies.[100] At almost the same moment that Lopo Gonçalves first crossed the equator in 1473, Paolo dal Pozzo Toscanelli wrote a letter to Fernão Martins, canon of Lisbon cathedral, on the subject of possible circumnavigation: 'You must not be surprised ... if I call the parts where the spices are west, when they usually call them east, because to those sailing west, those parts are found by navigation on the underside of the earth. But if by land on the upper side, they will always be found to the east.'[101] Written in order to be comprehensible to the layman, the childish simplicity of these instructions contrasts nicely with the complexity of the task at hand. This task consisted

---

[99] Juan Vives, *On Education*, quoted in Walter S. Gibson, *Mirror of the Earth. The World Landscape in Sixteenth-Century Flemish Painting* (Princeton, NJ: Princeton University Press, 1989), pp. 49–50.

[100] See Denis Cosgrove, 'Mapping New Worlds: Culture and Cartography in Sixteenth-Century Venice', *Imago Mundi*, vol. 44, 1992, pp. 65–89; Samuel Y. Edgerton, *The Renaissance Discovery of Linear Perspective* (New York: Basic Books, 1975); Thomas Goldstein, 'The Role of the Italian Merchant Class in Renaissance and Discoveries', *Terrae Incognitae*, vol. 8, 1976, pp. 19–27; Erwin Panofsky, *Perspective as Symbolic Form* (New York: Zone Books, 1995).

[101] Letter, 24 June 1474. Quoted in Goldstein, 'Geography', pp. 13–14.

of convincing the Portuguese elite of the validity of a new worldview which was clearly at odds with the educated lore of the day, prompting them to act urgently upon this new knowledge. But when both Martins and Alfonso V failed to respond, a copy of the same letter was sent to a more entrepreneurial spirit in Genoa who was soon to take action.[102]

There was a short step from claiming that the ocean was navigable, and foreign lands inhabitable in principle, to demonstrating that the whole world was in fact inhabited. Such demonstrations could take place in many ways, not infrequently by invoking observations which had earlier been dismissed as false or absurd when interpreted within the framework of the *orbis terrarum*. But as Copernicus scornfully remarked, there was now 'little reason to marvel at the existence of antipodes'.[103] Old but previously discounted geographical observations were supplemented by the enormous amount of new observations generated by the discoveries, and gradually assimilated into one and the same pool of geographical knowledge. Thus, in the very same year that *De revolutionibus* was published, the Venetian humanist Giovanni Battista Ramusio took upon himself the no less heroic task of bringing together all existing geographical knowledge into one organized body.[104] This resulted in what was to become a landmark achievement of Renaissance geography, the *Navigazioni e viaggi* (1550–9). In this work, Ramusio presented a series of arguments to the effect that the entire world was indeed inhabited by human beings:

The sun makes its course with such order that the inhabitants [at the north pole] live not as moles buried under the earth but as other creatures who are upon this terrestrial globe, illuminated so that they are able most profitably to maintain and provide for their livelihood ... Now, by the matter stated above I think there can be no longer any doubt that beneath the

---

[102] A copy of this letter was sent by Toscanelli to the young Christopher Columbus. See Norbert Sumien, *La correspondence du savant Florentin Paolo del Pozzo Toscanelli avec Christophe Colomb* (Paris, 1927), pp. 9ff.

[103] Copernicus, *Revolutions*, ch. 3.

[104] See Richard Helgerson, *Forms of Nationhood. The Elizabethan Writing of England* (Chicago: University of Chicago Press, 1992), p. 152.

equator and below both poles there is the same multitude of inhabitants that there are in all the other parts of the world.'[105]

When later prefacing the first volume, the printer Giunti summarized the upshot of this argument: 'it is clearly able to be understood that this entire earthly globe is marvellously inhabited, nor is there any part of it empty, neither by heat nor by cold deprived of inhabitants'.[106] In 1570, this new knowledge was synthesized and subsequently presented by Abraham Ortelius in the shape of an atlas which 'offered the synoptic vision that disengages one from local prejudice and promotes a cosmopolitanism based on the moral wisdom that comes from self-knowledge'.[107]

That parts of the world previously thought to be uninhabitable were indeed inhabited led to an expansion of the *oikoumene*. In the *orbis terrarum*, the world known by men had coincided nicely with the world inhabited by the same men. But the construction of a *rotunditate absoluta* and its gradual corroboration by empirical cartography brought an expansion of the *oikoumene* far beyond its former and ancient limits. In this new world the discipline of cosmography 'could reign as an absolute sovereign over the terraqueous globe. It manipulated at will the natural frontiers of rivers and mountains; determined the future of peoples by fixing their migrations and boundaries.'[108]

But how did this expansion of the *oikoumene* affect conceptions of human community? What happened to the idea of a universal humanity once the ocean was no longer its limit, when it had become a highway connecting different peoples on different continents with each other? As Headley has argued, 'this abruptly expanded ecumene with its variety of peoples, would in time create an increasingly secular, religiously neutral lens, gradually revealing the common biological and

---

[105] Giovanni Battista Ramusio, *Navigazioni e viaggi*, quoted in Headley, 'Venetian Celebration', p. 3.
[106] Ramusio, *Navigazioni e viaggi*, quoted in Headley, 'Venetian Celebration', p. 3.
[107] Denis Cosgrove, 'Globalism and Tolerance in Early Modern Geography', *Annals of the Association of American Geographers*, vol. 93, no. 4, 2003, pp. 852–70, at p. 866.
[108] Frank Lestringant, *Mapping the Renaissance World. The Geographical Imagination in the Age of Discovery* (Cambridge: Polity Press, 1994), p. 3.

moral unity of mankind'.[109] But the way there was hardly straight. As we shall see in the next section, while the revolutions in cartography and geography pushed forward an expansion of the known world, they also gave rise to a mismatch between this new world and existing visions of human community – a mismatch that could be handled either by assimilating newly discovered peoples into existing accounts of humanity, or by adjusting those accounts in the light of the actual diversity of customs and standards.

IV

I started this chapter by describing a vision of world of community according to which mankind as a whole constitutes one singular, universal and boundless community. According to this vision, particular communities of lesser scope – ranging from the *polis* to the kingdom – are essentially embedded in that universal community that is a primordial fact of all human coexistence. The existence of community is integral to what it means to be a human being and to share this condition with other human beings. Human beings are human precisely by virtue of being members of the same species, and since this species – however defined and demarcated from other species – is something more than the mere sum of its members, it also constitutes a kind of primordial community. Being members of the same species, human beings are able to communicate with each other, thus bringing this immanent community closer to completion in time and space.

While such visions of community were frequently based on the idea of a common descent of the human race, or on a communion by believers in the Christian faith, the idea of a universal community could also be defined with reference to Stoic and Roman sources. Most medieval conceptions of world community were assembled from a variety of sources that were not always prima facie compatible, but which nevertheless provided the philosophical justifications necessary. Most of these medieval and Renaissance visions of world community were based on a universalistic social ontology that prioritized unity and wholeness over difference and particularity. But as the example

---

[109] John M. Headley, 'Geography and Empire in the Late Renaissance: Botero's Assignment, Western Universalism, and the Civilizing Process', *Renaissance Quarterly*, vol. 53, 2000, pp. 1119–55, at p. 1132.

of Dante hopefully has made plain, these visions could be fleshed out with reference to an array of values and symbols which in turn could be distilled from Greek, Roman and Arabic sources, and which then were carefully blended with elements of Christian doctrine.

The geographical and cartographical revolutions made conceptions of a universal human community increasingly difficult to justify in these traditional terms. The unfamiliarity of newly discovered places had a destabilizing impact upon the foundations of medieval knowledge, as the things and living beings found there were hard to fit into existing categories and classificatory schemes. As Harrison has remarked, 'what had once been a coherent universal language was inundated by an influx of new and potentially unintelligible symbols'.[110] Most crucially, however, the idea of a common human descent made it difficult to account for the geographical dispersion of peoples across the dry surfaces of the globe. If this dispersion were to be consistent with the idea of a common origin, it was necessary to explain how different people had ended up in different places, as well as why the existence of these places had been forgotten.[111] As Headley has noted, 'The growing recognition of the earth's universal habitability could only make more acute the problem of squaring the Adamic origin of all mankind with the swelling contours and complexity of its membership.'[112] And since the newly discovered peoples could hardly be described as faithful Christians, this excluded them from the community of believers as well. Thus, to the extent that mankind had been rendered coextensive with the class of believers, such exclusion was bound to be problematic.[113]

This new predicament produced two different kinds of response. The first was to twist visions of universal community into justifications

---

[110] Harrison, *The Bible, Protestantism, and the Rise of Natural Science*, p. 91; Anthony Pagden, *European Encounters with the New World. From Renaissance to Romanticism* (New Haven, CT: Yale University Press, 1993), pp. 17–49; Joan-Pau Rubiés, 'Futility in the New World: Narratives of Travel in Sixteenth-Century America', in Elsner and Rubiés, *Voyages and Visions*, pp. 74–100.

[111] See Joan-Pau Rubiés, 'Hugo Grotius's Dissertation on the Origin of the American Peoples and the Use of Comparative Methods', *Journal of the History of Ideas*, vol. 52, no. 2, 1991, pp. 221–4.

[112] Headley, 'Venetian Celebration', p. 10.

[113] Cosgrove, *Apollo's Eye*, pp. 135–38.

of statehood and empire. As we shall note in the next chapter, this reversal was largely accomplished by grafting the inherited symbols and values of universal community onto a new and spatially demarcated context, another option made possible by the geographical and cartographical revolutions. The second response, which largely evolved in opposition to the first, was to redefine the concept of community in order to render it more inclusive and at least less obviously biased. The problem confronted by those efforts was how to reconcile the geographical diversity of peoples with received notions of a unified mankind. But even if it was difficult to conceptualize a common humanity outside a theological framework that presupposed either a common descent or a common faith, that framework had nevertheless come to incorporate conceptual elements that made it possible to redefine conceptions of community in order to accommodate a plurality of different peoples, without abandoning its underlying assumptions about the essential unity of mankind. Hence the encounter with new peoples on new continents led to several efforts to broaden the understanding of humanity and human community in terms increasingly independent of scriptural authority. While the universalistic conceptions of human community that resulted from these efforts never exercised much direct influence on the political practices of early modern states and empires, these ideas became part of the background understanding of early modern jurisprudence.[114]

In the rest of this section, I shall analyse one such effort in some detail, that of Bartolomé de Las Casas. This choice is motivated by the recent interpretations of his work by scholars like Todorov and Campbell. These authors have argued that his work ought to

[114] See, for example, John M. Headley, 'The Universalizing Principle and Process: On the West's Intrinsic Commitment to a Global Context', *Journal of World History*, vol. 13, no. 2, 2002, pp. 291–321; David Kennedy, 'Primitive Legal Scholarship', *Harvard International Law Journal*, vol. 27, no. 1, 1986, pp. 1–98; Richard Tuck, 'The "Modern" Theory of Natural Law', in Anthony Pagden, *The Languages of Political Theory in Early Modern Europe* (Cambridge: Cambridge University Press, 1987), pp. 99–119; Richard Tuck, *The Rights of War and Peace. Political Thought and International Order from Grotius to Kant* (Oxford: Oxford University Press, 1999), pp. 40–1; Benjamin Keen, 'The Legacy of Bartolomé de Las Casas', *Ibero-Americana Pragensia*, vol. 11, 1977, pp. 57–67.

be understood as implicitly apologetic for the conquest of America, despite the fact that it was written in explicit opposition to the dispossession and enslavement of the Indians. By disregarding the larger theological context within which this argument was developed, these authors have interpreted the insistence on equality as an implicit denial of human diversity.

Written in response to the claims advanced by Juan Gines de Sepúlveda, Las Casas's treatise *In Defense of the Indians* (1552–3) had originally been delivered as an oral disputation in Valladolid in 1550.[115] In this work, he proceeded to refute a series of arguments to the effect that war should be waged against the American Indians on account of their barbarous nature. That such a war was justified had been vigorously asserted by Sepúlveda, who argued that since the American Indians were not only natural slaves and practised cannibalism, but also made human sacrifices and were totally ignorant of the Christian religion, they ought to be dispossessed, enslaved and perhaps even killed. Arguments like these were not new or original, and had a long history within canon law. As Innocent IV had already made plain in the thirteenth century, the pope could not authorize intervention in the affairs of infidel societies on the sole grounds of them being infidel, but in order to enforce adherence to natural law in those instances when it had been broken by the sinful practices of those societies. According to this doctrine, secular rulers required papal authorization for their interventions in such communities, and such authorization in turn required clear evidence of actual violations of natural law. The debate between Las Casas and Sepúlveda must therefore be understood against the background of these prior discussions of the relationship between Christian and non-Christian societies – especially Muslim ones – and the demand for the systematic justification of wars undertaken by the former against the latter.[116]

---

[115] Bartolomé de Las Casas, *In Defense of the Indians. The Defense of the Most Reverend Lord, Don Fray Bartolomé de Las Casas, of the Order of Preachers, Late Bishop of Chiapa, Against the Persecutors and Slanderers of the Peoples of the New World Discovered Across the Seas*, trans. Stafford Poole (DeKalb: Northern Illinois University Press, 1992).

[116] The literature is extensive. See John G. A. Pocock, *Barbarism and Religion*, vol. IV, *Barbarism, Savages and Empires* (Cambridge:

Hence also the persuasiveness of the defence of the Indians to a large extent depended on the extent to which the concept of the barbarian could be redefined in such a way that arguments for excluding the Indians from membership in the universal human community could be effectively refuted. To this end, Las Casas drew on a variety of ancient and medieval sources that could be used to support a more inclusive view of human community than that of Sepúlveda.[117] Consequently, Las Casas argued, and contrary to appearances, the American Indians are neither natural slaves nor barbarians in any morally relevant sense of these terms. While the Indians certainly spoke a different language and were undoubtedly engaged in many sinful and abhorrent practices, they nevertheless displayed a wide range of virtues in their conduct towards each other, and were clearly in possession of rational faculties, as indicated by the nature of their social and political institutions. The Indians, writes Las Casas,

are not ignorant, inhuman, or bestial. Rather, long before they had heard the word Spaniard they had properly organized states, wisely ordered by excellent laws, religion, and custom. They cultivated friendship and, bound together in common fellowship, lived in populous cities in which

Cambridge University Press, 2005), pp. 157–226; Muldoon, *Popes, Lawyers, and Infidels*, pp. 132–52; James Muldoon, *The Americas in the Spanish World Order. The Justification for Conquest in the Seventeenth Century* (Philadelphia: University of Pennsylvania Press, 1994), pp. 15–37; James Muldoon, 'Solórozano's *De Indiarum Iure*: Applying a Medieval Theory of World Order in the Seventeenth Century', in James Muldoon, *Canon Law, the Expansion of Europe, and World Order* (Aldershot: Variorum, 1998), pp. 29–45; Anthony Pagden, 'Dispossessing the Barbarian: The Language of Spanish Thomism and the Debate over the Property Rights of the American Indians', in Pagden, *The Languages of Political Theory*, pp. 79–98; Anthony Pagden, 'The Forbidden Food: Francisco de Vitoria and José de Acosta on Cannibalism', *Terrae Incognitae*, vol. 13, 1981, pp. 17–29.

[117] For various influences on Las Casas, see Brian Tierney, *The Idea of Natural Rights. Studies on Natural Rights, Natural Law and Church Law 1150–1625* (Atlanta, GA: Scholars Press, 1997), pp. 272–87; Kenneth J. Pennington, 'Bartolomé de las Casas and the Tradition of Medieval Law', *Church History*, vol. 39, 1970, pp. 149–61; Pagden, *European Encounters*, pp. 51–5, 69–70; Anthony Pagden, 'Ius et Factum: Text and Experience in the Writings of Bartolomé de las Casas', *Representations*, vol. 33, 1991, pp. 147–62.

they wisely administered the affairs of both peace and war justly and equitably.[118]

The fact that the Indians are fully capable of forming political communities of their own not only indicates that they possess a sense of community among themselves, but also that they belong to the universal community of all mankind. The existence of such a social bond among the Indians implies that they should to be regarded as equal to the Spaniards, rather than as natural slaves or barbarians in the sense established by Aristotle and Aquinas. Judging by the functioning of their social and political institutions, the Indians are at least as sophisticated as the Spaniards. Therefore, the Indians ought to be treated as humanely as possible, and should enjoy the same rights to life and property as the Spaniards. Yet the fact remains indisputable that they are unbelievers. They know nothing of Christianity and its holy sacraments, 'for no matter how well governed a people may be or how philosophical a man, they are subject to complete barbarism ... if they are not imbued with the mysteries of Christian philosophy'.[119] But, as such, they must also be outside the jurisdiction of Christian authorities, and cannot therefore legitimately be punished for their sins by these authorities.[120]

To Las Casas, the fact that the Indians are ignorant of God is not a sufficient ground for denying them the basic rights of life and possession. Since the meaning of the term barbarian is wholly relative to the theological framework within which it has been defined and used, no class of people can properly be called barbarians. The only valid sense of these terms Las Casas recognizes applies to those 'who are sunk in insensitivity of mind, ignorant, irrational, lacking ability, inhuman, fierce, corrupted by foul morals and unsettled by nature or by reason of their depraved habits of sin'.[121] The true barbarians are those who are unable to form communities in the first place, and whose social practices hence cannot be comprehended within *any* theological or philosophical framework at hand. Such true barbarians cannot be identified with any particular community, for the

[118] Las Casas, *In Defense of the Indians*, pp. 42–3.
[119] Las Casas, *In Defense of the Indians*, p. 49.
[120] Las Casas, *In Defense of the Indians*, pp. 54–62.
[121] Las Casas, *In Defense of the Indians*, p. 53.

simple reason that they live outside all community, in a state of pure savagery.

But not even this kind of true barbarian is wholly beyond salvation, and should therefore not be excluded from the universal community of humanity. 'Even though these peoples may be completely barbaric', writes Las Casas, 'they are nevertheless created in God's image.'[122] It follows that if all men are profoundly equal by virtue of being thus created, faith cannot be a morally relevant attribute when allocating rights to individuals or peoples. This position is even more consistently advocated in his *Apologética historia* (*c.* 1550), in which further arguments were offered against Sepúlveda:

For all the peoples of the world are men, and the definition of all men, collectively and severally, is one: that they are rational beings. All possess understanding and volition, being formed in the image and likeness of God; all have the five exterior senses and the four interior senses, and are moved by the objects of these; all have natural capacity or faculties to understand and master the knowledge that they do not have; and this is true not only of those that are inclined toward good but those that by reason of their depraved customs are bad; all take pleasure in goodness and in happy and pleasant things and all abhor evil and reject what offends or grieves them ... Thus all mankind is one, and all men are alike in what concerns their creation and all natural things, and no one is born enlightened. From this it follows that all of us must be guided and aided at first by those who were born before us.[123]

According to Las Casas, the fundamental unity of mankind neither derives from a common descent, nor can it be derived from a communion of believers. Rather, the unity of mankind derives from the rationality of its members, a rationality whose nature remains unaffected by differences in customs and morals, however sharp these differences might appear from a Christian viewpoint. Hence the heinous vices and detestable practices of the Indians are not sufficient to disqualify them from full membership in the universal community of mankind, since the Indians are both sociable and rational.

---

[122] Las Casas, *In Defense of the Indians*, p. 39.
[123] Quoted in Benjamin Keen, *Latin American Civilization: History and Society, 1492 to the Present* (Boulder, CO: Westview, 1996), pp. 72–3.

Now it is possible to object that this essentially Stoic vision implies a denial of the moral relevance of cultural differences, and that by insisting on the sameness of all human beings, it also furnishes a rationale for assimilation.[124] But to my mind this criticism is based on an anachronistic interpretation of the conception of community we find in Las Casas. To him, that community is universal precisely by virtue of being *diverse* in its composition. Such a universal humanity is always present irrespective of whether concrete human beings actually share a common habitat, or whether they happen to subscribe to the same ethical standards. This insistence on absolute equality between Spaniards and Indians does not lead him to deny the existence and importance of the profound cultural differences between these peoples, but rather to affirm the fact that *being different is what they share in common*. This is most evident in the way Las Casas conceives of the relationship between community and faith. As a result of the encounter with the Indians, this relationship can no longer be understood as mutually implicating. While the Indians admittedly do not know anything about the Christian God, they nevertheless display an intensity of religious worship that indicates a relationship to divinity. Indeed, even those practices of worship which are truly detestable from a Christian point of view can be seen as expressions of a genuine religious sentiment among the Indians. In the final analysis, the practice of human sacrifice is at least as indicative of religious worship as are expressions of virtue among the Christians.[125] They are equally *human* practices, and therefore also equally expressive of the existence of human community: the message that transpires from the texts of Las Casas is one of toleration in the face of human diversity.[126]

But is this still religious belief in any meaningful sense? As Todorov has pointed out, 'What then remains common and universal is no longer the God of the Christian religion, to whom all should accede, but the very idea of divinity, of what is above us; the religious rather

---

[124] Tzvetan Todorov, *The Conquest of America: The Question of the Other* (New York: Harper and Row, 1992), p. 167; for a similar criticism, see also David Campbell, *Writing Security: United States Foreign Policy and the Politics of Identity* (Manchester: Manchester University Press, 1992), pp. 111–18.
[125] Las Casas, *In Defense of the Indians*, p. 39.
[126] Cf. Nederman, *Worlds of Difference*, pp. 99–115.

than religion.'[127] To Todorov, it appears as if the upshot of this Stoic appeal to divinity is merely to *secularize* the concept of community by disconnecting it from Christian theology, and instead turning the question of community into what looks like a problem of comparative anthropology. Different communities have different gods and cannot therefore be measured against the same standards: Christianity is but *one* among many equally valid claims on the human spirit.[128]

But Las Casas was not a secularist. His argument has a rather different significance when put into its proper context. To him, the problem is how to broaden the inherited Christian conception of community in order to be able to accommodate the rightful claims to life and property by the Indians who are in the process of being dispossessed and enslaved. His encounter with them made it plain that either this inherited conception of a universal human community had to yield, or the Indians could be dispossessed and killed without any further justification. Las Casas solves this difficult theological problem by first disconnecting the criteria of inclusion from their foundations in scriptural authority. He then reinterprets these criteria in Stoic terms, by making sociability, rationality and the worship of divinity the signs of a common humanity. He seems to imply that by widening the concept of community to include those ways of life clearly at odds with the *letter* of the Christian doctrine, the underlying *spirit* of a Christian community can better be preserved and more easily spread.

This consolidation of universal community at a new level presupposes a prior division of humanity into different communities which can subsequently be made subject to ecumenical practices precisely because of the actual differences between them. Since medieval conceptions of community were insufficiently flexible for this purpose, they were replaced by conceptions that carried much less obvious Christian commitments, and which therefore could accommodate more easily the new forms of political life encountered in the Americas

---

[127] Todorov, *Conquest of America*, p. 189.
[128] Todorov, *Conquest of America*, p. 190. For a similar interpretation, see Hayward R. Alker, 'The Humanities Movement in International Studies: Reflections on Machiavelli and Las Casas', *Alternatives*, vol. 36, no. 4, 1992, pp. 347–71. Compare also Roberto S. Goizueta, 'Bartolomé de Las Casas, Modern Critic of Modernity: An Analysis of a Conversion', *Journal of Hispanic/Latino Theology*, vol. 4, no. 4, 1996, pp. 6–19.

and elsewhere. In order to preserve the spirit of universal community in this new context, these newly discovered peoples would have to be known and evaluated according to their own immanent principles and standards. Singular humanity is thus broken up into a plurality of peoples. Each of these peoples reflect the universal facts of human community precisely by being different from each other. Las Casas thus succeeds in retaining what had become most dear to him since his own conversion – the spirit of community as exemplified by the teachings and life of Christ – by admitting that these differences between peoples might be of divine sanction. The implication is very simple: whereas before humanity was constituted as one single community, humanity is now constituted by a plurality of distinct communities.

While the communitarian visions of Dante and Las Casas are literally worlds apart, they nevertheless share a series of important assumptions in common. Their respective visions were articulated in different cosmological contexts and in response to very different problems, but are both indebted to the same ancient and medieval sources. Both these authors successfully recontextualized these sources in order to broaden existing notions of community to accommodate the most salient and controversial religious and social differences of their day. They both assumed that the scope of human community must necessarily coincide with the limits of the known world, and that it must encompass every single human being within that world. To both Dante and Las Casas, the presence of human beings necessarily implies the existence of community, a fact that must be inferred from the sometimes strange and abhorrent modes of intercourse prevailing within and between human societies.

But there is one important difference between Dante and Las Casas that bears witness to important differences in the cosmological context. To Dante, mankind constitutes one universal community by virtue of being singular, while to Las Casas mankind constitutes one universal community by virtue of being diverse. When the latter defends the notion of a common humanity against the challenges posed by the strange practices of newly discovered peoples, he does so by assuming that mankind is naturally divided into distinct peoples with different gods and moral standards, yet nevertheless partake in a common humanity. The medieval definition of mankind in the singular is thereby replaced by a definition of mankind in the plural. Such a conclusion was possible to reach only against the backdrop of the prior change in cosmological outlook brought about by the cartographic and geographic revolutions, a change which had given rise to the conviction that there were parts of the world to be found beyond the limits of the *orbis terrarum*, and that these parts were inhabited by human beings. The vantage point from which the geographic dispersion and subsequent intercourse between different peoples could be understood had thereby been relocated to a hypothetical point situated over and above the human abode. In this way, the communal vision of Las Casas seems more appropriate for the inhabitants of a *rotunditate absoluta*, who would have to contend with a plurality of human communities thus imagined. Yet this also represents a harbinger of its eventual demise, and its replacement with the particularistic conceptions of community we find in subsequent attempts to derive justifications for nations and empires out of this universalistic framework. It is to these attempts we now must turn.

4 | *Nationalizing community*

WITHIN the discipline of modern international relations, the existence of an international society of states has long constituted a point of departure for further inquiry. On those relatively rare occasions when scholars have felt compelled to inquire into the historical origins of this international society, they have argued that the peace of Westphalia constitutes a crucial turning point, when papal and imperial claims to boundless authority were finally and decisively replaced by a system of territorial states.[1] Yet it has been argued that this view of the origin of modern international society is nothing but a myth. According to the critique, this myth was created during the nineteenth century in order to endow the then emergent international order with a more noble ancestry.[2] But if the idea of an early modern international system is indeed a myth, what did the early modern world look like, and how did it come into being? As I will suggest in this chapter, the early modern world consisted of emergent nations and empires that were crafted out of universalistic conceptions of community by nationalizing a wide array of symbols and metaphors. This process was facilitated by cosmological changes

---

[1] For some recent examples, see Daniel Philpott, *Revolutions in Sovereignty. How Ideas Shaped Modern International Relations* (Princeton, NJ: Princeton University Press, 2001); Christian Reus-Smit, *The Moral Purpose of the State. Culture, Social Identity, and Institutional Rationality in International Relations* (Princeton, NJ: Princeton University Press, 1999); Hendrik Spruyt, *The Sovereign State and its Competitors* (Princeton, NJ: Princeton University Press, 1994); Heather Rae, *State Identities and the Homogenisation of Peoples* (Cambridge: Cambridge University Press, 2002), pp. 1–54.

[2] Andreas Osiander, 'Sovereignty, International Relations, and the Westphalian Myth', *International Organization*, vol. 55, no. 2, 2001, pp. 251–87; Stéphane Beaulac, *The Power of Language in the Making of International Law* (Leiden: Martinus Nijhoff, 2004).

which made spatial differentiation of political communities look natural, and which relocated the vantage point from which human affairs could be judged to sovereign authority.

When accounting for this transition, it has been common to consult early modern theorists of international law. Yet these theorists offer little guidance, since they were struggling hard to make sense of this world by means of concepts that were rapidly becoming outdated. To them, any division of mankind into distinct and bounded communities was inherently problematic since it appeared to contradict and undermine those universalistic foundations upon which the very edifice of natural law rested. For example, the concept of *ius gentium* was very hard to make coherent sense of in the context of a plurality of bounded and distinct communities, since it presupposed a united mankind. One way out of this dilemma was to turn the question of what is common to all men (*homines*) into a question of what is common to all nations (*gentes*).[3] But this only meant that the existence of particular communities somehow had to be reconciled with the inherited universalistic framework in order to preserve the integrity of the natural law tradition. The resulting explanations reflected these concerns, insofar as they frequently invoked exogenous causes of the division of mankind. To Grotius, particular communities had emerged for practical reasons, 'not with the intention of abolishing the society which links all men as a whole, but rather in order to fortify that universal society by a more dependable means of protection'.[4] To Locke, the division of humanity was a consequence of the Fall: 'Mankind are one Community ... one Society, distinct from all other Creatures. And were it not for the corruption, and vitiousness of degenerate Men, there would be no need of any other; no necessity that Men should separate from this, and by positive agreements combine into smaller and divided associations.'[5] To this explanation was added an acknowledgement

---

[3] Richard Waswo, 'The Formation of Natural Law to Justify Colonialism, 1539–1689', *New Literary History*, vol. 27, no. 4, 1996, pp. 743–59, at p. 745.

[4] Hugo Grotius, *De iure praedae commentarius (de Indis)* [c. 1609], Carnegie Endowment for International Peace (Oxford: Clarendon Press, 1950), p. 19.

[5] John Locke, *Two Treatises of Government*, vol. II, ed. Peter Laslett (Cambridge: Cambridge University Press, 1988), §128, p. 352. For the

of human diversity that made the existence of cultural differences the very starting point for Locke's moral theory.[6] Hence, to both Grotius and Locke, mankind was essentially *one* community, yet it had accidentally been divided into distinct peoples, with different customs and different standards of moral conduct. Both Grotius and Locke struggled to reconcile these conflicting assumptions about the nature of human community within the framework of natural law. And although they tried to explain why mankind had been divided into distinct communities, these explanations could also conveniently be drawn upon in order to justify the domination and dispossession of non-European peoples, thereby legitimizing various forms of colonialism and imperialism.[7]

Hence, if we want to understand the transition from universalistic to particularistic conceptions of community within political thought, we have to look to other sources for support. In this chapter, I will explore the early modern order by focusing on how the connection between memory and identity was established in accounts of nationhood and empire during the Renaissance and the French Revolution. This choice of episodes is motivated by my ambition to show that the modern tension between universalistic and particularistic conceptions of community first emerged when the concept of community had been fully nationalized, and that this did not happen until relatively late. Since the examples offered in

---

universalistic underpinnings of his argument, see Jeremy Waldron, *God, Locke, and Equality. Christian Foundations in Locke's Political Thought* (Cambridge: Cambridge University Press, 2002), p. 154.

[6] Daniel Carey, *Locke, Shaftesbury, and Hutcheson. Contesting Diversity in the Enlightenment and Beyond* (Cambridge: Cambridge University Press, 2006), pp. 14–33.

[7] See Edward Keene, *Beyond the Anarchical Society* (Cambridge: Cambridge University Press, 2002); James Tully, 'Rediscovering America: The Two Treatises and Aboriginal Rights', in James Tully, *An Approach to Political Philosophy: Locke in Context* (Cambridge: Cambridge University Press, 1993), pp. 147–76; Barbara Arneil, 'John Locke, Natural Law, and Colonialism', *History of Political Thought*, vol. 13, no. 4, 1992, pp. 587–603; Barbara Arneil, *John Locke and America. The Defence of English Colonialism* (Oxford: Clarendon Press, 1996), pp. 45–77; David Armitage, 'John Locke, Carolina, and the Two Treatises of Government', *Political Theory*, vol. 32, no. 5, 2004, pp. 602–27.

support of this argument are intended to illustrate the mechanisms through which this happened, the resulting historical account will necessarily be sketchy.

Existing research on identity construction also frequently assume that such processes take place within a world already divided into distinct peoples, with individual communities already being present in some rudimentary form.[8] These accounts can tell us how distinct communities take on a character of their own, but have very little to say about how these communities and the larger social whole of which they form part were created in the first place. In a remarkable essay published in 1986, James Clifford predicted that future historians of ideas may look back on the twentieth century noting that this was a time when Western intellectuals became preoccupied with culture and language.[9] What Clifford appears to be saying is not simply that things like national identities are social constructs by virtue of being constituted in and through language, but rather that the very notion of 'being constructed' might have a history of its own. Thus, as long as we take the connection between memory and identity for granted, we will be tempted to conclude that 'Societies are necessarily particular because they have members and memories. Humanity, by contrast, has members but no memory, and so it has no history and no culture.'[10] But what if the memory of humanity has simply been repressed and marginalized in the process of constituting particular communities? In this chapter, I would like to argue that the mechanisms of memory and forgetfulness provide important clues to how the particularization of community was carried out in political thought.

---

[8] Recent studies include M. Lane Bruner, *Strategies of Remembrance: The Rhetorical Dimensions of National Identity Construction* (Columbia: University of South Carolina Press, 2002), pp. 1–11; Rogers M. Smith, *Stories of Peoplehood: The Politics and Morals of Political Membership* (Cambridge: Cambridge University Press, 2003).

[9] James Clifford, 'On Ethnographic Self-fashioning: Conrad and Malinowski', in Thomas C. Heller, Morton Sisna and David E. Wellbery, eds., *Reconstructing Individualism. Autonomy, Individuality, and the Self in Western Thought* (Stanford, CA: Stanford University Press, 1986), pp. 140–62, at pp. 142–3.

[10] Michael Walzer, *Thick and Thin. Moral Argument at Home and Abroad* (Notre Dame, IN: University of Notre Dame Press, 1994), p. 8.

I

In order to understand how the connection between memory and identity has been instrumental in carrying out this transition, we must venture into the realm of *myths* and *monuments*. Doing this makes it possible to ask questions about how the distinction between the real and the constructed has been drawn and redrawn in order to support and debunk different conceptions of community.[11] To my knowledge, a recognizably modern connection between memory and identity first emerged as a result of efforts to redefine the category of the person to suit the needs of the early modern state. As John Locke explains in *An Essay Concerning Human Understanding* (1690), it is

> the same consciousness that makes a man be himself to himself, *personal identity* depends on that only, whether it be annexed only to the individual substance, or can be continued in a succession of several substances. For as far as any intelligent being can repeat the *idea* of any past action with the same consciousness it had of it at first, and with the same consciousness it has of any present action, so far it is the same *personal self*.[12]

To Locke, a memory that connects past and present within one uninterrupted sequence is a condition of a unitary consciousness, and a unitary consciousness is what makes an individual identical with himself throughout time and despite the corporeal and other changes the passing of time inevitably brings. Furthermore, when Locke described memory as constitutive of personal identity, he did so with the important proviso that it applied to sane men only, and argued that personal identity thus conceived was a necessary condition of autonomy and thus also of legal responsibility.[13] The concept of memory was crucial to the definition of man as a bearer of rights within the

---

[11] See Benedict Anderson, *Imagined Communities: Reflections on the Origin and Spread of Nationalism* (London: Verso, 1991), pp. 9–46; Paul Veyne, *Did the Greeks Believe in their Myths?* (Chicago: University of Chicago Press, 1988); William H. Sewell, 'The Concept(s) of Culture', in Victoria E. Bonnell and Lynn Hunt, eds., *Beyond the Cultural Turn* (Berkeley: University of California Press, 1999), pp. 35–61.

[12] John Locke, *An Essay Concerning Human Understanding* [1689] (London: Dent, 1976), p. 163.

[13] Locke, *Essay*, p. 171.

early modern state. Supposedly, to Locke, each man is master of his own memory in the sense that recollection itself is a conscious act undertaken by the subject, who thereby is also assembling himself, as it were. But how, then, can we possibly account for the identity of that subject *doing* the recollection without ending up in infinite regress by postulating an infinite series of consciousnesses?

Attempts to answer this question paved the way for Humean scepticism. This scepticism extends beyond induction into the realm of subjectivity and identity. 'I may venture to affirm of the rest of mankind', writes Hume, 'that they are nothing but a bundle or collection of different perceptions, which succeed each other with an inconceivable rapidity, and are in perpetual flux and movement.'[14] Out of this 'memory not only discovers the identity, but also contributes to its production, by producing the relation of resemblance among the perceptions'. Yet these relations are themselves of a fluid and transitory nature, so 'we have no just standard, by which we can decide any dispute concerning the time, when they acquire or lose a title to the name of identity'.[15] Mankind would thus be at a loss in the absence of a memory that can break down the chaotic totality of perceptions into *individual* bundles and arrange these in patterns according to the principles of resemblance and causation. To Hume, therefore, memory is as indispensable to identity as it is arbitrary in character.

When precariously extended to the categories of *collective* memory and *collective* identity, the above equations look like accurate descriptions of their actual interrelationship. This, at least, was what Nietzsche thought when he concluded that 'there is a degree of sleeplessness, of rumination, of the historical sense, which is harmful and ultimately fatal to the living thing, whether this living thing be a man a people or a culture'.[16] And, in a sense, he was right. When later incorporated into modern social theory, this symbiotic

---

[14] David Hume, *A Treatise of Human Nature* [1739–40] (London: Longmans, Green and Co., 1874), p. 534.
[15] Hume, *Treatise of Human Nature*, pp. 541–3.
[16] Friedrich Nietzsche, 'On the Uses and Disadvantages of History for Life' [1874], in his *Untimely Meditations* (Cambridge: Cambridge University Press, 1983), pp. 57–125, at p. 62. Compare Martin Hollis, 'Of Masks and Men', in Michael Carrithers, Steven Collins and Steven Lukes, eds., *The Category of the Person: Anthropology, Philosophy, History* (Cambridge: Cambridge University Press, 1985), pp. 217–33;

relationship between memory and identity itself became dependent on the *social context* of remembrance and forgetting. Thus, according to Halbwachs, 'it is in society that people normally acquire their memories. It is also in society that they recall, recognize and localize their memories ... and the groups of which I am part at any time give me the means to reconstruct them.'[17]

Thus, it only takes an empiricist account of the nature of personal memory coupled with a holistic understanding of society in order to create a short-circuit between the concepts of memory and identity that cuts across the distinction between individual and group, connecting all these concepts in one powerful recipe for communal belonging.[18] Following this recipe, we are inclined to believe that collective identities are produced out of collective memories as much as individual memories and identities are dependent on both. The relationship between collective memory and identity is always a two-way street: there is no community without a corresponding memory that records its trajectory in time, and no such trajectory without the active construction of a past order to support or debunk a given identity in the present.[19]

But it is important to remember that this idea that memory is constitutive of identity is an invention of modern philosophy and social theory, not a timeless feature of memory itself. Ancient and medieval writers regarded memory as part of the human soul, made up of mental pictures of past sense impressions. Since mental pictures were regarded as essential for all thinking, the accurate recollections of such past sensations were indispensable sources of knowledge. Much energy was devoted to inventing and perfecting methods of memorizing by means of different forms of imaginary. Later techniques were developed that codified these pictures in various contraptions. But while

---

T. L. S. Sprigge, 'Personal and Impersonal Identity', *Mind*, no. 385, 1988, pp. 29–49.

[17] Maurice Halbwachs, *On Collective Memory* [1940–8] (Chicago: University of Chicago Press, 1992), p. 38.

[18] For an analysis of the relationship between personal and collective memory, see Paul Ricoeur, *Memory, History, Forgetting* (Chicago: University of Chicago Press, 2004), pp. 93–132.

[19] For an overview, see Jeffrey K. Olick and Joyce Robbins, 'Social Memory Studies: From "Collective Memory" to the Historical Sociology of Mnemonic Practices', *Annual Review of Sociology*, vol. 24, 1998, pp. 105–40.

the capacity for remembrance was undoubtedly held in high esteem, the idea that the *content* of the mental pictures stored in the human mind would somehow condition the identity of its bearer appears foreign in this intellectual context.[20] But one feature of memory seems to recur across different contexts, and that is its association with spaces and places. Most of the mnemonic techniques developed by the ancients sought to facilitate remembrance by allocating its objects to spaces imagined within the mind, and many of the contraptions later conceived were built in order to allow for a spatial ordering of these objects.[21] As I shall argue in the rest of this chapter, it is this association with space and places that paves the way for the modern connection between memory and identity. When the space of memory becomes equated with that of the territorial state, then it also becomes possible to construct the identity of a nation on the basis of that very memory. Therefore, if we want to understand the role of memory in the nationalization of community, we must pay close attention to how memorial space is gradually rendered coextensive with the territory of emergent states, and how this simultaneously brings a repression of all those memories that cannot be tailored to fit the needs of the national community.[22]

II

When modern nation-states were created, it was by means of resources already available within the world in which they emerged. In this world, visions of a community of all mankind blended with visions of monarchy or empire, both being based on similar symbolic foundations. Both visions were universalistic in aspiration and inherently

---

[20] See Frances Yates, *The Art of Memory* (Chicago: University of Chicago Press, 1966), pp. 17–62; Janet Coleman, *Ancient and Medieval Memories* (Cambridge: Cambridge University Press, 1993); Mary Carruthers, *The Book of Memory: A Study of Memory in Medieval Culture* (Cambridge: Cambridge University Press, 1990).

[21] Yates, *Art of Memory*, pp. 163–330.

[22] Jonathan Boyarin, 'Space, Time and the Politics of Memory' in Jonathan Boyarin, ed., *Remapping Memory: The Politics of Timespace* (Minneapolis: University of Minnesota Press, 1994), pp. 1–37; Pierre Nora, 'Between Memory and History: Les Lieux de Mémoire, *Representations*, no. 26, 1989, pp. 7–24.

boundless in scope. But although this world was populated by peoples who knew little or nothing of territorial differentiation, it supposedly had a centre, embodied in the legal and political institutions of early Rome. This world constituted the symbolic backdrop for subsequent European state formation, and provided the ideological impetus behind further imperial expansion by European powers.[23] As Yates has argued, 'The symbolism of the empire of Charles V, which seemed able to include the whole world as then known and to hold out the promise of a return to spiritual unity through a revival of the cementing power of the Christianized imperial virtues, was a comforting phantom in the chaotic world of the sixteenth century.'[24] Campanella provides us with an interesting example of the ease with which such phantoms were created in the fluid context of Renaissance political thought. Written within a cosmological framework similar to that of Copernicus, his *Monarchia di Spagna* (*c.* 1600) contains a plan for the creation of a world community, if only in order to sustain the successful global expansion of Spanish imperial power. The best way to secure lasting domination over foreign lands is through the gradual *hispanization* of all peoples, by forcing everyone within the empire to adopt Spanish laws, language, and customs.[25]

Those who tried to justify state-building faced the formidable task of reinterpreting and recontextualizing the rich world of signs, symbols and metaphors that had been handed down to them from the ancients and medieval Christianity, and which had been filtered through

---

[23] See Anthony Pagden, *Lords of all the World: Ideologies of Empire in Spain, Britain and France, c.1500–1800* (New Haven, CT: Yale University Press, 1995), pp. 29–102; David Armitage, *The Ideological Origins of the British Empire* (Cambridge: Cambridge University Press, 2000), pp. 1–23; David Armitage, 'The Elizabethan Idea of Empire', *Transactions of the Royal Historical Society*, vol. 14, 2004, pp. 269–77.

[24] Frances A. Yates, *Astraea. The Imperial Theme in the Sixteenth Century* (London: Routledge, 1975), p. 27.

[25] See Frances A. Yates, *Giordani Bruno and the Hermetic Tradition* (London: Routledge, 1964), pp. 360–97; John M. Headley, *Tommaso Campanella and the Transformation of the World* (Princeton, NJ: Princeton University Press, 1997), pp. 197–245; Anthony Pagden, *Spanish Imperialism and the Political Imagination. Studies in European and Spanish-American Social and Political Theory* (New Haven, CT: Yale University Press, 1990), pp. 37–64.

Renaissance attempts to appropriate the same sources in support of city-states. Since these symbols and metaphors had been tailored to fit boundless forms of political community, the task at hand was how to restrict their range of applicability in such a way that they could be used to reinforce those particularistic forms of political identity needed to sustain emergent territorial states. In order to achieve this, certain things had to be remembered in order to bestow the emergent territorial order with intelligibility and legitimacy. Other things had to be forgotten, and for much the same reasons. Thus, in this section I shall argue that the modern order of states was indeed crafted out of a set of resources whose origin constantly threatened this creation, and that this origin therefore had to be carefully repressed within collective social memory. This was commonly done by making crucial symbols and metaphors appear to be new and exclusive inventions of particular peoples, while concealing the fact that they constituted parts of a cultural heritage common to the entire West, and sometimes even to a wider world than that.

As I argued earlier, similar moves had been undertaken during the Italian Renaissance, and then notably in the political context of city-states and their quest for survival in an increasingly hostile environment. Thanks to the peculiarities of Renaissance modes of knowing and writing, ancient sources could be reappropriated and important political insights distilled from them by means of the use of the esoteric doctrines of resemblance and *exempla*. Provided that the underlying conception of time was cyclical, history was bound to repeat itself infinitely. Against the backdrop of such a cosmology, it was fully possible to argue by means of examples derived from ancient sources when legitimating different forms of rule or different lines of action against one's opponents. What once applied in Athens or Sparta now apparently applied in quattrocento Milan or Florence, without the slightest degree of anachronism being felt as long as certain rules had been obeyed in the selection and sampling of classical texts. In other words, there was no firm divide separating past and present, simply because the concept of secular and linear time (*tempus*) could not claim to be the sole legitimate foundation of historiography.[26] Perhaps the best example of the resulting propensity for

---

[26] Jens Bartelson, *A Genealogy of Sovereignty* (Cambridge: Cambridge University Press, 1995); Coleman, *Ancient and Medieval Memories*, pp. 541–62.

time travelling is found in Petrarch's letters in support of Cola di Rienzo's effort to reestablish the Roman Republic in 1344, in which Petrarch seems to assume that the past millennium had done nothing to change the identity of the Roman people, and its capacity to endow the emperor with legitimacy.[27] And while the Roman concept of *patria* was used to describe such secular communities during the Middle Ages, and while the term *natio* had been used to denote common birth and ancestry among their members, these secular communities were intrinsically hard to make sense of outside the universalistic framework of medieval legal theory.[28]

By the sixteenth century, similar rhetorical strategies were redeployed in order to make sense of a kind of entity that had not yet been conceptualized in fully independent terms before. This new entity was premised on the actual or desired *coincidence* between a sufficiently homogeneous people and a continuous territory, and was most frequently created through the assimilation of ancient myth. These efforts to justify the congruence between peoples and territories in mythical terms represent the first steps towards the nationalization of political community. Not surprisingly, the first authors to tell stories that purported to explain the spatio-temporal trajectory and gradual triumph of distinct peoples were from that corner of Europe that had the strongest reasons for doing so, given their experience of conquest and discovery. For this purpose, they vernacularized predominantly Latin sources, and used those sources to create poetic defences of their achievements.

Thus, when Luís Vaz de Camões wrote his poem *Os Lusíadas* (1572), it was not only to celebrate the discoveries of Vasco da Gama, but also to instil a sense of peoplehood in the ancient races of Lusitania. Thus, in *Os Lusíadas*, the triumph of the Portuguese

---

[27] Francesco Petrarca, 'Letter to Cola di Rienzo and the Roman People' (Variae 48, Horatorio) in Petrarch, *The Revolution of Cola di Rienzo* (New York: Italica Press, 1996), pp. 10–36; Yates, *Astraea*, pp. 13–16; Coleman, *Ancient and Medieval Memories*, p. 558. See also Åsa Boholm, 'Reinvented Histories: Medieval Rome as a Memorial Landscape', *Ecumene*, vol. 4, no. 3, 1997, pp. 247–72.

[28] See Ernst Kantorowicz, '*Pro Patria Mori* in Medieval Political Thought', *American Historical Review*, vol. 56, no. 3, 1951, pp. 472–92; Liah Greenfeld, *Nationalism: Five Roads to Modernity* (Cambridge, MA: Harvard University Press, 1992).

discoveries is intimately connected not only to the glory and bravery of those who achieved it, but also, and more importantly, to the formation of the Portuguese people, their independence from the Castilian Crown, their expulsion of the Moors, and the dynastic legitimacy of their crown.[29] Connecting all the above in one single epic, Camões assimilates and compares the Portuguese experience to that of other glorious empires in the past. Skilfully redrawing the line between fact and fiction, the gods of those empires are now on the side of Portugal, the legitimate heir to their imperial greatness. Thus none less than Jupiter sets the stage in Canto One:

Eternal dwellers in the starry heavens, you will not have forgotten the great valour of that brave people of the Portuguese. You cannot therefore be unaware of that it is the fixed resolve of destiny that before their achievements those of Assyrians, Persians, Greeks and Romans shall fade into oblivion. Already with negligible forces ... they have expelled the Moslem ... while against the redoubtable Castilians they have invariably had heaven on their side.[30]

This task also required a shift in vantage point from the global perspective conveyed by Copernicus and the Venetian cartographers. Instead of viewing the whole world from a hypothetical point above it, Camões views this new world from a point *within* it:

Proud Europe lies between the tropic of Cancer and the Arctic zone, where cold is as intense as the heat is here on the equator. To the north and west it is bounded by the ocean, to the south by the Mediterranean Sea. And if Spain is the Head of Europe, Portugal, set at its western extremity, where land ends and sea begins, is as it were the crown on the head.[31]

Camões succeeds in mobilizing a wide range of mythological sources in his celebration of the Portuguese discoveries. Yet this might strike a more inquisitive reader as strange, since these glorious

---

[29] For an analysis of the rhetorical structure of *Os Lusíadas*, see Richard Helgerson, *Forms of Nationhood. The Elizabethan Writing of England* (Chicago: University of Chicago Press, 1992), pp. 149–63.
[30] Luís Vaz de Camões, *The Lusiads* (Harmondsworth: Penguin, 1952), p. 42.
[31] Camões, *Lusiads*, pp. 78–80.

battles also include Viriato's guerrilla-like war against the Romans. But why so daringly count on the support of Roman deities while taking so much pride in their victory *against* the Romans? Would not that most likely upset the same deities, and tempt them to withdraw their support because of the obvious hubris of the Portuguese? But *Os Lusíadas* is built on a strategy of textual assimilation. Everything that is foreign to the Portuguese in time and space is gradually swallowed up in the course of their providential march to unity and grandeur. Memory traces of earlier empires and their gods are visible and intelligible only to the extent that they condition the formation of the Portuguese people, and can be used to justify its achievements. Portugal and the Portuguese become real only to the extent that the Romans are forgotten other than as a distant yardstick of military valour and aristocratic virtue. But in order to institute this forgetfulness in a persuasive way, the Romans must be confronted and beaten on their mythological home ground, as it were. This is done by the fearsome creature of Adamastor, who introduces himself in the following way in Canto Five:

I am that mighty hidden cape, called by you Portuguese the Cape of Storms, that neither Ptolemy, Pomponius, Strabo, Pliny nor any other of past times ever had knowledge of. This promontory of mine, jutting out towards the South Pole, marks the southern extremity of Africa. Until now it has remained unknown: your daring offends it deeply. Adamastor is my name. I was one of the giant sons of earth, brother of Enceladus, Briareus, and the others. With them I took part in the war against Jupiter, not indeed piling mountain upon mountain but as a sea-captain, disputing with Neptune's squadrons the command of the deep.[32]

It seems as though Vasco da Gama has finally met somebody in the same trade from whom he has things to learn. The discovery of Adamastor by Vasco marks the final poetic victory over the Romans, since this bizarre innovation by Camões is a potent newcomer in the Western gallery of mythological creatures. His claim to fame is to have fought none other than Jupiter himself, if only in order to be turned into a rock as a punishment. Yet, as we might recall from Matthew's gospel, being turned into a rock is not necessarily a bad thing, since

---

[32] Camões, *Lusiads*, p. 131.

both empires and churches can be built on them.[33] And through this double move, Vasco da Gama is now admitted to the same aristocratic hall of fame, closely followed by his men, 'since no trial, however great, has caused them to falter in that unshakable loyalty and obedience which is the crowning quality of the Portuguese'.[34]

Thus, Camões succeeded in creating a veritable poetic vortex that sucked up what was of value in both Roman and Christian symbolic heritage, and twisted all those memory fragments into a poetic defence of Portuguese peoplehood and imperial ambition.[35] In a gesture that would later find its full justification in Vico's attempt to shed light on the 'deplorable obscurity' of the origin of nations, Camões established a mnemonic practice that could make sense of a desired future of a people in terms of a past which could then be made to look increasingly alien and easily forgotten.[36] Doing this, he could draw on an established tradition of rhetorical prophecy which had earlier been used to boost dynastic claims against the Castilians.[37] This was the final victory of the Portuguese over the Romans, a victory which made it possible for Camões to find his place alongside the other heroes of the discoveries.

But the same tactics of assimilation could be used in cross-cultural comparisons as well. When the illustrious Fernão Mendes Pinto, 'who in twenty-one years was five times shipwrecked, thirteen times taken captive, and seventeen times sold as a slave',[38] posthumously had his work defended against popular disbelief by the Lisbon editors of his *Peregrinaçam* (1614), they did so by appealing to the impeccable nature of Pinto's memory.[39] Whether his memory was impeccable or

---

[33] Matthew 16:18–19. [34] Camões, *Lusiads*, p. 134.
[35] For an analysis, see David Quint, *Epic and Empire. Politics and Generic Form from Virgil to Milton* (Princeton, NJ: Princeton University Press, 1993), pp. 113–25.
[36] Giambattista Vico, *The New Science* [1746] (Ithaca, NY: Cornell University Press, 1976), pp. 102–3.
[37] See Helder Macedo, 'The Rhetoric of Prophecy in Portuguese Renaissance Literature', *Portuguese Studies*, vol. 19, 2003, pp. 9–18.
[38] Joseph Addison, 'Frozen Voices', *Tatler*, no. 254, 23 November 1710, adapted from *The Voyages and Adventures of Fernand Mendez Pinto*, translated into English by H. Cogan [1653] (facsimile London: Dawsons of Pall Mall, 1969), p. 1.
[39] *Voyages and Adventures of Fernand Mendez Pinto*, preface, folio A.

not, his book certainly exemplified a structure that would prove fruitful to subsequent imperial exploits by both the Portuguese and the British. Pinto carefully chronicles his experiences and impressions of Africa, India, China and Japan, and compares local customs in those places with those of the Portuguese and its nobility. Not surprisingly, Pinto frequently finds the virtues of the latter reflected in the demeanour of local princes, and is often greeted with hospitality by them.[40]

Pinto's narrative is based on a chronological recall of events. But before it was published, the manuscript had been entrusted to the chronicler Francisco de Andrade who subdivided it into chapters. This subdivision was done according to the principles of contemporary cartography, so that each chapter eventually came to narrate experiences specific to distinct places as the voyage proceeded. Although somewhat cumbersome, the resulting division makes the *Peregrinaçam* look akin to the index of an atlas or a modern guidebook. Consequently, in the English translation of 1653, names of places are consistently italicized, as are brief orations. Much in the same vein, Damião de Góis – a friend of Erasmus – had published his *Urbis olisiponis descriptio* in 1554, which applied similar geographical principles when describing the features of Renaissance Lisbon and its surroundings, while still subscribing to Strabo's view that the city had been founded by Ulysses.[41]

The works of Pinto and Góis reflect other Portuguese concerns at that time – navigation and cartography. As a result of their collaboration with Italian cartographers, the Portuguese were now using sophisticated maps and instruments to assist navigation, and hence to further imperial ambitions. In 1478, Abraham Zacuto had circulated his *Almanach perpetuum*, which made it possible to calculate latitude on the basis of the position of the sun. Other solar tables were published by Valentim Fernandes in his *Reportório dos tempos*

---

[40] *Voyages and Adventures of Fernand Mendez Pinto*, pp. 21–3.
[41] Damião de Góis, *Lisbon in the Renaissance. A New Translation of the Urbis Olisiponis Descriptio by Jeffrey S. Ruth* (New York: Italica Press, 1996). For an analysis, see Elisabeth Feist Hirsch, 'The Discoveries and the Humanists', in John Parker, ed., *Merchants and Scholars. Essays in the History of Exploration and Trade* (Minneapolis: University of Minnesota Press, 1965), pp. 33–46.

(1518) in order to further facilitate maritime explorations.[42] The gradual accumulation of knowledge in these areas led to the establishment of a hydrographical repository within the Armazem da Guine e Indias in order to keep this knowledge from falling into the hands of competitors.[43] Maps and globes also became 'prized possessions, not only keeping their owners informed of the latest discoveries and commercial ventures, but also providing them with a sense of security as to their own identity within such an ever-changing world'.[44] In the larger context of maritime exploration, this meant that the ocean, 'previously seen as an impassable barrier, by the last third of the fifteenth century had … become an intercontinental highway for those impious ships'.[45] Thus, in Portugal and elsewhere, dreams of unlimited territorial power 'found the beginnings of its realization in the map or sphere that was dedicated to the monarch, framed by his arms and traversed by his ships, and that opened up to his dreams of empire a space of intervention stretching to the limits of the terraqueous globe'.[46] In the process of expansion, the Portuguese empire had to digest all new knowledge it encountered, since it was indispensable

[42] Jerry Brotton, *Trading Territories. Mapping the Early Modern World* (London: Reaktion Books, 1997), p. 54.
[43] J. B. Harley, 'Silences and Secrecy. The Hidden Agenda of Cartography in Early Modern Europe', in Paul Laxton, ed., *The New Nature of Maps. Essays in the History of Cartography* (Baltimore, MD: Johns Hopkins University Press, 2001), pp. 84–107, at p. 93. See also A. Texeira da Mota, 'Some Notes on the Organization of Hydrographical Services in Portugal before the Beginning of the Nineteenth Century', *Imago Mundi*, vol. 28, 1976, pp. 51–60.
[44] Brotton, *Trading Territories*, p. 75.
[45] John M. Headley, 'The Sixteenth-Century Venetian Celebration of the Earth's Total Habitability: The Issue of the Fully Habitable World for Renaissance Europe', *Journal of World History*, vol. 8, no. 1, 1997, pp. 1–27, at p. 9.
[46] Frank Lestringant, *Mapping the Renaisasance World. The Geographical Imagination in the Age of Discovery* (Cambridge: Polity Press, 1994), p. 23. See also Denis Cosgrove, *Apollo's Eye. A Cartographic Genealogy of the Earth in the Western Imagination* (Baltimore, MD: Johns Hopkins University Press, 2001), pp. 79–101; David Turnbull, 'Cartography and Science in Early Modern Europe: Mapping the Construction of Knowledge Spaces', *Imago Mundi*, vol. 48, 1996, pp. 5–24; Mark Neocleous, 'Off the Map. On Violence and Cartography', *European Journal of Social Theory*, vol. 6, no. 4, 2003, pp. 409–25.

to its success and consolidation. Hence the appropriation of space on a global scale was as much a source of knowledge as it was a source of sovereignty.[47]

But before these imperial sensibilities led to a lust to dominate everything foreign, the response to the unknown was largely one of marvel. Thus Pinto's narrative is not so much a tale of subjugation and conquest as one of hardship and friendship, and of the practical problems involved in getting to know foreign people and foreign places. But first you have to get there: in his hands, the concept of *peregrination* locates this enterprise of knowing firmly in the spatial realm, so that cultural and spatial barriers appear to be more or less coextensive. In their new use, the equivalents of the Latin term *peregrinatus* came to mean something akin to aimless wandering rather than pilgrimage. As such, it was a way of travelling that was different from that denoted by the same term earlier, until pilgrimage was discredited during the sixteenth century.[48] And this is exactly what Pinto says he does: he wanders as a foreigner from place to place, his own chosen status as a foreigner permitting him to discover sameness wherever he goes. The harder it is to get to a place, the harder it is to get to know it and its inhabitants, Pinto seems to say. Yet the harder it is, the bigger the eventual payoff in terms of recognition. Whereas the Muslims encountered along the established trade routes allow for few real surprises and appear to corroborate standard prejudices against the Moor, the Chinese and Japanese are close to being unreachable, and are therefore less comprehensible but all the more fascinating. The deluge in Canton and the reaction of its inhabitants is a good example: Pinto takes their panic and hysteria to be indicative of their special devotion to God.[49]

---

[47] Brotton, *Trading Territories*, p. 83; Vitorino Magalhães Godinho, 'Entre myth et utopie: les grandes découvertes. La construction de l'espace et l'invention de l'humanite aux XVe et XVIe siècles', *Archives Européenes de Sociologie*, vol. 32, 1991, pp. 3–52.

[48] The de-legitimization of pilgrimage was largely the responsibility of Erasmus and Montaigne. See C. R. Thompson, *The Colloquies of Erasmus* (Chicago: University of Chicago Press, 1965), and Wes Williams, '"Rubbing up Against Others": Montaigne on Pilgrimage', in Jas Elsner and Joan-Pau Rubiés, *Voyages and Visions. Towards a Cultural History of Travel* (London: Reaktion Books, 1999), pp. 101–23.

[49] *Voyages and Adventures of Fernand Mendez Pinto*, p. 309.

Japan marks the spatial horizon of early Portuguese imperial experience in the same way Rome constituted its temporal horizon in Camões. It is in the encounter with this extreme otherness that the Portuguese attain collective identity. When Pinto and his companion Father Belquior eventually arrive in Japan, having survived a series of disasters in China, Pinto sets out to the Fortress of Osquy in order to meet the 'king' just to discover that the king has gone fishing on the isle of Xequa, 'entertaining himself in the catching of a great Fish, whereof the name was not known, and which has come thither from the bottom of the Sea, with a great number of other little fishes'. Pinto's curiosity is momentarily relieved by a sumptuous feast, whereupon he receives an invitation to go fishing with the king, 'for on thy coming, and on the death which I hope to give to this Fish, my perfect content depends'.[50] This done – whale killed and all – Pinto explains this act of hospitality in terms of the esteem enjoyed by the Portuguese, 'for all the inhabitants held it for most certain, that the King of Portugal was indeed the only Prince, which might term himself the Monarch of the world, as well as for the large extent of his territories, as for his power, and mighty treasure'.[51] The same enthusiasm was obviously shared by the king himself, since he, upon hearing about the military strength of Portugal, said 'I sware truly unto you, that I should desire nothing so much in the world, as to see the Monarchy of this great Country, whereof I have heard such wonderful things'.[52] It was accounts like these that were responsible for Pinto's reputation as a liar, at home as well as abroad. To be sure, the *Peregrinaçam* is sprinkled with other fantastic events, yet it lacked those chapters on mermaids and tritons that were more or less mandatory in the chorography of the day.[53] Nonetheless, it was Pinto – rather than Camões or Góis – that came to be known as the epitome of a liar.[54]

As a consequence of his method of assimilation, Pinto simply failed to make exotic places appear sufficiently strange to command

---

[50] *Voyages and Adventures of Fernand Mendez Pinto*, p. 311.
[51] *Voyages and Adventures of Fernand Mendez Pinto*, p. 312.
[52] *Voyages and Adventures of Fernand Mendez Pinto*, p. 314.
[53] See for example Góis, *Lisbon in the Renaissance*, pp. 10–12.
[54] William Congreve, *Love for Love* [1695] (London: Macmillan, 1967), II:5: 'Fernando Mendez Pinto was but a type of thee, thou liar of the first magnitude.'

the credence of his contemporaries. With this in mind, Pinto's *Peregrinaçam* could safely be shuffled into the recesses of libraries in Coimbra and Oxford as an entertaining travelogue. His tale of colonial experience could be celebrated as a masterpiece of vernacular prose, and compared with the poetry of Camões, but with little factual accuracy attributed to its content. Yet *Peregrinaçam* contains a recipe for remembrance that would continue to resonate throughout the coming centuries. As we have seen above, the radically new meaning attributed to the concept of pilgrimage brings a silent revolution in the art of travelling, permitting the traveller to assimilate different experiences by virtue of casting *himself* rather than the Other as the foreigner: where those chroniclers who had gone to the Americas had found little but insurmountable otherness, Pinto is shaking hands with people all over the East.[55]

When the spatial grid of Renaissance geography was superimposed on this story of hardship and friendship, the flow of memory is broken up and confined to episodes taking place at distinct places at distinct times, as if the act of remembering itself was a matter of navigating the seas of past experience. To assimilate within a framework of spatial differentiation means making difference relative to space, and then making similarity contingent on the ability to move across the geographical boundaries erected by the same practice of differentiation. Moving across these boundaries is tantamount to finding infinite points of similarity, while effectively repressing all difference that cannot be understood as being conditioned by spatial distance. As we have seen in the case of Pinto, this is accomplished through a peregrination that takes us across the surface of the planet, while keeping the range of resources used for explaining these differences constant: Christian virtue and natural accident. To Pinto, other worlds exist only to the extent that they can be incorporated into the tale of Portuguese identity and its ultimate mastery of the world.

---

[55] Compare Tzvetan Todorov, *The Conquest of America: The Question of the Other* (New York: Harper and Row, 1992); Anthony Pagden, *European Encounters with the New World* (New Haven, CT: Yale University Press, 1993), pp. 17–49; Joan-Pau Rubiés, 'The Oriental Voices of Mendes Pinto, or the Traveller as Ethnologist in Portuguese India', *Portuguese Studies*, vol. 10, 1994, pp. 24–43.

But the Portuguese were not to be left alone in their quest for global mastery. Similar efforts to create a nation and an empire on the basis of ancient myths produced similar results in England during the same period. While this quest for identity was motivated in part by the need for domestic legitimacy, it also fuelled overseas expansion and dreams of global empire. Again the geographical and cartographical revolutions provided these ambitions with critical momentum. As Hakluyt claims in his *Principal Navigations* (1589), he was the first 'that produced and shewed both the olde imperfectly composed, and the new lately reformed Mappes, Globes, Spheares, and other instruments of this Art for demonstration in the common schooles, to the singular pleasure, and generall contentment of my auditory ... I meddle in this worke with the Nauigations onely of our owne nation.'[56] The conceptual resources with which this nation was built were drawn from a variety of ancient and medieval sources, making Tudor imperialism 'a blend of nascent nationalism and surviving medieval universalism'.[57] In order to achieve this precious blend, authors like Davenant and Drayton transferred symbols and images from the Roman Empire and Christianity to the new context of the territorial state.[58] True to this ambition, Drayton warns against staying local in the quest for nationhood in his *Poly-Olbion* (1613). Those who remain content to do this are, '[p]ossest with such stupidity and dulnesse, that rather then thou wilt take pains to search into ancient and noble things, choosest to remaine in the thicke fogges and mistes of ignorance, as neere the common Lay-stall of a Citie; refusing to walker forth into the Tempe and Feelds of the Muses'.[59]

---

[56] Richard Hakluyt, *Principal Navigations, Voyages, Traffiques and Discoveries of the English Nation* (London, 1589), dedicatory epistle and preface. See Armitage, *Ideological Origins of the British Empire*, pp. 61–99.

[57] Yates, *Astraea*, p. 87; Helgerson, *Forms of Nationhood*, pp. 107–47; Armitage, 'Elizabethan Idea of Empire'.

[58] Patricia Springborg, 'Global Identity: Cosmopolitan Localism', paper presented at IPSA, Seoul, 17–21 August 1997. Cited by kind permission of the author.

[59] Michael Drayton, *Poly-Olbion, or a chorographicall description of the tracts, riuers, mountaines, forests, and other parts of this renowned Isle of Great Britaine*, quoted in Springborg, 'Global Identity', p. 29.

In order to actually manifest the kind of identity that this poem so eloquently celebrates, nascent nationalism had to be disseminated to the populace in order to stir the right sentiments in them. Thus Davenant speculated about how to turn his own proto-nationalist poetry into popular entertainment. In his *Proposition for the Advancement of Moralities* (1651), this was to be done through a spectacle, 'in which shall be presented severall ingenious Arts, as Motion and transposition of Lights; to make a more naturall resemblance of the great and virtuous actions of such as are eminent in Story; and chiefly of those whose famous Battails and Land and Sea by which this Nation is renown'd'.[60] That the theatre was chosen as the preferred channel of dissemination is perhaps no coincidence, since the way in which theatres were constructed closely reflected simultaneous developments in the art of memory during the Renaissance.[61] Ultimately, the purpose of this reappropriation and assimilation of the Roman and Christian heritage was not only to create a sense of common identity, but also to reinforce the legitimacy of their monarchy by wrapping the English crown in mythical splendour.[62] As Selden commented on Drayton's efforts, 'If in Prose and Religion it were justifiable, as in Poetry and Fiction, to invoke a *Locall Power* (for anciently both *Jewes, Gentiles & Christians* have supposed to every Countrey a singular *Genius*) I would therein joyne with the Author.'[63]

In this section, we have seen how early modern political identities were created by means of strategies of remembrance that assimilated everything useful in the past, while simultaneously erasing the traces of this act of assimilation. These strategies made it possible to transfer symbols from boundless visions of community first to the emergent world of empires, and then to states. What was deemed of value in the past was dug up from ancient sources, reinterpreted and then attributed to the guardians of early modern order, the crown, the nobility and the church. It was then a truly monumental task to disseminate this collective memory to the people and make it stick in an age when literacy was still a privilege of the few. Poetry presupposed a degree

---

[60] William Davenant, *Proposition for the Advancement of Moralities*, quoted in Springborg, 'Global Identity', p. 30.
[61] Yates, *The Art of Memory*, pp. 310–54.
[62] Yates, *Astraea*, pp. 59–87.
[63] John Selden, 'Illustrations', quoted in Springborg, p. 30.

of literacy that made it impractical for this purpose if not staged into spectacles, a fact which confined much of the knowledge of 'national traditions' to the elites that had invented them. But the early modern strategy par excellence had been to create spatial symbols of identity that could be deciphered in terms of those virtues that had been appropriated from the ancients.[64] Cathedrals, royal palaces and public buildings were erected with remarkable stylistic uniformity throughout Europe during this period, drawing on similar principles of construction and decoration.

When we reach the end of the seventeenth century, the substratum of modern nationhood had been created, with or without the aid of singular geniuses. This had little to do with what happened or did not happen in Westphalia, but more to do with the shift in cosmological perspective that occurred at the beginning of this century when geographical and cartographical knowledge was being harnessed for the purposes of state-building and imperial expansion. The vantage point from which human affairs could be contemplated was then literally brought down to earth. It was no longer located over and above the terrestrial globe, but at a series of discrete points on the planetary surface, each gradually corresponding to a claim to territorial sovereignty.

It was then but a short step to particularizing existing historical memories, by assimilating the whole array of symbols, metaphors, and tropes within emergent vernacular literary traditions. This process was greatly facilitated by the philosophical contention that historical memory is constitutive of identity, implying that those parts of the past that could not be tailored to fit present requirements of political identity ought simply to be forgotten. Not only were parts of a more universalistic and boundless past now recycled to boost claims to territorial authority and the particularistic identities of hopefully congruent nations, but they were also providing fresh justifications of imperial expansion. In this process, medieval and Renaissance visions

---

[64] See, for example, Anne-Marie Lecoq, 'The Symbolism of the State. The Images of the Monarchy from the Early Valois Kings to Louis XIV', in Pierre Nora, *Rethinking France: les lieux de mémoire*, vol. I: *The State* (Cambridge, MA: Harvard University Press, 2001), pp. 217–67; Françoise Choay, *The Invention of the Historic Monument* (Cambridge: Cambridge University Press, 2001), pp. 40–62.

of world community were translated into recipes for nationhood and ideologies of empire, their constituent concepts having their range of applicability firmly delimited by territorial boundaries. It was then left to others to provide the theoretical justification for what had now largely been accomplished in practice, and, by consistent omission, help readers *forget* the fact that the early modern state had been crafted out of prior and boundless conceptions of human community. Yet the plurality of territorial states thus constituted did not form an international society in any recognizably modern sense of the term, since states were still essentially embedded within the universal order of a *Respublica Christiana*, however difficult it had become to make sense of this order after the Reformation.

III

After this formative phase, the nationalization of community continued, driven forward by similar mechanisms in different contexts. Although both the Dutch Revolt and the English Civil War were prolonged disputes about the locus and scope of sovereign authority, the eventual resolution of these disputes brought new definitions of the corresponding conceptions of community. These new conceptions were tailored to fit the more successful claims to sovereignty, and came to emphasize the bounded and historically specific character of the community in question, irrespective of whether it was conceived of in religious or secular terms.[65]

But what was to become the most conclusive step towards nationalizing the concept of community was taken after the French Revolution, and in response to the problems of legitimacy that the revolutionaries had created for themselves by abolishing the old order. With the old

---

[65] Scholarship here is enormous, but for some inspiring accounts, see Graham Darby, ed., *The Origins and Development of the Dutch Revolt* (London: Routledge, 2001); Martin van Gelderen, *The Political Thought of the Dutch Revolt 1555–1590* (Cambridge: Cambridge University Press, 1992); Laura Cruz, 'The 80 Years' Question: The Dutch Revolt in Historical Perspective', *History Compass*, vol. 5, no. 3, 2007, pp. 914–34; D. Alan Orr, 'Sovereignty, Supremacy and the Origins of the English Civil War', *History*, vol. 87, no. 288, 2002, pp. 474–90; Quentin Skinner, 'Hobbes on Representation', *European Journal of Philosophy*, vol. 13, no. 2, 2005, pp. 155–84.

Nationalizing community 109

sources of authority and community so thoroughly discredited, from where was the young republic to derive legitimacy in the absence of a pre-constituted *demos*? As Rousseau formulated this problem:

For a young people to be able to relish sound principles of political theory and follow the fundamental rules of statecraft, the effect would have to become the cause; the social spirit, which should be created by those institutions, would have to preside over their very foundation; and men would have to be before the law what they should become by means of law. The legislator therefore, being unable to appeal to either force or reason, must have recourse to an authority of a different order, capable of constraining without violence and persuading without convincing.[66]

The solution to this problem proposed by Emmanuel de Sieyès may seem evident to those of us who have been accustomed to take it for granted, but it was not at all obvious to his contemporaries. As he explained, 'The nation is prior to everything. It is the source of everything. Its will is always legal; indeed it is the law itself.'[67] This called for a complete conversion of the French. As Robespierre expressed it, 'I am convinced of the need to effect a complete regeneration, and, if I may so express it, to create a new people'.[68] And indeed, such a conversion was attempted through cultural policies that 'derived their fundamental unity from their goal of transforming the French people

---

[66] Jean-Jacques Rousseau, The Social Contract [1762] in *The Social Contract and Discourses* (London: Dent, 1990), p. 216.
[67] Emmanuel de Sieyès, *What is the Third Estate?* [1789] (London: Pall Mall Press, 1963), p. 124. For an analysis, see Istvan Hont, *Jealousy of Trade. International Competition and the Nation-State in Historical Perspective* (Cambridge, MA: Harvard University Press, 2005), pp. 447–528. See also Robert Wokler, 'The Enlightenment and the French Revolutionary Birth Pangs of Modernity', in Johan Heilbron, Lars Magnusson and Björn Wittrock, eds., *The Rise of the Social Sciences and the Formation of Modernity* (Dordrecht: Kluwer, 1998), pp. 22–40; Lucien Jaume, 'Citizen and State under the French Revolution', in Bo Stråth and Quentin Skinner, eds., *States and Citizens* (Cambridge University Press, 2003), pp. 131–44.
[68] Robespierre, speech 13 July 1793, quoted in David A. Bell, *The Cult of the Nation in France. Inventing Nationalism, 1680–1800* (Cambridge, MA: Harvard University Press, 2001), p. 156. As Bell notes, this speech was given on the very day of Marat's assassination.

as a whole and giving them new unity and uniformity'.[69] But creating that kind of particular whole required a forceful intervention into the realm of collective memory, an intervention which brought a further tightening of the link between memory and identity.

As Choay and Arrhenius have shown, the French Revolution brought a renewed focus on monuments and their historicity. The Latin term itself, *monumentum*, derives from the verb *monere*, to recall: the restorative practices of the French Revolution amplified this function while imposing a systematic forgetfulness on the original symbolic meaning of the monuments thus restored. As Arrhenius argues, 'Spatial operations participated not just in constituting the monument but also in changing its significance ... it is shown how the monument, through spatial intervention, is transformed from an instrument of power into an object of knowledge and finally into a site of sentiment.'[70] In the French context, this was a way of undoing the symbolic meaning vested in monuments by the *ancien régime*, and to bestow on them new meanings more consonant with the aspirations of the Revolutionaries. In this process, contexts were altered, and objects were moved and reclassified according to new criteria. Indeed, this entire drive towards the restoration of monuments could later be celebrated as one of the significant achievements of the revolutionary age.[71]

But before these buildings and other objects could be recontextualized, they had to be appropriated, and rendered into one homogeneous class of monuments. A first step in this direction was taken in November 1789 when the Assemblée Nationale decided to dispossess the church of its property. What then ensued was the giant task of cataloguing the confiscated objects by preparing careful inventories of statues, paintings, books and manuscripts. Consequently, a Commission des Monuments was appointed in November 1790 to take care of the inventory.[72] The outcome of these efforts was the notion of a *patrimoine*, and the revolutionaries subsequently debated how this enormous collection of objects should be handled. Whereas

---

[69] Bell, *Cult of the Nation*, pp. 160–1.
[70] Thordis Arrhenius, *The Fragile Monument: On Conservation and Modernity* (Stockholm: Royal Institute of Technology, 2003), p. 10.
[71] Arrhenius, *The Fragile Monument*, p. 52.
[72] Arrhenius, *The Fragile Monument*, p. 53.

some were in favour of selling most of it in order to cancel the substantial national debt inherited from the *ancien régime*, others advocated restriction because many of these objects constituted *historical monuments*. Such objects should not be valued as religious artefacts or in terms of their mere material value, but should rather be inserted into a grand narrative of French history leading up to the events of the Revolution itself. As Arrhenius has noted, 'the notion of *monuments historiques* would turn the historical monument into a site of reflection in which the success or failure of the present epoch could be mirrored'.[73]

Eventually, those parts of ecclesiastical property that were not sold, melted down and moulded into canon-balls, or used as quarries for limestone and marble, were reclassified and rearranged as symbolic pieces of a collective memory that could legitimize the Revolution and its outcome. Practices of conservation and restoration become integral to this entire process of rebuilding the banks of collective memory to cater to a new political agenda, while effectively erasing traces of the former authority of monarchy, nobility and church.[74] Yet, as Arrhenius points out, this left the revolutionaries with the difficulty of explaining how they could claim to support the arts while condemning its former protagonist, the *ancien régime*. After all, the Revolution posed as a child of the Enlightenment.[75]

The invention of the *museum* became the solution to this dilemma, since within its walls, 'iconoclasm was achieved without destruction'.[76] A member of the Revolutionary Commission des Arts, Alexandre Lenoir, transplanted sculptures from the recently deconsecrated royal tombs at the church of Saint-Denis to the *dépôt* of Petits-Augustins, and in 1793, this was opened up to the public, being formally granted the status of Musée des Monuments Français in 1795, and then becoming a branch of the Louvre.[77] In order to delete memories of an absolutist past while recontextualizing its leftovers, this museum employed

---

[73] Arrhenius, *The Fragile Monument*, pp. 55–6.
[74] Choay, *Invention of the Historic Monument*, pp. 63–81.
[75] Arrhenius, *The Fragile Monument*, p. 60.
[76] Stanley J. Idzerda, 'Iconoclasm during the French Revolution', *American Historical Review*, vol. 60, 1954, pp. 13–26. Quoted in Arrhenius, *The Fragile Monument*, p. 68.
[77] Arrhenius, *The Fragile Monument*, p. 69.

a series of techniques not unlike those proposed by Davenant for the popular dissemination of English nationalist poetry. The monuments thus recovered were grouped together in chronological order, and put on display in rooms decorated to convey the ambience of different centuries. In the first room – illustrating the thirteenth century – the fragments collected from the tombs of Saint-Denis were on display in virtual darkness. As the visitor progressed through rooms and centuries, the amount of light gradually increased until it reached its peak in the age of Enlightenment. The progress of history, so dear to that age, was thus reflected in the sequential ordering of rooms and in the way daylight was distributed within them. The Revolutionary museum thus solved the conflict between conservation and destruction: 'Evicted from the re-generated space of the Revolutionary city, re-assembled and confined to the museum, the monuments of the *ancien régime* represented the tangible evidence of a new form of knowledge: the History of the Nation.'[78]

Thus, at the very same time as the concept of the nation made its first modern appearance in Sieyès, this invention was supplemented and sustained by a field of visibility generated by the didactic layout of the Revolutionary museum. The reality of the French nation, in all its historicity, became hard to doubt against the backdrop of these monuments and fragments, neatly lined up in order in front of the spectator. In the process, memories of the absolutist past and the identities that had corresponded to *its* ways of remembering were repressed, and later gradually forgotten. A new world of symbolic significance had been created, and another seemingly irretrievably lost. At the level of tactics, this meant that the revolutionaries had successfully escaped the 'thicke fogges and mistes of ignorance' that had previously been associated with going local in the quest for identity. Indeed, these 'fogges and mistes' were now deviously sprayed back onto that past as a means of escaping it.

Yet underlying this profound change we find a disturbing continuity, since the *strategies* of remembrance had remained fairly intact during the Revolutionary transition. The revolutionaries had succeeded in doing to the absolutist state, the church, and the nobility more or less what these prior forces had done to the symbols of universal

---

[78] Arrhenius, *The Fragile Monument*, p. 71.

community that they reappropriated for themselves. To be sure, new mnemonic techniques were developed and used by the revolutionaries, as well as new and more advanced methods for disseminating memories thus retrieved to the populace. But at the level of strategic imperatives, few things had changed. Indeed, the connection between memory, identity and territoriality seems to have been *reinforced* in this process, since collective memory was not only expressed in a spatial context – the museum – but also rendered instrumental in codifying a collective historical experience within a bounded portion of space. Memory was thereby coupled to a historical and collective subject – the nation – that could finally be made congruent with the territory of a state. The coincidence of state and nation that we normally take to be the culmination of a successful process of state formation had virtually been *remembered* into existence. But what was conveniently forgotten in this process was not only the *ancien régime*, but also the entire legacy of universal community which had furnished this process with the conceptual raw material essential to its completion.

Thus, the firmly territorialized connection between memory and identity forged by the revolutionaries was the end of a cumulative series of strategic interventions in the field of social memory. In this process, myths were gradually replaced by monuments as the main carriers of collective memory during modernity.[79] With this in mind, it seems as though Hume had caught the Enlightenment spirit of remembrance very well, as he insisted on both its constitutive relation to identity and its arbitrary character. Memory and identity had indeed been rigorously connected in practice, but in a way that was as philosophically arbitrary as were the attempts to create a *demos* on the basis of this connection. Nevertheless, that there was such a connection had become increasingly hard to doubt. As Renan summarized the end result in 1882, 'A nation is a soul, a spiritual principle. Two things, which in truth are but one, constitute this soul or spiritual principle. One lies in the past, one in the present. One is the possession in common of a rich legacy of memories; the other is present-day consent, the desire to live together, the will to perpetuate the value of

---

[79] Nuala Johnson, 'Cast in Stone: Monuments, Geography, and Nationalism', *Environment and Planning D: Society and Space*, vol. 13, no. 1, 1995, pp. 51–65.

the heritage that one has received in an undivided form.'[80] Thus, the concept of community, from having been defined and used in universalistic terms by medieval and Renaissance scholars, had now found a new and paradigmatic expression in the nation-state. This nationalization also brought an international society composed of such bounded communities, fully in accordance with the prophecies of the *ius naturalists*, albeit later than we have been led to believe by the Westphalian myth. We must now turn our attention to the responses that such nationalization provoked among those who reflected upon its consequences.

---

[80] Ernest Renan, 'What is a Nation?' in Geoff Eley and Ronald Grigor Suny, eds., *Becoming National: A Reader* (Oxford: Oxford University Press, 1996), pp. 41–55, at p. 52. On the institutionalization of these ideas in the French context, see Sudhir Hazareesingh, *The Saint-Napoleon. Celebrations of Sovereignty in Nineteenth-Century France* (Cambridge, MA: Harvard University Press, 2004).

5 | Reinventing mankind

IN the previous chapter, we saw how early modern states and empires were created and legitimized with reference to myths and symbols which had previously been used to justify universal and boundless forms of human association. As a consequence, although each group of people derived its alleged uniqueness from common sources, it had become increasingly difficult to understand these groups as parts of a wider human community, since the concept of community had its range of applicability equally restricted by territorial boundaries. The fictitious state of nature invented in order to justify this transition to bounded forms of association was thereby ironically realized *between* emergent territorial states.[1]

But during the eighteenth century dreams of a universal empire based on conquest and conversion become harder to sustain. New ideologies of empire based on the virtues of trade and manufacture emerged, leading to intensified economic and political competition between these trading states.[2] To those critical of this new order, the division of mankind into distinct peoples was increasingly regarded as the main cause of both domestic despotism and political rivalry between states. Although key figures of eighteenth-century political thought were engaged in this critical enterprise, many of them were also responsible for propagating and perpetuating the same very particularistic conceptions of community which made the hopes of escaping the international state of nature look futile. Few authors reflect this ambivalence better than Rousseau: to him, the division

---

[1] See Richard Tuck, *The Rights of War and Peace. Political Thought and International Order from Grotius to Kant* (Oxford: Oxford University Press, 1999), pp. 6–14.

[2] Anthony Pagden, *Lords of all the World: Ideologies of Empire in Spain, Britain, and France, c.1500–1800* (New Haven, CT: Yale University Press, 1995), pp. 120ff.

of mankind into distinct societies had taken place long ago, and its outcome was both irreversible and tragic.[3] As we learn from *Discours sur l'origine d'inégalité* (1754), mankind becomes divided the very moment it enters the social state, since this transition unbridles the most destructive of human passions:

Civil right having thus become the common rule among the members of each community, the law of nature maintained its place only between different communities ... and serve as a substitute for natural compassion, which lost, when applied to societies, almost all the influence it had over individuals, and survived no longer except in some great cosmopolitan spirits, who, breaking down the imaginary barriers between different peoples, follow the example of our Sovereign Creator, and include the whole human race in their benevolence.[4]

The very establishment of bounded communities led to a situation in which 'bodies politic, remaining thus in a state of nature among themselves, presently experienced the inconveniences which had obliged individuals to forsake it'.[5] Yet the only source of hope that Rousseau is able to identify resides in 'some great cosmopolitan spirits', who hope but are unlikely to be able to restore the lost unity of mankind. Thus, in Rousseau we encounter a first and tentative formulation of the modern tension between universalistic and particularistic viewpoints.[6]

In this chapter, I shall describe how this tension emerged as an unintended consequence of the Enlightenment critique of despotism

---

[3] On Rousseau and the natural law tradition, see Robert Wokler, 'Rousseau's Pufendorf: Natural Law and the Foundations of Commercial Society', *History of Political Thought*, vol. 15, no. 3, 1994, pp. 373–402.

[4] Jean-Jacques Rousseau, 'A Discourse on the Origin of Inequality', in Jean-Jacques Rousseau, *The Social Contract and Discourses* (London: Dent, 1990), p. 99.

[5] Rousseau, 'Discourse on the Origin of Inequality', p. 99.

[6] Robert Wokler, 'The Enlightenment: The Nation-State and the Primal Patricide of Modernity', in Norman Geras and Robert Wokler, eds., *Enlightenment and Modernity* (London: Routledge, 2005), pp. 161–83. See also Robert Wokler, 'Isaiah Berlin's Enlightenment and Counter-Enlightenment', in Joseph Mali and Robert Wokler, eds., 'Isaiah Berlin's Counter-Enlightenment', special issue of *Transactions of the American Philosophical Society*, vol. 93, no. 3.

and imperialism. As I do this, I shall focus on how the *concept of mankind* was redefined and redeployed for critical purposes in eighteenth-century political thought.[7] As I shall argue, this reinvention of mankind is best understood in the context of contemporary cosmological beliefs and the change these underwent during this period. While the first phase of European expansion had mainly been a matter of maritime exploration, the second phase was more focused on the continental interiors. The cartographical knowledge generated during the first phase was now supplemented by the findings of natural history and anthropology generated during the second phase, both these disciplines being devoted to the documentation and classification of all forms of life found on foreign shores.[8] The massive influx of reports from expeditions to exotic places indicated that mankind was even more diverse than previously thought, again fuelling speculation as to whether all the peoples of the earth were indeed members of the same species. Much of this speculation had profound implications for the possibility of conceptualizing human community in universalistic terms.[9] Those who struggled to articulate visions of

---

[7] Enlightenment cosmopolitanism makes sense only against the backdrop of this reconceptualization of humanity. See, for example, Pauline Kleingeld, 'Six Varieties of Cosmopolitanism in Late-Eighteenth-Century Germany', *Journal of the History of Ideas*, vol. 60, no. 3, 1999, pp. 505–24; Ursula Vogel, 'Cosmopolitan Loyalties and Cosmopolitan Citizenship in the Enlightenment', in Michael Waller and Andrew Linklater, eds., *Political Loyalty and the Nation-State* (London: Routledge, 2003), pp. 17–26.

[8] See, for example, Mary Louise Pratt, *Imperial Eyes. Travel Writing and Transculturation* (London: Routledge, 1992), pp. 15–37; Robert Wokler, 'Anthropology and Conjectural History in the Enlightenment', in Christopher Fox, Roy Porter and Robert Wokler, eds., *Inventing Human Science: Eighteenth Century Domains* (Berkeley: University of California Press, 1996), pp. 31–52; Denis Cosgrove, *Apollo's Eye. A Cartographic Genealogy of the Earth in the Western Imagination* (Baltimore, MD: Johns Hopkins University Press, 2001), pp. 189–204; Ursula Vogel, 'The Sceptical Enlightenment: Philosopher Travellers Look Back at Europe', in Geras and Wokler, *Enlightenment and Modernity*, pp. 3–24.

[9] David N. Livingstone, 'Geographical Inquiry, Rational Religion, and Moral Philosophy: Enlightenment Discourses on the Human Condition', in David N. Livingstone and Charles W. J. Withers, *Geography and Enlightenment* (Chicago: University of Chicago Press, 1999), pp. 93–119.

world community thus had to reconcile the seemingly infinite diversity of human customs and moral standards found in all those recently discovered corners of the earth with their inherited universalistic conceptions of humanity. In Enlightenment social thought, the concept of *race* and theories of racial differences between people on different continents provided one way of handling this difficult dilemma. As Buffon argued, 'every circumstance concurs in proving, that mankind are not composed of species essentially different from each other; that, on the contrary, there was originally but one species, who, after multiplying and spreading over the whole surface of the earth, have undergone various changes by the influence of climate, food, mode of living, epidemic diseases, and the mixture of dissimilar individuals'.[10] Yet insisting on the basically unitary character of mankind posed a further problem, since it was hard to make sense of mankind without reference to something sacred located above the temporal and terrestrial existence of mortal human beings. In response to these problems, eighteenth-century conceptions of mankind tend to be both *holistic* and *secular* in outlook. Mankind is conceived of as something more than the sum of its individual parts, and individual human beings are considered human precisely by virtue of being members of mankind. Mankind is in turn understood as one single and immanent community firmly located in the temporal realm, yet subdivided into races whose characteristics were explained by differences in climate and social context. Although most of these conceptions assumed a natural hierarchy between races, the issue was no longer whether human beings encountered on other continents were in fact human or not. Thus, given the context within which such conceptions of mankind and humanity were articulated, I think we should be careful not to reduce them to attempts to justify imperial expansion by means of an appeal to universal reason.[11] In the following sections, I shall describe

---

For humanity as an object of knowledge during this period, see Michel Foucault, *The Order of Things. An Archaeology of the Human Sciences* (London: Routledge, 1989), pp. 303–87; Roy Porter, *The Enlightenment* (Houndmills: Palgrave, 2001), pp. 11–21.

[10] Georges-Louis Leclerc, comte de Buffon, 'The Geographical and Cultural Distribution of Mankind', in Emmanuel Chukwudi Eze, ed., *Race and the Enlightenment. A Reader* (Oxford: Blackwell, 1997), pp. 14–28, at p. 27.

[11] Anthony Pagden, 'Human Rights, Natural Rights, and Europe's Imperial Legacy', *Political Theory*, vol. 31, no. 2, 2003, pp. 171–99; Sankar

how the critique of the natural law tradition by Shaftesbury and Vico pushed forward a redefinition of mankind in such holistic and secular terms. In the third section, I shall analyse how such conceptions of mankind were translated into essentially critical visions and projected onto a global political space by Turgot, Diderot and Raynal.

I

One of the main ambitions of Enlightenment political thought was to explain and justify the existence of political authority without any explicit reference to theological concepts or religious authority. This aspiration had been inaugurated by Grotius and Hobbes, and expectations of its completion were to animate political reflection during the coming centuries as well.[12] Although a secular account of political authority was indispensable to any critique of early modern statecraft, such an account was also fraught with danger since it might easily spill over into a de-legitimization of the very ideas in whose name this criticism was undertaken. Enlightenment criticism of absolutist political authority had to be undertaken in the name of a community of free human beings in order to have the desired impact, yet this concept of a community of free human beings was initially very hard to separate from the Christian framework within which it had originated, and from which absolutist rule also derived much of its legitimacy.[13]

The critics of the early modern state were thus faced with a dilemma. In order to be able to de-legitimize despotism and imperialism, they needed recourse to a conception of human community that allowed them to build a strong case in favour of human equality and dignity, but without accepting the validity of scriptural doctrine. Now the basics of such an account had been provided by Locke in his *Two*

Muthu, *Enlightenment Against Empire* (Princeton, NJ: Princeton University Press, 2003), pp. 72–209.

[12] See Quentin Skinner, 'Hobbes's Changing Conception of Civil Science', in Quentin Skinner, *Visions of Politics*, vol. III (Cambridge: Cambridge University Press, 2002), pp. 66–86; Richard Tuck, *Philosophy and Government 1572–1651* (Cambridge: Cambridge University Press, 1993), pp. 279–348.

[13] For the dilemmas of early Enlightenment criticism, see Reinhart Koselleck, *Critique and Crisis. The Pathogenesis of Modern Society* (Oxford: Berg, 1988), pp. 53–123.

Treatises of Government. While his view of human nature undeniably rested on Christian foundations, it was hard to reconcile with other parts of his philosophy where he had taken the existence of a divided mankind for granted.[14] To Locke, all human beings are equal by virtue of being members of the same species, but in practice this equality is compromised by the existence of national boundaries that effectively separate communities from each other, politically as well as morally.[15] Most of the critics of the early modern state thus faced the difficult choice between retaining conceptions of a common humanity along with their unmistakably religious foundations, or becoming secular while losing sight of anything commonly human over and above the plurality of distinct peoples. This problem was further aggravated by a growing sense of moral difference between cultures, as the penetration of new continents yielded a constant stream of accounts that seemed to vindicate such conclusions. Enlightenment critics tried to formulate holistic and secular conceptions of humanity that could render such diversity as meaningful and fully legitimate expressions of one and the same underlying humanity, thereby widening the range of applicability of this latter concept to include peoples previously excluded. Yet some of these assumptions were hard to reconcile with the fact that the nationalization of the concept of community was among the undeniable outcomes of the French Revolution, threatening to relegate notions of a universal humanity and visions of world community to the status of unattainable utopias.[16]

But, I would like to suggest, many of our seemingly secular ideals of a universal humanity owe more to religious discourse than some of its modern proponents have been willing to admit. In making this point,

---

[14] Daniel Carey, *Locke, Shaftesbury, and Hutcheson. Contesting Diversity in the Enlightenment and Beyond* (Cambridge: Cambridge University Press, 2006), pp. 1–97.

[15] John Locke, *Two Treatises of Government*, vol. II, ed. Peter Laslett (Cambridge: Cambridge University Press, 1988), §45. For an excellent study of the religious foundations of his doctrine of equality, see Jeremy Waldron, *God, Locke, and Equality. Christian Foundations of Locke's Political Thought* (Cambridge: Cambridge University Press, 2002), esp. pp. 126–30.

[16] See Istvan Hont, *Jealousy of Trade. International Competition and the Nation-State in Historical Perspective* (Cambridge, MA: Harvard University Press, 2005), pp. 447–528.

I shall draw on the works of two authors who have not received much attention within the study of political thought: Shaftesbury and Vico. Some of this neglect is due to the fact that these authors can hardly be described as *political* philosophers in the narrow sense of the term, since they had very little to say about questions of sovereign authority and its legitimacy. Another reason why their works have received so little attention is their ambiguous attitude to reason, which has disqualified both authors from full membership in the Enlightenment canon.[17] By contrast, both Shaftesbury and Vico were more interested in the question of human community, and appealed more to sentiment and myth in their attempts to understand its foundations. This is also precisely what makes these authors interesting in the present context. Both of them tried to make sense of human community in opposition to the standard accounts of their age, and by doing this they provided the conceptual foundations upon which later conceptions of world community were built.[18]

These standard accounts were based either on providence or universal reason. According to the providential view, the nature and historical trajectory of human communities ought to be understood as a manifestation of divine design and intervention. For example, Cardinal Bossuet's best-selling *Discourse on Universal History* (1681) explained political change in terms of historical providence: 'What is coincidence to our uncertain foresight is concerted design of a higher foresight, that is, to the eternal foresight which encompasses all causes and all effects in a single plan.'[19] During the eighteenth century, this view was challenged by an account that held that human communities are but expressions of human reason, and since human reason is of universal scope, so is the nature of human community. As Hume summarized this view in *An Enquiry Concerning Human Understanding*

---

[17] For a background, see Isaiah Berlin, *Vico and Herder. Two Studies in the History of Ideas* (New York: Vintage, 1976), pp. 3–142; Gertrude Himmelfarb, *The Roads to Modernity. The British, French, and American Enlightenments* (New York: Knopf, 2004), pp. 23–52. See also Jerome B. Schneewind, *The Invention of Autonomy* (Cambridge: Cambridge University Press, 1998), pp. 261–309.

[18] For their influence on Diderot and Kant, see Schneewind, *Invention of Autonomy*, pp. 466–70, 483–530.

[19] Jacques Bénigne Bossuet, *Discourse on Universal History* [1681] (Chicago: University of Chicago Press, 1976), p. 374.

(1748), 'Mankind are so much the same, in all times and places, that history informs of nothing new or strange … Its chief use is only to show men in all varieties of circumstances and situations, and furnishing us with materials from which we may form our observations and become acquainted with the regular springs of human action and behaviour.'[20] To many Enlightenment philosophers, such uniformity of human nature was an essential prerequisite for a secular morality. Such a secular morality could hopefully be extracted from actually existing human communities by means of scientific observation, thus gradually undoing the need for religious authority to support it.

Shaftesbury and Vico accepted none of these views of human community. Rejecting rationalistic accounts of moral authority, they also rejected the contractual view of society along with its implications for relations between communities: to the *ius naturalists*, individual communities coexisted in a state of nature to the effect that violent conflict between them appeared to be an inescapable part of the human condition. Shaftesbury opposed this view on several grounds. First, he objected to the atomistic conception of the individual that provided the foundation of the social contract in Hobbes and Locke. Instead, he understood human beings to be profoundly sociable, to such an extent that they could not be meaningfully thought of apart from the community in which they live. It is thus 'ridiculous to say that there is any obligation on man to act sociably or honestly in a formed government and not in that which is commonly called the state of nature', since man is 'made rational and sociable and can not otherwise increase or subsist than in that social intercourse and community which is his natural state'.[21] Second, Shaftesbury found himself in equally sharp disagreement with the way the division of mankind into distinct communities had been explained in the natural law tradition. The division of mankind was not the outcome of a series of multiple social compacts, but rather the result of the natural sociability of men. If 'natural affection and the care and nurture of the offspring be natural … it follows that society must also be

---

[20] David Hume, *An Enquiry Concerning Human Understanding* (Oxford: Oxford University Press, 1902), p. 84.
[21] Anthony Ashley Cooper, third earl of Shaftesbury, *Characteristics of Men, Manners, Opinions, Times* [1711/14] (Cambridge: Cambridge University Press, 1999), pp. 51, 283.

natural to him and that out of society and community he never did, nor ever can, subsist'.[22] Men are thus 'naturally and necessarily united for each other's happiness and support'. And without this general society of mankind, 'The division of climates and regions is fantastic and artificial, much more the limits of particular countries, cities, or provinces.'[23] Third, even if Shaftesbury believed that the particular communities are formed as a result of the natural affection between human beings, he implicitly denied that the particular community ever could be the ultimate source of moral sentiment or judgement. Instead, he regarded mankind as a whole to be the proper frame of reference when judging human affairs, since 'a public spirit can come only from a social feeling or sense of partnership with humankind'.[24] Yet as he readily admits, 'that greater community falls not easily under the eye'.[25] This left Shaftesbury with the difficulty of inferring moral precepts from this rather vague notion of a universal mankind, and without appealing to religious authority or universal reason. The only moral category comprising all mankind is the *sensus communis*, which denotes 'a sense of public weal, and of the common interest, love of the community or society, natural affection, humanity, obligingness, or that sort of civility which rises from a just sense of the common rights of mankind, and the natural equality there is among those of the same species'.[26]

Thus, Shaftesbury understands humanity in a way that is both universalistic and communitarian: being sociable is what makes human beings *human* in all times and in all places. In his view, man is not only inseparable from the concrete community in which he finds himself out of necessity and affection, but each man is also a member of mankind as a whole, to which he owes his very *capacity* for a social life and moral virtue. Within the Stoic view that he struggles so hard to reinvigorate, mankind is only comprehensible within the context of a larger cosmos, reflecting a purposeful design of both nature and

---

[22] Shaftesbury, *Characteristics*, p. 287.
[23] Shaftesbury, *Characteristics*, p. 401. For an interesting discussion of his criticism of Locke's account of human diversity, see Carey, *Locke, Shaftesbury, and Hutcheson*, pp. 98–149.
[24] Shaftesbury, *Characteristics*, p. 50.
[25] Shaftesbury, *Characteristics*, p. 52.
[26] Shaftesbury, *Characteristics*, p. 48.

society, which mutually and harmoniously sustain and reinforce each other within the same order. While there is no clear conception of world community to be found in Shaftesbury, he cultivates the notion that human beings are first and foremost members of mankind, and that this membership is necessary in order to attain belonging within the particular community. Mankind thus constitutes one immanent moral community upon which all human beings depend for their existence. This was an idea that would continue to resonate in later Enlightenment political thought.

But how should we handle the undesirable consequences of the division of mankind into particular communities? Again Shaftesbury has no answer that would satisfy a modern political theorist. The moral framework he proposes is limited to the boundless *sensus communis*. This common sense is inherent in the moral capacity of men, and also an integral part of their sociability. While such common sense can never be the final arbiter of truth, it is capable of acting as a mediating instance in those cases where the moral standards of particular communities or their members happen to come into conflict. It thus refers to the sense of civility that can be manifested among human beings within as well as across communities, and which ideally would provide a touchstone of human thought and action. As such, the *sensus communis* makes it possible for human beings to create concrete universals out of what otherwise would remain their purely particularistic and idiosyncratic standards of judgement.[27] As we shall note in this chapter and the next, this proposition would be further developed by some of his successors.

II

The next step towards a reinvention of humanity was taken by Vico. Although written in a different context and from a very different perspective, Vico's *Scienza nuova* (1725) is equally critical of the natural law tradition. Starting from the assumption that mankind is uniform and men sociable, Vico tries to uncover the generic principles

---

[27] For an analysis see Valentina Gueorguieva, 'La connaissance de l'indéterminé. Le sens commun dans la théorie de l'action', unpublished dissertation (Université Laval, Quebec: Faculté des Sciences Sociales, 2004), ch. 1.

underlying all known human communities, in order to formulate a general account of human community that is both universal and open to variation across time and space. He then sets out to explain the actual division of mankind into distinct communities in terms of such spatio-temporal variation. As Vico begins by stating, 'The philosophers have not yet contemplated His providence in respect of that of it which is most proper to men, whose nature has this principal property: that of being social ... It will be shown in the present work that this is the true civil nature of man, and that law exists in nature.'[28] This social nature further implies that 'the world of civil society certainly has been made by men, and that its principles are therefore to be found within the modifications of our own human mind'.[29] Consequently, in order to attain knowledge of this world, Vico proposes the development of a rational civil theology which, 'studying the common nature of nations in the light of divine providence, discovers the origins of divine and human institutions among the gentile nations, and thereby establishes a system of the natural law of the gentes'.[30] This new science will investigate the history of 'the ideas, the customs, and the deeds of mankind. From these three we shall derive the principles of the history of human nature, which we shall show to be the principles of universal history.'[31] Thus, in order to understand these former ideas, customs, and deeds we need to know their origins, and this knowledge is by its very nature historical in character. Social and political institutions cannot be understood with reference to timeless principles of human nature, and since human nature develops in tandem with those institutions, both are expressive of the same underlying patterns in history. Our science, writes Vico, 'comes to describe at the same time an eternal history traversed in time by the history of every nation in its rise, development, maturity, decline, and fall'.[32]

To Vico, the fact that the human race has always lived and still lives in societies is enough to resolve the question whether laws exist by nature or by convention, since to him, *physis* and *nomos*

---

[28] Giambattista Vico, *The New Science* (Ithaca, NY: Cornell University Press, 1976), §2, p. 3–4.
[29] Vico, *New Science*, §331, p. 96.   [30] Vico, *New Science*, §31, p. 20.
[31] Vico, *New Science*, §368, p. 112.
[32] Vico, *New Science*, §349, p. 104

are necessarily inseparable.[33] Vico thus opposes both Grotius and Pufendorf, according to whom universal law is the product of human reason alone, being duly instantiated in the laws of particular communities.[34] To Vico, these laws rather derive from the *sensus communis* of men, which he defines as 'judgement without reflection, shared by an entire class, an entire people, an entire nation, or the entire human race'.[35] In his interpretation, the *sensus communis* not only provides the foundation of law *within* distinct communities, but also of the relationship between distinct communities. This is so since 'uniform ideas originating among entire peoples unknown to each other must have a common ground of truth'. This in turn 'establishes the common sense of the human race as the criterion taught to the nations by divine providence to define what is certain in the natural law of the gentes'. Different nations then 'reach this certainty by recognizing the underlying agreements which, despite variations of detail, obtain among them all in respect of this law'.[36] Legal principles can therefore be embodied in different ways in different communities, yet beyond all these superficial differences there is a universal law of all humanity.

But provided that there is such a universal law of all mankind, how was this law able to spread if mankind had already been divided into distinct communities and dispersed into different places? Admittedly, this natural law 'had separate origins among the several peoples, each in ignorance of the others, and it was only subsequently, as a result of wars, embassies, alliances, and commerce, that it came to be recognized as common to the entire human race'.[37] Vico suggests that 'There must in the nature of human institutions be a mental language common to all nations, which uniformly grasps the substance of things feasible in human social life and expresses it with as many diverse modifications as these same things may have diverse aspects.'[38] The main task of the *Scienza nuova* is to decipher this mental language in order to gain an understanding of the most general principles of the

---

[33] Vico, *New Science*, §135, p. 62.
[34] John D. Schaeffer, *Sensus Communis. Vico, Rhetoric, and the Limits of Relativism* (Durham, NC: Duke University Press, 1990), p. 82.
[35] Vico, *New Science*, §142, p. 63.
[36] Vico, *New Science*, §144–5, pp. 63–4.
[37] Vico, *New Science*, §146, p. 64.   [38] Vico, *New Science*, §161, p. 67.

sensus communis, thereby laying bare the foundations upon which *all* human community ultimately must rest. To this end, Vico outlines a comprehensive teleology that purports to explain the transition from primitive to more advanced forms of human association. While each such stage of human development is represented as a cohesive convergence of linguistic, social and legal elements, the transition between them is explained with reference to principles of providential progress. While being divinely ordained, this progress is propelled by the more unsociable traits of mankind: 'Out of ferocity, avarice, and ambition, the three vices which run throughout the human race, it creates the military, merchant, and governing classes, and thus the strength, riches and wisdom of commonwealths. Out of these three great vices, which could certainly destroy all mankind on the face of the earth, it makes civil happiness.'[39]

To Vico, mankind consists of a plurality of different communities, each of them being a particular and integrated whole with a moral life of its own. Yet all these communities are variations on a common underlying theme – that of human community in the universal sense. As Gadamer has argued in this context, 'what gives the human will its direction is not the abstract universality of reason but the concrete universality represented by the community of a group, a people, a nation, or the whole human race'.[40] Hence, the actual differentiation of mankind into distinct communities only makes sense against the backdrop of a common humanity, and the concept of a common humanity only takes on meaning in relation to the actual diversity of human communities. In order to make sense of the fact that mankind constitutes one single community despite the fact of being divided into distinct groups, Vico gives the concept of *sensus communis* a meaning slightly different from that found in Shaftesbury. As Gadamer has remarked, 'the *sensus communis* is the sense of what is right and of the common good that is to be found in all men ... it is a sense that is acquired through living in the community and is determined by its structures and aims'.[41] So rather than being merely a way of describing what is common to members of one particular community, the

---

[39] Vico, *New Science*, §132, p. 62.
[40] Hans-Georg Gadamer, *Truth and Method* (New York: Continuum, 1989), p. 21.
[41] Gadamer, *Truth and Method*, p. 22.

sensus communis is what actually constitutes groups of peoples into communities by providing them with a common language, this language being a repository of their founding myths.[42]

To Vico, mankind as a whole is not categorically distinct from the lesser communities that compose it, since both are but instantiations of the same underlying principles. The universal community constituted by mankind as a whole as well as by particular communities rests on the same foundation, that of the *sensus communis*, being expressive of the common mental language that is the foundation of communal life among all human beings.[43] As Mali has remarked, 'What is true and common among all people ... is only the immanent process of "being social", a truly universal process which indeed produces many kinds of human nature and reason and society.'[44] And, as he further observes, this quest for a common mental language also amounts to a rehabilitation of myth as a category constitutive rather than merely descriptive of human experience. This implies that we must inquire into their founding myths if we want to explain how human societies have been created and sustained.

This ambition to turn myth into an object of inquiry in its own right distinguishes Vico from many of his predecessors. While authors like Dante and Camões were content to draw on existing myths in order to justify their visions of community, Vico turns the study of myth into a prerequisite for understanding the historical formation of communities. He does not dismiss myths as false or irrational, but rather tries to understand their function in political life by asking what those myths may have meant to their makers, and, even more importantly, what has been made *by means* of them. The answers he provides indicate a new way of viewing myth as an inescapable part of what it means to be a human and social being. Since human societies are repositories of myths, a proper understanding of their function would provide a key to the common features of all human societies. The moment we fully understand the constitutive function of myth in social and political life, we would be emancipated from the spell it has exercised upon our political imagination: we would then

---

[42] See Joseph Mali, *The Rehabilitation of Myth. Vico's New Science* (Cambridge: Cambridge University Press, 1992), pp. 45–50.
[43] Schaeffer, *Sensus Communis*, pp. 80–99.
[44] Mali, *The Rehabilitation of Myth*, p. 52.

also be effectively inoculated against another cunning replay of the tricks of Virgil.[45] That would mark the end of empire and the beginning of true human community.

To sum up: both Shaftesbury and Vico struggled to articulate conceptions of human community that were based on notions of the universal sociability of men, rather than on providential history or on abstract reason. Since men are social beings, the conditions of existence of individual human beings are inseparable from those of the particular community in which they live. Yet both individual human beings and these particular communities can only be fully understood as manifestations of a common humanity. Both Shaftesbury and Vico explain the actual division of mankind into distinct communities as the outcome of historical processes of differentiation, and explain all subsequent changes that these communities have undergone by assuming that providence is gradually replaced by reason as the driving force in human affairs. Since both assume that humanity is sufficiently uniform to constitute one single moral community, they also assume that the transitions experienced by individual communities conform to a universal pattern.[46] As we shall see in the next section, from here it was a short step to posit different stages of human development, and then project these stages onto the global space opened up by continental exploration.

But beyond these similarities we find two very different accounts of the unity of mankind. While both Shaftesbury and Vico would have agreed that 'the moral and historical existence of humanity ... is itself decisively determined by the *sensus communis*', they attributed different meanings to this concept. Whereas Shaftesbury defines the *sensus communis* as a social virtue that derives from human sociability, Vico regards the *sensus communis* as a condition of possible community.[47] Yet both authors regard the *sensus communis*

---

[45] Mali, *Rehabilitation of Myth*, pp. 136–209.
[46] For an analysis of such assumptions and their significance during the eighteenth century, see Reinhart Koselleck, 'The Eighteenth Century as the Beginning of Modernity', in *The Practice of Conceptual History. Timing History, Spacing Concepts* (Stanford, CA: Stanford University Press, 2002), pp. 154–69.
[47] Gadamer, *Truth and Method*, p. 22. For other comparisons, see Gueorguieva, 'La connaissance de l'indéterminé', ch. 1; Bo Petterson, 'Exploring the Common Ground: *Sensus communis*, Humor and the

as boundless and universal. The concept is used to demarcate a sphere of collective meaning and experience that transcends different stages of development. The concept is used to bridge the gap between the actual diversity of human customs and moral standards made plain by the constantly proliferating accounts of newly discovered cultures, and the assumption of a universal humanity which had deep roots in the traditions they drew upon. We would thus be entitled to speak of a moral community of all mankind to the extent that the thoughts and actions of its members can be better explained by a *sensus communis* than by their nationalities.

III

As Muthu has recently argued, the Enlightenment critique of early modern imperialism was conditioned by efforts to articulate notions of a common humanity that could incorporate the cultural diversity made obvious by imperial penetration.[48] This will help us to understand how the concept of mankind became independent of a transcendental point of reference, and how mankind *itself* thereby becomes the ultimate source of political authority. Understanding this will in turn help us to understand how the socio-religious conceptions of humanity discussed in the previous section were translated into secular visions of world community which then enabled the Enlightenment critique of despotism and imperialism.

In the third chapter, we saw how the assumption of a fully navigable and inhabitable planet constituted the background against which visions of world community were articulated. These assumptions also made it possible to imagine a vantage point situated above the terrestrial globe from which the totality of human affairs could be comprehended and judged. In Chapter 4, we saw how this vantage point was relocated to the territorialized political community and identified with the point of view of its sovereign. In the rest of this chapter, we shall see how the fact that the earth was fully inhabitable was taken to imply that historical development would most likely bring about the unification of mankind, thus relocating the vantage

---

Interpretation of Comic Poetry', *Journal of Literary Semantics*, vol. 33, 2004, pp. 155–67.

[48] Muthu, *Enlightenment Against Empire*.

point from which human affairs could be comprehended to the end point of that development. As Arendt was to remark, 'Precisely when the immensity of available space on earth was discovered, the famous shrinkage of the globe began, until eventually in our world ... each man is as much an inhabitant of the earth as he is an inhabitant of his country.'[49]

Few authors illustrate this ambition better than the young Turgot, who early on had taken a strong interest in both natural history and geography. In a lecture held at the Sorbonne in December 1750, he argued that 'the human species, considered since its origin, appears to the eye of a philosopher as one immense whole'. Having formed distinct and later discordant societies, mankind would nevertheless ultimately be reunited as an inevitable consequence of its gradual progress. This would happen as 'isolated nations draw closer to each other, and commerce and politics finally reunite all parts of the globe, and the total mass of the human species ... marches towards the utmost perfection'.[50] In his *Plan d'un ouvrage sur la géographie politique* (1751), these ideas were further developed and related to the contemporary findings of natural history and geography.[51] Turgot now boldly suggested that the cultural division and the spatial dispersion of mankind were in fact the outcome of parallel processes. Consequently, he argued, increased commerce between different parts of the world would not only gradually lessen the differences between peoples at different stages of economic development, but would also make natural boundaries easier to surmount. This view led him further to assume that all stages of human development from the primitive to the more advanced are indeed represented

---

[49] Hannah Arendt, *The Human Condition* (Chicago: University of Chicago Press, 1958), p. 250.

[50] Anne Robert Jacques Turgot, *Tableau philosophique des progrès successifs de l'esprit humain*, in *Œuvres de Turgot et documents le concernant*, ed. Gustave Schelle (Paris: Félix Alcan, 1913), vol. I, p. 215. See also Michael Heffernan, 'On Geography and Progress: Turgot's *Plan d'un ouvrage sur la géographie politique* (1751) and the Origins of Modern Progressive Thought', *Political Geography*, vol. 13, no. 4, 1994, pp. 328–43.

[51] Compare Anne Robert Jacques Turgot, *Lettre à Buffon sur son système de formation de la terre*, in *Œuvres de Turgot et documents le concernant*, vol. I, pp. 109–13.

within the same homogeneous global space, and hence also that progress would take place sequentially on a planetary scale. Thus the differences result from, 'the movement of nations, to the greater or lesser degree of facility in overcoming the barriers by which nature ... has assigned different societies their part of the terrestrial globe, to communications, to the greater or lesser degree of facility with which peoples are blended together'.[52] From this followed a series of implications for the universal history of mankind, and how to understand the process of division and dispersion. As Turgot went on to explain in his *Discourses sur l'histoire universelle* (1751), 'particular customs and dialects give rise to diverse nations. Every obstacle that diminishes communication, and consequently also distance, which is one of these obstacles, fortify the nuances which separate nations, but, in general, the peoples of one continent are blended together.'[53] As exchange between peoples in different continents increased, and physical barriers became less important obstacles to human intercourse, the blending together of people could now occur on a global scale, eventually leading to the formation of one single global civilization.

While Turgot was trying to make sense of the division of mankind by positing different stages of evolution, some of his friends were critical of the claim to European superiority inherent in such theories of sequential progress. One response characteristic of these critics was to turn the notion of progress on its head, thereby inverting the relationship between barbarism and civilization. The *Supplément au voyage de Bougainville* (1772) by Diderot is a case in point. Diderot starts this fictitious travelogue by noting that the discoveries have given us 'a better understanding of this old earth and its inhabitants, greater safety on the seas ... and more accuracy in our charts', before going on to criticize their corrupting impact on the innocent cultures thus discovered, the native Tahitian being 'close to the origin of the world and the European near its old age'.[54] As Pagden has noted, this critique 'is an argument about the integrity and ultimate incommensurability of all cultures ... and about the reliance of "Enlightenment" and

---

[52] *Œuvres de Turgot*, vol. I, p. 259.
[53] *Œuvres de Turgot*, vol. I, p. 281.
[54] Denis Diderot, *Political Writings*, ed. John Hope Mason and Robert Wokler (Cambridge: Cambridge University Press, 1992), pp. 36–8, 40.

civility upon diversity'.[55] And indeed, many authors took an interest in exotic cultures in order to be able to argue that such diversity was constitutive of humanity. Geographical inquiry came to incorporate a comparative analysis of human cultures along with accounts of the dispersion of humanity. This knowledge also paved the way for a systematic critique of imperial practices, since it could now be argued that those practices represented a threat to the precious diversity so characteristic of mankind. But when these authors projected their accounts of mankind onto the new dimension of existence opened up by the fusion of geography and natural history, they found it difficult to explain how humanity could possibly be reunited within one and the same community.[56]

Perhaps there is no better example of this problem than the *Histoire philosophique et politique des établissements et du commerce des Européens dans les deux Indes* (1770–80) by the Abbé Guillaume-Thomas Raynal.[57] Largely based on anonymous contributions from leading figures of the Enlightenment such as Diderot, this popular work embodied many of the critical aspirations and inner limitations of Enlightenment historiography.[58] Being global in its geographical

[55] Anthony Pagden, *European Encounters with the New World. From Renaissance to Romanticism* (New Haven, CT: Yale University Press, 1993), p. 143.
[56] See Charles W. J. Withers, 'Eighteenth-Century Geography: Texts, Practices, Sites', *Progress in Human Geography*, vol. 30, no. 6, 2006, pp. 711–29; Clarence J. Glacken, *Traces on the Rhodian Shore. Nature and Culture in Western Thought from Ancient Times to the End of the Eighteenth Century* (Berkeley: University of California Press, 1967), pp. 501–50; Michael T. Bravo, 'Ethnographical Navigation and the Geographical Gift', in Livingstone and Withers, *Geography and Enlightenment*, pp. 199–235.
[57] There is no standard edition of this work, although the 1780 edition is widely used. For reasons of availability, I have used the fifth edition (The Hague, 1776). Since there is no consistency between editions as to the subdivision of volumes and chapters, I shall refer to book and page only. All translations are mine unless otherwise indicated. For an account of its popularity, see Robert Darnton, *The Forbidden Best-sellers of Pre-revolutionary France* (New York: Norton, 1995).
[58] See John G. A. Pocock, *Barbarism and Religion*, vol. IV: *Barbarians, Savages and Empires* (Cambridge: Cambridge University Press, 2005), pp. 229–331. For the complex relationship between the contributions of Diderot and Raynal, see Yves Benot, 'Diderot–Raynal: l'impossible

scope, the *Histoire des deux Indes* reads like a sequel to the great works of Renaissance cosmography. It provides the reader with an update on what has happened since the beginning of the discoveries, since 'there has not been an equally interesting event for the human race in general'.[59] But while Renaissance cosmographers had been content to describe the geographical features of the newly discovered continents, Raynal provides the reader with dense accounts of the customs of foreign peoples, and how they have been affected by their encounter with Europeans. His philosophical framework also allows him to pass moral judgement on these peoples and their customs, as well as to provide a moral balance-sheet of European expansion. As such, the *Histoire des deux Indes* is a critical history of European imperialism, backed by detailed descriptions of the places and peoples brought under European control. Since his criticism of imperialism has already received extensive and competent treatment, in the rest of this section I shall focus on the underlying conception of a global society within which this history and critique play themselves out.[60]

To Raynal, the existence of a global society antedates the formation of the states system in Europe. This global society consists of distinct peoples grouped together in nations, together representing the totality of human customs and values, therefore also reflecting all possible stages of human development. To Diderot and Raynal, the existence of such manifold communities is the outcome of concrete historical processes, all of them propelled by the innate sociability of men, yet conditioned by variations in climate. As Diderot goes on to explain, 'National character is the result of a large number of causes, some of them constant and some variable. The constant causes are determined by the part of the earth which they inhabit. The variable causes are recorded in their annals, and are evident from their effects.'[61] The very notion of a world society within which these

---

divorce', in Yves Benot, *Les lumières, l'esclavage, la colonisation*, ed. Roland Desné and Marcel Dorigny (Paris: Éditions la Découverte, 2005), pp. 138–53.

[59] Raynal, *Histoire*, book I, p. 1.

[60] See Koselleck, *Critique and Crisis*, pp. 175–83; Muthu, *Enlightenment Against Empire*, pp. 72–121; Yves Benot, 'Diderot, Pechmeja, Raynal et l'anticolonialisme', in Benot, *Les Lumières*, pp. 107–23.

[61] Diderot, *Political Writings*, p. 177. See also Pagden, *European Encounters*, pp. 143–53.

processes take place presupposes the existence of such a primordial plurality of peoples being culturally different from each other but morally equal. Beyond all their differences, human communities are built on the same foundation, that of human sociability. 'The need to associate', reads another passage written by Diderot, 'derives the need to have laws relative to that condition, that is to say, by combining all common and individual instincts, a general combination which maintains the mass and plurality of individuals'.[62] All human communities are therefore profoundly equal by virtue of being composed of individual human beings themselves being equal: it is hard to doubt the fact that it was Diderot who translated Shaftesbury into French.[63]

This attempt to model the moral equality of particular communities upon the equality of individuals is reminiscent of the view of the general will that Diderot had already proposed in the *Encyclopédie* in 1755. According to this view, the general will of the species 'forms the rule binding the conduct of an individual towards another in the same society, together with the conduct of an individual towards the whole society to which he belongs, and of that society itself towards other societies ... submission to the general will is the bond which holds all societies together'.[64] In this usage, the concept of a general will is applicable to all communities including the community of all mankind. Indeed, this general will is precisely what makes mankind one single moral community, and the existence of such a universal community is necessary in order for smaller groups of people to constitute themselves into communities of their own.

Some commentators have interpreted these passages as an attempt to globalize the notion of a general will which we find in *Du contrat social*.[65] But as Wokler showed some time ago, there are strong reasons to believe that the reverse holds true, and that the universalistic conception of the general will both antedated and influenced

---

[62] Raynal, *Histoire*, book XIX, pp. 155–6. Translation in Diderot, *Political Writings*, p. 205.
[63] Schneewind, *Invention of Autonomy*, p. 466; Jerrold Seigel, *The Idea of the Self. Thought and Experience in Western Europe since the Seventeenth Century* (Cambridge: Cambridge University Press, 2005), pp. 187–8.
[64] Diderot, *Political Writings*, p. 21
[65] Koselleck, *Critique and Crisis*, pp. 175–86.

Rousseau's account.[66] When used in the *Encyclopédie*, the concept of a general will was articulated with reference to mankind as a whole. It was this reference that made it possible to conceptualize humanity as if it constituted one single community, yet simultaneously being composed of lesser communities. In the way Diderot uses the concept of a general will, this concept cuts across all forms of human association, irrespective of their complexity and size. In a similar way as the concept of the general will provided Rousseau with the means to reformulate the foundations upon which all virtuous political communities must rest, so it is possible for Diderot to conceive of mankind as being constituted by analogous concerns of political virtue. As Diderot states in the *Histoire des deux Indes*, morality 'is in effect a science, the object of which is the preservation and common happiness of the human race ... Their constant and eternal principle is in man himself.'[67]

Since the general will will also be the benchmark of all legitimate governance, the community of all mankind is also necessarily a *political* community by virtue of the fact that it can be said to possess such a will of its own. Any prospective world government would have to obey the general will, lest it should ruin itself from within: as Raynal goes on to argue, 'to act without consulting the general will ... is to estrange the hearts and spirit and even to discredit the good and the honourable'.[68] The general will of mankind make it possible to establish a chain of equivalences that takes us from mankind as a whole all the way down to individual human beings. These individuals cannot be separated from the communities they happen to inhabit, any more than those communities can meaningfully be separated from the universal community to which they belong. Since both this overarching community and all lesser communities must be

---

[66] Robert Wokler, 'The Influence of Diderot on the Political Theory of Rousseau: Two Aspects of a Relationship', in Theodore Besterman, ed., *Studies on Voltaire and the Eighteenth Century*, vol. 132, 1975, pp. 55–112; Jean-Jacques Rousseau, *The Social Contract*, in Rousseau, *Social Contract and Discourses*, p. 203. For the evolution of the concept of the general will, see Patrick Riley, *The General Will Before Rousseau* (Princeton, NJ: Princeton University Press, 1986).

[67] Raynal, *Histoire*, book XIX, p. 302. Translation from Diderot, *Political Writings*, p. 211.

[68] Raynal, *Histoire*, book XIX, p. 187.

expressive of the general will, there cannot be any conflict between the will of all mankind and the will of particular communities in *principle*. If these wills appear to contradict each other, this is merely the result of a *misinterpretation* of the general will, since its very universality precludes any *real* conflict between its different expressions. Hence, the concept of general will was a defining characteristic of a universal and boundless human community before it was nationalized by Rousseau, to whom 'moral rights could be established only in those communities that were formed by the agreement of their members'.[69]

But how is this general will to become manifest in practice? The *Histoire des deux Indes* contains an account of the emergence of the European society of states and its outward expansion. Raynal begins this analysis by dividing the art of government into two main forms: legislation and politics proper. While the former has primarily taken place *within* communities, the latter has largely played itself out in the relationship *between* them. As we learn from the *Histoire des deux Indes*, there was little communication and interaction among ancient and medieval societies to warrant anything but the most primitive codes of legal conduct, since at that point in time 'justice was decided by force'.[70] Gradually, more civilized political relations started to evolve in the Middle Ages, the papacy establishing itself as a supranational centre of communication. A truly modern system of politics emerges when individual sovereigns become preoccupied with what takes place within their respective states, and gradually lose interest in the changes that take place on the outside, until they suddenly wake up to find themselves stuck in petty rivalries, accusing each other of trying to create a universal monarchy.[71] These rivalries are then given additional momentum by the rise of despotism and intensified international commerce. When absolutist states started to regard trade as a means of increasing their political and military power, it led to jealousy of trade between states, a 'secret conspiracy to ruin everybody without enriching anybody'.[72]

---

[69] Wokler, 'Influence of Diderot', p. 108.
[70] Raynal, *Histoire*, book XIX, p. 190.
[71] Raynal, *Histoire*, book XIX, p. 192.
[72] Raynal, *Histoire*, book XIX, p. 233. Hume had formulated the conditions of economic competition: 'Nothing is more usual, among states which have made some advances in commerce, than to look on the

This volatile combination of despotism and economic nationalism also generated a constant push for territorial expansion in order to satisfy the insatiable appetites of the metropolis and its aristocratic elites. Despotism and imperialism reinforce each other, and domestic abuses of power are made possible by imperial expansion and domination, as well as conversely.[73]

To Raynal, this arrangement was inherently immoral since it was not in the general interests of humanity. Although law and politics had tragically been torn apart, they should ideally be brought to coincide again. Raynal shows very little confidence in the ability to establish a lasting peace between states by relying on balances of power. Instead he pins some of his hope on the invisible hand of free trade, which could 'lead unnoticeably to this universal peace'.[74] But in order to liberate trade from mercantile constraints, absolutist monarchies must first be replaced by republican governments. Only then are peaceful relations possible between European states, since when 'authority resides in the mass of people ... the public principles and interests dominate negotiations'. Then 'The general spirit that lives and perpetuates itself in every nation is the only rule of intercourse.'[75] Then the general will will come to prevail in the society of states, and thereby also for the ultimate benefit of all mankind.

In the final analysis, the *Histoire des deux Indes* is a piece of revolutionary rhetoric with a distinctive global twist. In order to realize the general will on a global scale, it has to be liberated from all constraints, so that it can flourish within as well as between communities, until it finally becomes embodied in republican institutions. But such emancipation necessitates a global revolution in order to break the destructive connection between despotism and imperialism that has kept the peoples of both the new and the old world enslaved by the

---

progress of their neighbours with a suspicious eye, to consider all trading states as their rivals, and to suppose that it is impossible for any of them to flourish, but at their expense.' David Hume, 'Of Jealousy of Trade' [1758] in Hume, *Essays, Moral, Political, and Literary*, available at http://oll.libertyfund.org/title/704/137536 (accessed 21 April 2009). For an excellent account of this problem in eighteenth-century political and economic thought, see Hont, *Jealousy of Trade*.

[73] Raynal, *Histoire*, book XIX, pp. 223–37.
[74] Raynal, *Histoire*, book XIX, p. 237.
[75] Raynal, *Histoire*, book XIX, p. 201.

same corrupt masters. Since this revolution ought to be undertaken in the name of a united mankind, it finds justification in the same general will that it promises to realize in historical time. As Koselleck has remarked on this somewhat circular account, 'In Raynal, overseas and the future were the fictive area of exculpation that indirectly guaranteed the triumph of morality.'[76] But Raynal cannot tell us how to get from the present into that desirable future: there is no clear concept of progress to be found in the *Histoire des deux Indes*, only scattered remarks that indicate a faith in human reason and a belief in the inevitability of revolution.[77] As Condorcet later formulated this article of faith in the aftermath of the Revolution:

We shall demonstrate how nature has joined together indissolubly the progress of knowledge and that of liberty, virtue and respect for the natural rights of man; and how these ... must ... become inseparable from the moment when enlightenment has attained a certain level in a number of nations, and has penetrated the whole mass of great people whose language is universally known and whose commercial relations embrace the whole area of the globe. Once such close accord had been established between all enlightened men, from then onwards all will be friends of humanity, all will work together for its perfection and happiness.[78]

In this chapter, we have seen how criticism of the natural law tradition provided the starting point for a critique of the despotism and imperialism of early modern states. While Grotius, Hobbes and Locke accepted the division of mankind into distinct communities as an inescapable part of the human condition, authors like Shaftesbury, Vico, Turgot and Diderot sought to recover the patterns underlying this differentiation, and hence also the foundations of a united mankind. These authors tried to formulate an alternative to the particularistic social ontology of Hobbes and Locke by arguing that human beings are profoundly sociable, and that all human communities must be understood as expressions of such sociability.

[76] Koselleck, *Critique and Crisis*, p. 183.
[77] See Reinhart Koselleck, 'The Unknown Future and the Art of Prognosis', in *The Practice of Conceptual History*, pp. 131–53, at pp. 137–8.
[78] Marie-Jean-Antoine Nicolas de Caritat, marquis de Condorcet, *Sketch for a Historical Picture of the Progress of the Human Mind* [1795] (London: Weidenfeld and Nicolson, 1955), p. 10.

Since human communities have all been formed on the basis on the common capacities of their members, particular communities cannot be understood in isolation from the concerns of mankind as a whole. Since each particular community derives its existence from such a universal community, relations between such lesser communities must be understood as fundamentally embedded within this larger whole.

The idea that mankind is something more than the sum of its parts became an indispensable starting point for the critique of the practices of the early modern state. While many of these conceptions allowed for a hierarchical understanding of racial differences that would strike us as racist today, the category of mankind had been broadened to include human beings previously excluded, albeit admittedly in an inferior position. Projecting their secular and holistic conceptions of humanity onto the continental depths of what was now a fully inhabitable and navigable planet, Diderot and Raynal took the plurality of customs encountered to be evidence of the intrinsic and constitutive diversity of mankind. This made it possible for them to criticize both domestic despotism and imperial expansion for being contrary to the general will of all mankind. While this critique led to a plea for a global revolution in the name of this unified mankind, it also gave rise to the difficult question of how its precepts could be translated into viable legal and political institutions on a global scale. It is to the answers to those questions that we must now turn our attention.

6 | *Globalizing community*

THE critics of the *ancien régime* regarded domestic despotism as a cause of both war and imperialism, and argued that popular sovereignty combined with free trade would bring an end to these destructive practices. But while this criticism was undertaken in the name of a universal human community, most of these writers could present no viable alternative to the system of states which was emerging in Europe. Old universalistic proposals were rapidly becoming obsolete, and the idea of any legal or political authority over and above that of individual states was becoming increasingly difficult to defend in this new context.[1]

But how, then, could the idea of a unified mankind be translated into political practice, and reconciled with the existence of a plurality of sovereign states? While the authors discussed in the previous chapter were struggling to overcome the undesirable consequences of the division of mankind into distinct peoples, they had little to say about the political relations between particular communities, and how these should be arranged for the benefit of mankind as a whole. And while these authors articulated conceptions of a universal humanity and then projected these conceptions onto a global space, they found it difficult to explain how such a world community could be realized in historical time. This difficulty was largely due to the fact that the underlying cosmological framework made it hard to reconcile the classificatory ambitions of geography and natural history with the ideas of historical evolution and progress. Also, providential history did not lend any automatic support to secular visions of a

---

[1] Stéphane Beaulac, *The Power of Language in the Making of International Law* (Leiden: Martinus Nijhoff, 2004), pp. 128–79. See also Francis H. Hinsley, *Power and the Pursuit of Peace. Theory and Practice in the History of Relations between States* (Cambridge: Cambridge University Press, 1963), pp. 13–61.

world community, and theories of sequential progress were hard to combine with the ideals of human equality and moral unity.

In this chapter, I shall focus on how Immanuel Kant tried to overcome these difficulties by redefining geographical space and historical time in a way that made progress towards a world community look inevitable. Much of the impetus behind this effort was provided by the shortcomings of existing legal doctrine. One of the most influential attempts to reconcile the idea of a united mankind with its actual division into distinct communities during this period had been undertaken by Christian Wolff. In his *Jus gentium methodo scientifica pertractatum* (1749), Wolff had outlined a comprehensive doctrine that rendered individuals as well as communities parts of a higher moral and political order, yet without appealing to any of the traditional sources of moral and legal authority of his day.[2] Wolff started this treatise by noting that a nation 'consists of a multitude of men united into a state'. Such nations 'must be regarded in relation to each other as individual free persons living in a state of nature'.[3] Yet the existence of such a state of nature among nations does not imply the absence of community, since even 'after the human race was divided into nations, that society which before was between individuals continues between nations … so likewise individual men do not cease to be members of that great society which is made up of the whole human race, because several have formed together a particular society'.[4] Thus, individuals as well as the particular communities which they inhabit are all members of the same primordial society of all mankind, in which all men are united to each other.[5] Particular nations are therefore compelled by nature to enter into a political association which 'binds the human race or all nations on to

---

[2] Christian Wolff, *Jus gentium methodo scientifica pertractatum*, vols. I–II (Oxford: Clarendon Press, 1934). I have used the English translation by Joseph H. Drake, which I have checked against the Latin text of 1764. In this process, I have also benefited greatly from Nicholas Greenwood Onuf, '*Civitas Maxima*: Wolff, Vattel and the Fate of Republicanism', *American Journal of International Law*, vol. 88, no. 2, 1994, pp. 280–303.

[3] Wolff, *Jus gentium*, §1.   [4] Wolff, *Jus gentium*, §7.

[5] For the context in which this argument was developed, see Jerome B. Schneewind, *The Invention of Autonomy* (Cambridge: Cambridge University Press, 1998), pp. 438–42.

Globalizing community 143

the other, since moreover it is assumed that others will unite in it, if they know their own interests'.[6] Wolff terms this association of both nations and individuals a *civitas maxima*: 'Inasmuch then as nations are understood to have combined in a [*civitas maxima*], individual nations also are understood to have bound themselves to the whole, because they wish to promote the common good, and the whole to the individuals.'[7] To Wolff, the international society of states is naturally and necessarily embedded within the community of all mankind, and the political relations within the former must therefore be subordinated to the interests of the latter and its individual members. Yet while Wolff justified this order with reference to its human purpose, the ontological status of the *civitas maxima* remained obscure to his contemporaries, and Wolff himself had very little to say about the conditions of its realization.[8]

I

Reconciling the actual division of humanity into distinct peoples with the ideal of a world community required a simultaneous change in cosmological outlook. What was needed was a philosophical synthesis that could explain how both the cultural division and the geographical dispersion of mankind could be overcome in historical time. Such a synthesis in turn presupposed that knowledge of the spatial and temporal dimensions of human existence could be integrated within one and the same framework. To Kant, such an understanding of the human condition was only possible through a prior and systematic juxtaposition of geographical and historical knowledge. While geography provided the means to integrate all knowledge into a coherent system, history provided the explanation of its progressive development. As he stated in *Physische Geographie* (c. 1775):

Geography and history fill out the whole extent of our knowledge; geography namely that of space, history on the other hand that of time ... Here the whole is the world, the stage on which we shall present all experience.

---

[6] Wolff, *Jus gentium*, §9.   [7] Wolff, *Jus gentium*, §12.
[8] For an analysis, see Nicholas Greenwood Onuf, *The Republican Legacy in International Thought* (Cambridge: Cambridge University Press, 1998), pp. 58–109.

Travels, and intercourse with people, broaden the extent of our knowledge. Each contact teaches us to know mankind but demands much time if this goal is to be reached. If we are already prepared by instruction we already have a whole, a framework of knowledge which teaches us to know mankind. Now we are in a position to classify each experience and to give it its place in this framework.[9]

Such a spatio-temporal framework is necessary in order to understand the world, since all phenomena and relations found on the surface of the earth are but parts of the same single whole. But his cosmology is also profoundly *anthropocentric*: not only does mankind belong to the earth, but the earth belongs to mankind.[10] The accidental division and dispersion of mankind does not alter this primordial bond between the earth and its inhabitants, since to belong to this world is also to belong to a world of one's own making. This being so, the spatio-temporal framework necessary for attaining knowledge of the world ultimately resides nowhere else but in the human mind. Hence the vantage point from which to contemplate human affairs is no longer situated above or within territorial space, but in mankind itself, enabling its collective sovereignty over the terraqueous globe.

The moral corollary of this cosmology was that human beings are autonomous and rational subjects, insofar as they are capable of imposing laws upon themselves, and able to find the reasons for obeying these laws within reason rather than in any outside authority. Such moral autonomy is constitutive of the idea of right, if we by right mean 'the sum total of the conditions within which the will of one person can be reconciled with the will of another in accordance

---

[9] Immanuel Kant, *Physische Geographie, Gesammelte Schriften, Preussiche Akademie Ausgabe*, quoted in Paul Richards, 'Kant's Geography and Mental Maps', *Transactions of the Institute of British Geographers*, no. 61, 1974, pp. 1–16, at p. 7. See also Charles W. J. Withers and David N. Livingstone, 'Introduction. On Geography and Enlightenment', in Charles W. J. Withers and David N. Livingstone, eds., *Geography and the Enlightenment* (Chicago: University of Chicago Press, 1999), pp. 1–28.

[10] Richard Hartshorne, 'The Concept of Geography as a Science of Space: From Kant and Humboldt to Hettner', *Annals of the Association of American Geographers*, vol. 48, no. 2, 1958, pp. 97–108; D. N. Livingstone and R. T. Harrison, 'Immanuel Kant, Subjectivism and Human Geography: A Preliminary Investigation', *Transactions of the Institute of British Geographers*, vol. 6, no. 3, 1981, pp. 359–74.

with a universal law of freedom'. The universal law of right thus dictates that 'your external actions be such that the free application of your will can co-exist with the freedom of everyone in accordance with a universal law'.[11] As Yovel has summarized this argument, the rational will first constitutes the good and then adopts what it has constituted in order to progressively expand itself into the world of human affairs.[12]

Kant explicates this moral autonomy by defining reason and humanity in terms of each other. The moral agency of human beings requires universal freedom as its condition of possibility, and this moral autonomy in turn presupposes that human beings are rational beings, since this is what makes them ends in themselves rather than mere means to something external to them. The universality of the moral law thus presupposes the prior recognition of each human being as a moral subject in its own right. To some commentators, this emphasis on the principles of individuality and freedom would seem to rule out the possibility that human beings derive their moral status from their belonging in any human community at all.[13] Yet I believe that the concept of moral autonomy should be interpreted as a *condition* of such belonging, since the way in which Kant understands the self arguably presupposes constitutive relations to other human beings.[14] This makes even more sense once we realize that Kant indeed regarded mankind as one single moral community, and that moral autonomy of the self is the very foundation of that community. Such moral autonomy is the result of an evolutionary process

---

[11] Immanuel Kant, 'The Metaphysics of Morals', in Hans Reiss, ed., *Kant: Political Writings* (Cambridge: Cambridge University Press, 1991), pp. 131–75, at p. 133.
[12] Yirmiyahu Yovel, 'Kant's Practical Reason as Will: Interests, Recognition, Judgment, Choice', *Review of Metaphysics*, vol. 52, no. 2, 1998, pp. 267–94, at p. 269.
[13] See, for example, Alasdair MacIntyre, *A Short History of Ethics* [1967] (London: Routledge, 1998), pp. 183–91.
[14] Compare Andrea T. Baumeister, 'Kant: The Arch-Enlightener', in Norman Geras and Robert Wokler, eds., *Enlightenment and Modernity* (London: Routledge, 2005), pp. 50–65. See also Jerrold Seigel, *The Idea of the Self. Thought and Experience in Western Europe since the Seventeenth Century* (Cambridge: Cambridge University Press, 2005), pp. 295–331.

through which man distinguishes himself from the animals through the gradual development of his reason.[15] Through this 'transition from a rude and purely animal existence to a state of humanity ... man had attained a position of equality with all rational beings ... because he could claim to be an end in himself, to be accepted as such by all others, and not to be used by anyone else simply as a means to other ends'.[16]

The fact that human beings have come to possess reason makes them free, yet also restricts that very freedom by turning their very humanity into the ultimate limit of that freedom. The concept of humanity figures in at least two distinct senses in Kant's political writings. On the one hand, humanity is an ideal state that must be attained by human beings as a condition of their moral autonomy and full membership in the moral community of mankind. On the other, humanity is an attribute of every human being simply by virtue of being a member of the human species. In order to account for the possibility of a world community, Kant has to find a way to mediate between these conceptions by explaining how the transition from the latter to the former takes place in history. This he does by assuming that the ideal of humanity can only be actualized through the gradual unfolding of the rational capacities of the species as a whole. Within this view, all mankind as well as all individual human beings will only be able to attain the status of moral subjects together, never in isolation from each other. Therefore, to disregard the human potential in other human beings by treating them as a means rather than as an end in themselves is simultaneously to undermine the universal freedom upon which all humanity ultimately rests.[17]

Taken together, these assumptions have profound implications for the way Kant conceives of the possibility of a world community. To Kant, mankind has been dispersed across the surface of the earth by natural forces, and has likewise been divided into distinct peoples

---

[15] As Yovel has argued, Kant's teleological view of history is indispensable to our understanding of his morality. See Yovel, 'Kant's Practical Reason as Will', pp. 267–94.

[16] Immanuel Kant, 'Conjectures on the Beginning of Human History', in Reiss, *Kant: Political Writings*, pp. 221–33, at p. 226.

[17] For an analysis of this relationship, see Louis Dupré, 'Kant's Theory of History and Progress', *Review of Metaphysics*, vol. 51, no. 4, 1998, pp. 813–28.

through natural accidents. This dispersion and division reflect an inherently purposeful nature, since it has also provided mankind with the means necessary to overcome any obstacles in order to facilitate intercourse between different peoples in different places.[18] Such intercourse is also a necessary condition of further progress. As we learn from *Idee zu einer allgemeinen Geschichte in weltbürgerlicher Absicht* (1784), nature has endowed mankind as a whole with rational capacities, but left men with the troubling task of using these capacities for their own benefit. In order for these innate capacities to develop, nature cunningly employs antagonism within human societies, the 'unsocial sociability of men, that is, their tendency to come together in society, coupled, however, with a continual resistance which constantly threatens to break this society up'.[19] It follows that the further development of human reason only can be accomplished within a society 'which has not only the greatest freedom, and therefore continual antagonism among its members, but also the most precise specification and preservation of the limits of this freedom in order that it can co-exist with the freedom of others'.[20] In order for such society to be possible, however, its external relationship with other states must in turn be subjected to law, since the 'same unsociability … gives rise in turn to a situation whereby each commonwealth … is in a position of unrestricted freedom'.[21]

Eventually and hopefully, 'The history of the human race as a whole can be regarded as the realisation of a hidden plan of nature to bring about an internally – and for this purpose also externally – perfect political constitution within which all natural capacities of mankind can be developed completely.'[22] Kant tells us that even if his critical philosophy does not allow us to infer any such purpose directly from the course of events, such an 'attempt to work out a universal history of mankind in accordance with a plan of nature aimed at a perfect

---

[18] Immanuel Kant, *The Critique of Judgment* (New York: Hafner, 1951), p. 215. For the context of this argument, see Clarence J. Glacken, *Traces on the Rhodian Shore. Nature and Culture in Western Thought from Ancient Times to the End of the Eighteenth Century* (Berkeley: University of California Press, 1967), pp. 530–7.
[19] Immanuel Kant, 'Idea for a Universal History with a Cosmopolitan Purpose', in Reiss, *Kant: Political Writings*, pp. 41–53, at p. 44.
[20] Kant, 'Universal History', p. 45.   [21] Kant, 'Universal History', p. 47.
[22] Kant, 'Universal History', p. 50.

civil union of mankind, must be regarded as possible and even as capable of furthering the purpose of nature itself'.[23] Thus, the gradual perfection of political institutions is driven forward by the very human unsociability that simultaneously threatens to destroy them; yet this development looks purposeful from the vantage point of the expected end result. Even if we are not allowed to infer such purpose from history itself, we are nevertheless obliged to operate with such a postulate in mind, if only to make sense of what otherwise would be nothing but a chaotic manifold of disparate events in history: as Kant states, 'if we assume a plan of nature, we have grounds for greater hopes'.[24]

But how can such a postulate be warranted, and wherein does this hope ultimately reside? These questions have long puzzled commentators.[25] Most of those who are sympathetic to the Kantian vision of world community have been reluctant to interpret his theory of history in teleological terms, since taking such an interpretation seriously would appear to undermine the scientific credibility of his views. Consequently, both Nussbaum and Muthu have argued that the grounds for hope exist independently of the question of whether history is inherently progressive or not. To them, the Kantian philosophy of history is a narrative crafted in order to inspire precisely the kind of liberal hope Kant himself alludes to.[26] Yet I do not think that this interpretation is very helpful when situating the Kantian vision in its proper cosmological context. Instead, I think we should keep in mind that those teleological views of history which we today find hard to

---

[23] Kant, 'Universal History', p. 52.
[24] Kant, 'Universal History', p. 52.
[25] See, for example, William A. Galston, *Kant and the Problem of History* (Chicago: University of Chicago Press, 1975); Yirmiyahu Yovel, *Kant and the Philosophy of History* (Princeton, NJ: Princeton University Press, 1980). For recent discussions, see Otfried Höffe, *Kant's Cosmopolitan Theory of Law and Peace* (Cambridge: Cambridge University Press, 2006), pp. 159–76; Howard Williams, '*Metamorphosis* or *Palingenesis*? Political Change in Kant', *Review of Politics*, vol. 63, no. 4, 2001, pp. 693–722 and Seigel, *The Idea of the Self*, pp. 315–17.
[26] See Martha Nussbaum, 'Kant and Stoic Cosmopolitanism', *Journal of Political Philosophy*, vol. 5, no. 1, 1997, pp. 1–25; Sankar Muthu, *Enlightenment Against Empire* (Princeton, NJ: Princeton University Press, 2003), pp. 168–9.

accept were once integral parts of a larger cosmological framework, and that in many respects we still remain indebted to that framework. I am therefore more inclined to follow Arendt and Lyotard, by taking other parts of Kantian philosophy into consideration to make better sense of his idea of historical progress.[27]

Thus, in the *Kritik der Urteilskraft* (1790), Kant provides an answer to the question of progress by invoking the concept of judgement. To Kant, judgement is derivative of the *sensus communis*, a concept which is now provided with yet another layer of meaning. Under the *sensus communis* we must include, writes Kant, 'a faculty of judgment which, in its reflection, takes account a priori of the mode of representation of all other men in thought, in order ... to compare its judgment with the collective reason of humanity'.[28] The active use of judgement makes it possible to recognize something as an example of a rule, but also to create the necessary concepts under which a particular example might be subsumed. The exercise of judgement is as much a matter of identifying examples of a given rule as it is a matter of identifying the rule of a given example.[29] When applied to the realm of historical experience, progress cannot be inferred directly, but the reflective judgement allows us to postulate such a purpose in the interests of increasing human knowledge.[30] The reflective judgement, writes Kant, 'must subsume

---

[27] See Hannah Arendt, *Lectures on Kant's Political Philosophy* (Chicago: University of Chicago Press, 1982); Jean-François Lyotard, *L'enthousiasme. La critique kantienne de l'histoire* (Paris: Galilée, 1986). For a useful commentary, see David Ingram, 'The Postmodern Kantianism of Arendt and Lyotard', *Review of Metaphysics*, vol. 42, 1988, pp. 51–77. For a discussion of these problems in the context of international relations theory, see Jens Bartelson, 'The Trial of Judgment: A Note on Kant and the Paradoxes of Internationalism', *International Studies Quarterly*, vol. 39, no. 2, 1995, pp. 255–79; Mark F. N. Franke, *Global Limits. Immanuel Kant, International Relations, and Critique of World Politics* (Albany: State University of New York Press, 2001), pp. 111–53.

[28] Kant, *Critique of Judgment*, p. 136.

[29] Kant, *Critique of Judgment*, p. 15; Hans-Georg Gadamer, *Truth and Method* (New York: Continuum, 1989), pp. 30–4.

[30] See Rudolf A. Makkreel, *Imagination and Interpretation in Kant. The Hermeneutical Import of the Critique of Judgment* (Chicago: University of Chicago Press, 1990), pp. 131–40.

under a law which is not yet given, and is therefore in fact only a principle of reflection upon objects, for which we are objectively quite in want of a law or of a concept of an object that would be adequate as a principle for the cases that occur'.[31] The reflective judgement cannot claim any absolute validity for itself, but can provide us with the conceptual resources necessary to understand what would otherwise remain incomprehensible. It permits us to 'judge concerning the possibility of these things and their production in no other fashion than by conceiving for this a cause working according to design'.[32] Thus, the assumption that the political world is orderly cannot be *inferred* from that world strictly speaking, but has to be *imposed* upon that world in order to render it intelligible. We are only entitled to assume that history is purposive as a regulative idea, as a heuristic principle by means of which we can bring order into a multitude of events which otherwise would fail to make any sense. As soon as we are able to discern patterns that are indicative of moral progress, it becomes our moral obligation to stick to this interpretation.

This brings us to the moral basis of this hope. As we learn from *Der Streit der Fakultäten* (1798), we need only to identity a single event that indicates that mankind is improving. 'This inference could then be extended to cover the history of former times so as to show that mankind has always been progressing ... It might then serve to prove the existence of a tendency within the human race as a whole, considered not as a series of individuals ... but as a body distributed in states and national groups.'[33] Thus, the ultimate source of liberal hope lies in the possibility that men will let ideas of progress guide not only their understanding of the political world, but their conduct within this world as well. Here we must bear in mind that the concept of judgement was devised by Kant in order to bridge the gap between theoretical and practical reason: if the regulative idea of progress is allowed to inform both thought and action, then moral progress will become a self-fulfilling prophecy. As Kleingeld has argued, such progress is warranted by the very harmonious unity of

---

[31] Kant, *Critique of Judgment*, p. 232.
[32] Kant, *Critique of Judgment*, p. 245.
[33] Immanuel Kant, 'The Contest of the Faculties', in Reiss, *Kant: Political Writings*, pp. 176–90.

reason, a fragile unity within which the concerns of practical reason must always take priority whenever theoretical reason fails to supply the conditions of valid knowledge.[34] I therefore believe the answer to the question of historical progress towards a politically united mankind lies in a reflexive view of human autonomy. Mankind is constantly in the process of constituting itself as autonomous by moulding the world in its image, and the social and political world becomes a world of our own making the very moment we define the spatio-temporal conditions of our coexistence.[35]

In this section, I have described how Kant tried to overcome the division of mankind by articulating the conditions of possible progress within the spatial limits posed by his account of geography. Set against this backdrop, mankind is constantly progressing towards completion and perfection by means of reason alone. Yet the ultimate warrant of this progress lies in the fact that the very spatio-temporal framework within which this progress takes place is a condition of possible knowledge. In the next section, I shall focus on how this benign circularity is used in order to justify the idea of a world community.

II

As we saw in the previous chapter, to the critics of absolutism, international trade had become subordinated to the corrupt ends of absolutist rulers. In an age when economic competition was still conceived of in zero-sum terms, trade rivalries often escalated to the brink of war.[36] Thus critics responded by advocating popular sovereignty and free trade in the hope that this would bring more peaceful relations between states. As Thomas Paine famously argued in *The Rights of Man* (1791–2), popular sovereignty was necessary in order to push

---

[34] See Pauline Kleingeld, 'Kant on the Unity of Theoretical and Practical Reason', *Review of Metaphysics*, vol. 52, no. 2, 1998, pp. 311–39.

[35] For the Kantian roots of contemporary constructivism, see Nicholas Greenwood Onuf, *World of Our Making. Rules and Rule in Social Theory and International Relations* (Columbia: University of South Carolina Press, 1989), pp. 38–9, 188–95.

[36] For a brilliant analysis, see Istvan Hont, *Jealousy of Trade: International Competition and the Nation-State in Historical Perspective* (Cambridge, MA: Harvard University Press, 2005), pp. 1–156.

interstate relations in a more civilized direction.³⁷ By contrast, to the supporters of the *ancien régime*, sovereign states were already united within a commonwealth whose legitimacy was based on principles of dynastic succession.³⁸ Given this complex ideological context, it was very difficult to defend any conception of world community without thereby implicitly invoking ideas that seemed to belong to an increasingly discredited past. Consequently, while many of those who argued in favour of popular sovereignty were naturally suspicious of the idea of a world community, they found it hard to envisage any viable alternative once it had been accepted that Europe consisted of sovereign states, and that no legitimate authority existed over and above them.³⁹

Such was the immediate ideological context in which the Kantian vision of world community was articulated. Before proceeding to this vision, I shall briefly engage two influential interpretations of Kantian international thought. The first of these is found in theories of *democratic peace*. According to this kind of interpretation, the ideal international order envisaged by Kant consists of sovereign states entertaining peaceful relations with each other by virtue of being internally democratic.⁴⁰ But I would like to suggest that it makes little

---

[37] Thomas Paine, *The Rights of Man* (Ware, Hertfordshire: Wordsworth, 1996), pp. 121–63; for an analysis, see Thomas C. Walker, 'The Forgotten Prophet: Tom Paine's Cosmopolitanism and International Relations', *International Studies Quarterly*, vol. 44, no. 1, 2000, pp. 51–72. See also 'Letter to the Abbé Raynal' (1782) in D. E. Wheeler, ed., *Life and Writings of Thomas Paine*, vol. VIII (New York: Vincent Park, 1908), pp. 180–5.

[38] See Edmund Burke, *Letters on a Regicide Peace II, Genius and Character of the French Revolution* (1796), in *Select Works of Edmund Burke* (Liberty Fund, IN: Indianapolis, 1999), pp. 153–89. For dicussions of his international theory, see Jennifer Welsh, *Edmund Burke and International Relations* (London: Macmillan, 1995); David Armitage, 'Edmund Burke and Reason of State', *Journal of the History of Ideas*, vol. 61, no. 4, 2000, pp. 617–34.

[39] A nice example of such despair is Jean-Jacques Rousseau, 'L'état de Guerre', in C. E. Vaughan, ed., *The Political Writings of Jean-Jacques Rousseau*, vol. I (Cambridge: Cambridge University Press, 1915), pp. 297–306.

[40] For some examples of this enormous debate, see Michael W. Doyle, 'Kant, Liberal Legacies, and Foreign Affairs', in Michael E. Brown, Sean M. Lynn-Jones and Steven E. Miller, eds., *Debating the Democratic Peace*

sense to saddle Kant with such a theory of democratic peace, whether in order to interpret Kantian writings on the topic, or in order to provide this theory with a more noble ancestry. I can think of at least three reasons. First, even if Kant indeed did assume a positive correlation between popular sovereignty and peaceful relations between states, such emphasis on popular sovereignty was one of the commonplaces of eighteenth-century political thought.[41] Second, such an interpretation would also be anachronistic, since Kant was hardly a democrat in any recognizably modern sense of this term. Rather, the international order he envisaged was based on principles of republican freedom rather than on modern ideas of democratic representation. Third, while Kant places certain requirements on the domestic structure of states, theorists of democratic peace have assumed that Kant was exclusively interested in the European states system. Yet while Kant certainly regarded sovereign states as a permanent feature of the international order, he also tried to integrate communities at different stages of development within a wider community of all mankind. Many of those who have turned to Kant to find support for the theory of democratic peace have thus distorted crucial parts of his argument in the process.

Another interpretation has been proposed by the advocates of *cosmopolitan democracy*. According to this interpretation, what Kant had in mind was a world society comprising the totality of human beings within a single framework of cosmopolitan right. Kant is believed to have argued that the international society of states ought to be replaced by a global society of autonomous individuals.[42]

(Cambridge, MA: MIT Press, 1996), pp. 3–57; Christopher Layne, 'Kant or Cant: The Myth of Democratic Peace', in Michael E. Brown, Sean M. Lynn-Jones and Steven E. Miller, eds., *Debating the Democratic Peace* (Cambridge, MA: MIT Press, 1996), pp. 157–201. For a more recent critique, see Sebastian Rosato, 'The Flawed Logic of the Democratic Peace Theory', *American Political Science Review*, vol. 97, no. 4, 2003, pp. 585–602. Also Mikkel Vedby Rasmussen, *The West, Civil Society and the Construction of Peace* (Houndmills: Palgrave, 2003).

[41] Hont, *Jealousy of Trade*, pp. 447–528.
[42] See, for example, Andrew Linklater, *Men and Citizens in the Theory of International Relations* (London: Macmillan, 1982); Daniele Archibugi, 'Immanuel Kant, Cosmopolitan Law and Peace', *European Journal of International Relations*, vol. 1, no. 4, 1995, pp. 429–56; David Held,

First, while this reading helps us to understand how individual human beings could fit into a world community, it fails to account for the fact that Kant regarded individual political communities as integral parts of such a world community as well. Second, to the extent that this interpretation takes these individuals into serious consideration, it does not understand them as essentially embedded, either in those particular communities where they happen to live, or in a wider world community.[43] Thus, if we want to make full sense of his conception of world community, we must understand how Kant tried to integrate both particular communities and individual human beings within a larger social whole represented by the totality of mankind. In the rest of this section, I shall argue that this was accomplished by positing a single universal community as the proper end result of human intercourse on a global scale. I shall then go on to discuss the relationship between the European society of states and this wider community of all mankind in some detail.

The Kantian vision of world community is essentially a geographical vision. Since humanity has been dispersed across the inhabitable surfaces of the planet by natural forces, the relations between different peoples are *global* in character. As Kant formulated this idea in the *Metaphysik der Sitten* (1797):

The rational idea ... of a peaceful ... international community of all those of the earth's peoples who can enter into active relations with one another, is not a philanthropic principle of ethics, but a principle of right. Through the spherical shape of the planet they inhabit, nature has confined them all within an area of definite limits. Accordingly, the only conceivable way in which anyone can possess habitable land on earth is by possessing a part within a determinate whole in which everyone has an original right to share.[44]

'Cosmopolitan Democracy and the Global Order: Reflections on the 200th Anniversary of Kant's "Perpetual Peace"', *Alternatives*, vol. 20, no. 4, 1995, pp. 415–29.

[43] For an analysis, see Antonio Franceschet, 'Sovereignty and Freedom: Immanuel Kant's Liberal Internationalist Legacy', *Review of International Studies*, vol. 27, no. 2, 2001, pp. 209–28; Antonio Franceschet, 'Popular Sovereignty or Cosmopolitan Democracy? Liberalism, Kant, and International Reform', *European Journal of International Relations*, vol. 6, no. 2, 2000, pp. 277–302.

[44] Kant, 'The Metaphysics of Morals', p. 172.

Kant's claim to have started a Copernican revolution in philosophy should therefore be taken in a very literal sense. His vision of a united mankind is a corollary of his geographical assumption of inhabitable continents being interconnected by fully navigable oceans. Most other theories of international order at this time were concerned exclusively with relations between European states, and they rarely bothered to discuss non-European communities other than as possible targets for conquest and exploitation by European powers.[45] By contrast, Kant's concept of a world community includes *all* human communities, irrespective of their degree of political and economic development, and regards them as indispensable parts of the same overarching community. The only boundaries morally relevant to such a community are those of the planet as a whole, since 'through the spherical shape of the planet they inhabit (*globus terraqueus*), nature has confined them all within an area of definite limits'.[46]

This world community is constituted through intercourse between human beings. Not only have natural forces compelled people to spread across the surface of the globe, but since the available space is limited, different peoples have been forced to interact with each other: 'since the earth is a globe, they cannot disperse over an infinite area, but must necessarily tolerate one another's company'.[47] As Kant further states in *Zum Ewigen Frieden* (1796), the 'community of man is divided by uninhabitable parts of the earth's surface such as oceans and deserts, but even then, the ship or the camel ... make it possible for them to approach their fellows over these ownerless tracts, and to utilize as a means of social intercourse that *right to the earth's surface* which the human race shares in common'.[48] Similarly, 'the oceans may appear to cut nations off from the community of their fellows. But with the art of navigation, they constitute the greatest natural incentive to international commerce, and the greater the number of neighbouring coastlines there are ... the livelier this commerce will

---

[45] A case in point is Saint-Pierre, whose 'peace project' actually recommended a crusade against the Turk. See Tomaz Mastnak, 'Abbé Saint-Pierre: European Union and the Turk', *History of Political Thought*, vol. 19, no. 4, 1998, pp. 570–98.
[46] Kant, 'Metaphysics of Morals', p. 172.
[47] Kant, 'Perpetual Peace', in Reiss, *Kant: Political Writings*, pp. 93–115, at p. 106.
[48] Kant, 'Perpetual Peace', p. 106.

be'.[49] Kant uses the term commerce (*commercium*) mainly to describe the economic aspects of human intercourse, but this concept also carries connotations of the mutual respect this intercourse is capable of generating between peoples.[50] To Kant, the interaction between peoples has intensified, and is gradually facilitated by technological innovations. This has made it increasingly possible for people from different continents to enter into contact with each other, so that a once divided mankind is now in the process of reconstituting itself into one single community.

Out of this intercourse common norms and rules gradually evolve. The fact that different peoples now interact on a global scale requires a distinct set of *cosmopolitan rights* (*ius cosmopoliticum*) to regulate their intercourse for the maximum benefit of this emergent community of all mankind.[51] As Kant goes on to explain, 'the peoples of the earth have thus entered in varying degrees into a universal community, and it has developed into a point where a violation of rights in *one* part of the world is felt *everywhere*'.[52] The actual diversity of communities ought therefore to be respected rather than abolished in the name of one single standard of civilization. Consequently, Kant refuses to regard European culture as a benchmark of civilization: the 'main difference between the savage nations of Europe and those of America is that while some American tribes have been entirely eaten up by their enemies, the Europeans know how to make better use of those they have defeated than merely by making a meal of them'.[53] Given the view of history described in the previous section, and even if the very finiteness of global space will inevitably give rise to disagreement over moral standards and basic principles of justice, such disagreements will eventually evolve into reciprocal respect between different peoples.[54]

Thus, and in contrast to Grotius and Locke, Kant did not believe that the Europeans enjoyed rights of settlement and dominion in those places where the local population – being hunters or gatherers – had

---

[49] Kant, 'Metaphysics of Morals', p. 172.
[50] Muthu, *Enlightenment Against Empire*, p. 195.
[51] Kant, 'Perpetual Peace', p. 98.   [52] Kant, 'Perpetual Peace', pp. 107–8.
[53] Kant, 'Perpetual Peace', p. 103.
[54] For this suggestion, see Jeremy Waldron, 'What Is Cosmopolitan?', *Journal of Political Philosophy*, vol. 8, no. 2, 2000, pp. 227–43.

raised no prior claims to property. Kant neither argued nor implied that the differences between settled and non-settled peoples were of any profound moral relevance, let alone that the former were justified in dominating or forcing the latter to conform to European standards of civilization. Since the earth is the common property of all mankind, there can be no automatic right of settlement, only rights of hospitality and resort, since 'all men are entitled to present themselves in the society of others by virtue of their right to communal possession of the earth's surface'.[55] To Kant, attempts to settle on foreign shores 'with a view to linking them with the motherland, can also occasion evil and violence in one part of the globe with ensuing repercussions which are felt everywhere else'.[56] But even if all 'nations are originally members of a community of the land', this community is not a legal one, it is 'a community of reciprocal action, which is physically possible, and each member has constant relations with all the others'.[57] As long as these basic rights of hospitality and resort are respected, 'continents distant from each other can enter into peaceful mutual relations which may eventually be regulated by public laws, thus bringing the human race nearer and nearer to a cosmopolitan constitution'.[58] So while Kant at times seems to assume that global interaction will gradually compel people outside Europe to abandon their state of natural freedom and enter into civil societies of their own creation, nothing strictly *obliges* these peoples to conform to the ways of political life adopted by the Europeans. To Kant, the principle of reciprocal freedom applies not only to individuals, but also to the relations between communities, compelling us to respect the rights of unsettled societies to remain in this condition should they choose to. We are therefore urged to acknowledge the fact that different human communities might embody incommensurable moral standards simply by virtue of being *human* communities. Kant seems to believe that such diversity is indeed constitutive of humanity, and he also takes such diversity into account by advocating the independence of all peoples irrespective of their degree of development.[59]

---

[55] Kant, 'Perpetual Peace', p. 106.
[56] Kant, 'Metaphysics of Morals', p. 172.
[57] Kant, 'Metaphysics of Morals', p. 172.
[58] Kant, 'Perpetual Peace', p. 106.
[59] Muthu, *Enlightenment Against Empire*, pp. 191–209.

These observations make it possible to confront a recent objection by Tully, which is symptomatic of the contemporary critique of visions of world community. According to him, the Kantian vision is not cosmopolitan in any ethically relevant sense, but instead profoundly Eurocentric. Its claim to universal validity is merely a way of concealing the fact that it is nothing but an imperial ideology, since 'the Kantian idea of free states and federation is not culturally neutral but is the bearer of processes of a homogenizing or assimilating European cultural identity'.[60] To Tully, this bias is evident in the way in which Kant classifies cultures according to their different stages of development, thus implying a moral hierarchy which can easily be used to justify imperial expansion and colonial domination. But if my analysis is correct, this critique overlooks the complex way in which Kant understood the relationship between Europe and the rest of the world, and the often ironic ways he used the concepts of barbarism and civilization in order to *subvert* their contemporary meanings in the interest of criticizing colonial practices. To Kant as to many of his contemporaries, the only true barbarians were to be found at Versailles.[61] Yet many of those things that Tully has to say about Kant's legacy in international affairs are unfortunately true, his theories having been used to justify a range of interventionist practices which Kant himself found highly objectionable.[62]

III

Let us now take a closer look at the European society of states, as well as its relationship to the rest of mankind. The situation in question, writes Kant in *Metaphysik der Sitten*, 'is that in which one state, as a moral person, is considered as existing in a state of nature in relation

---

[60] James Tully, 'The Kantian Idea of Europe: Critical and Cosmopolitan Perspectives', in Anthony Pagden, ed., *The Idea of Europe: From Antiquity to the European Union* (Cambridge: Cambridge University Press, 2002), pp. 331–58, at p. 339.
[61] See John G. A. Pocock, *Barbarism and Religion*, vol. IV: *Barbarians, Savages and Empires* (Cambridge: Cambridge University Press, 2005), pp. 277–93.
[62] See Beate Jahn, 'Kant, Mill and Illiberal Legacies in International Affairs', *International Organization*, vol. 59, no. 1, 2005, pp. 177–207.

Globalizing community

to another state, hence in a condition of constant war'.[63] Since the state of nature among peoples for moral reasons ought to be abandoned in favour of a state of law, a federation of peoples should be established 'in accordance with the idea of an original social contract, so that states will protect one another against external aggression while refraining from interference in one another's internal disagreements'.[64]

From these formulations, it would seem that a lasting peace between European powers would be possible only with the establishment of a common government. Such a solution had indeed been proposed by Condorcet, who believed a universal state to be desirable, 'as truth, reason, justice, the rights of man, the interests of property, of liberty, of security, are in all places the same; we cannot discover why all the provinces of a state, should not have the same civil and criminal laws, and the same laws relative to commerce'.[65] But Kant did not agree. As the creation of such an international state would necessitate the abolition of state sovereignty, such a union may prove hard to govern, and the 'multitude of corporations this would require must again lead to a state of war'.[66] Whenever the ideal of peace is based on the abolition of state sovereignty, it becomes difficult to realize since the very same condition that this ideal is intended to abolish – international anarchy – is the prime obstacle to its successful implementation. A lasting peace thus necessitates that we find a way out of this pragmatic paradox.

If we instead return to *Zum Ewigen Frieden*, the prospects of a lasting peace are not prey to such perversity, since 'it can be shown that the idea of federalism, extending gradually to encompass all states and thus leading to perpetual peace, is practicable and has objective reality … if the concept of international right is to retain any meaning at all, reason must necessarily couple it with a federation of this kind'.[67] Yet to Kant the establishment of a pacific federation is only

---

[63] Kant, 'Metaphysics of Morals', p. 165.
[64] Kant, 'Metaphysics of Morals', p. 165.
[65] Marie-Jean-Antoine Nicolas de Caritat, marquis de Condorcet, 'Observations on the Twenty-ninth Book of the *Spirit of the Laws*, by the Late M. Condorcet', in Antoine Louis Claude Destutt de Tracy, *A Commentary and Review of Montesquieu's Spirit of Laws* [1798] (Philadelphia: William Duane, 1811), pp. 261–82, at p. 274.
[66] Kant, 'Metaphysics of Morals', p. 171.
[67] Kant, 'Perpetual Peace', pp. 104–5.

possible between states whose internal constitution is in accordance with the principles of civil right. The principles of civil right demand that the members of society should enjoy reciprocal freedom and equality under a common constitution based on the idea of an original contract. If the consent of the citizens is required in order to decide whether war is to be declared or not, 'it is very natural that they will have great hesitation in embarking on so dangerous an enterprise'.[68] Kant goes on to distinguish this form of popular sovereignty from some of its contemporary contenders. This is done by insisting that a republican government has to be representative if it is to chime with the doctrine of right. Yet far from being democratic in any modern sense, the kind of government that Kant thought most conducive to peace was a constitutional republic based on a firm separation between legislative and executive powers in order to safeguard individual liberties, rather than a constitutional arrangement based on full popular control over these powers.[69] In order to explain under what conditions such a pacific federation is likely to emerge in Europe, Kant reiterates the teleological view of history discussed in the previous section, but gives it a distinctive moral twist. While we cannot observe or infer the presence of any agency above that of human beings, writes Kant, 'we can and must supply it mentally in order to conceive of its possibility by analogy with human artifices. Its relationship to and conformity with the end which reason directly prescribes to us ... makes it our duty to work our way towards this goal, which is more than an empty chimera.'[70] Therefore, a lasting peace in Europe would best be served by the establishment of a federation of constitutional republics.[71]

Let us now turn to the relationship between the European society of states and the wider community of all mankind discussed in the previous section. At first glance, there seems to be a considerable tension between the precepts of international right and those of cosmopolitan

---

[68] Kant, 'Perpetual Peace', p. 100.
[69] See Onuf, *Republican Legacy*, pp. 220–46. For Kant's concept of republicanism, see also Allen D. Rosen, *Kant's Theory of Justice* (Ithaca, NY: Cornell University Press, 1996); Patrick Riley, *Kant's Political Philosophy* (Totowa, NJ: Rowman and Littlefield, 1983).
[70] Kant, 'Perpetual Peace', pp. 109 and 114.
[71] For an elaboration of this argument, see Garrett Wallace Brown, 'State Sovereignty, Federation and Kantian Cosmopolitanism', *European Journal of International Relations*, vol. 11, no. 4, 2005, pp. 495–522.

right, since they are based on entirely different modes of association and intercourse. While the former is based on a contractual relationship between constitutional republics that have entered into a federation for pacific purposes, the latter is based the evolution of respect and reciprocity between human communities irrespective of their different stages of development. This tension has been further aggravated by a common way of reading Kant within academic international relations. According to this interpretation, the establishment of republican (or, when assimilated to late modern concerns, democratic) governments of states is a necessary condition for international peace, and such international peace is in turn necessary for the implementation of the principles of cosmopolitan right between peoples. This reading is not without textual support, and there is a compelling logic to the argument: once a pacific federation has been created among a few republican states, it is expected to attract new members by virtue of the economic and political advantages membership would bring. By the same token, as unsettled peoples outside the European system realized the advantages of European civilization and thus entered into settled conditions of civility, they could also be expected to join this federation at some later stage. This interpretation also seems plausible given that the prior abolition of despotism was widely perceived by his contemporaries to be a necessary step towards international peace.[72]

Another reason why this reading has been so prevalent within academic international relations has more to do with concerns internal to this discipline, however. To some theorists of international relations, an important question has been whether the causes of war are to be found in human nature, in the makeup of individual states, or in the structure of the international system itself. If this typology is taken to be exhaustive of available explanations, it becomes hard to make sense of Kantian international thought in ways that do not turn his theory into an example of any of these three images.[73]

But given that Kant takes the existence of mankind as a whole as the starting point for his political philosophy, I would like to reverse

---

[72] See, for example, Kenneth N. Waltz, 'Kant, Liberalism and War', *American Political Science Review*, vol. 56, no. 3, 1962, pp. 331–40.
[73] Kenneth N. Waltz, *Man, the State, and War: A Theoretical Analysis* (New York: Columbia University Press, 1959); also Hidemi Suganami, *On the Causes of War* (Oxford: Oxford University Press, 1996).

this reading and instead read the Kantian vision of world community from the *outside in*, by starting at the most comprehensive level of analysis and then working inwards, as it were. The way he conceived of the relationship between the European society of states and the wider community of all peoples will then start to make more sense, especially since his views of geography and human community antedate his thoughts on international and cosmopolitan right. More importantly, however, there are formulations which indicate that Kant believed that the different levels at which political rights could manifest themselves are actually *inseparable*, and in a way that reminds us of his great predecessor Wolff. As he explains with reference to the scope of international law,

a state of nature among individuals and families ... is different from a state of nature among entire nations, because international right involves not only the relationship between one state and another within a larger whole, but also the relationship between individual persons in one state and individuals in the other or between such individuals and the other state as a whole.[74]

Thus, even if Kant held that these levels should be distinguished in the interests of formulating a theory of international law, they are nevertheless interdependent since both individuals and the communities which they inhabit are parts of the same overarching world community, whose legitimacy in turn derives from the same underlying conception of right.

This would imply that the Kantian vision of world community cannot meaningfully be assimilated to the distinction between different levels of analysis conventionally drawn within academic international relations. To Kant, historical agency ultimately resides in humanity as a whole, being something more than the sum of its individual parts. This further entails that the Kantian vision of world community represents a fourth level of analysis, insofar as it focuses on the *totality* of social relations on a global scale. If this interpretation is correct, the ultimate sources of human concord should be sought at this level as well, rather than in the constitutional makeup of individual states or in the structure of the international system. In legal terms, this means that those principles of cosmopolitan right that would regulate human

---

[74] Kant, 'Metaphysics of Morals', p. 165.

intercourse within a world community would have to derive *directly* from the idea of moral autonomy, which tells us that 'every action which by itself or by its maxim enables the freedom of each individual's will to coexist with the freedom of everyone else in accordance with a universal law is right'.[75] From this perspective, there is no categorical difference between the rights of communities and the rights of individuals. The fact that Kant does not distinguish categorically between the rights of individuals and the rights of communities indicates that he thought that a world community ought to encompass both, and that he consequently regarded both kinds of political subjects as being equally entitled to be bearers of these rights, since 'individuals and states, coexisting in an external relationship of mutual influences, may be regarded as citizens of a universal state of mankind'.[76] Kant thus regards European states as fundamentally embedded within a more comprehensive community of communities, within which individual communities have equal legal status irrespective of their level of development.

This argument is similar to the views articulated by Diderot, but with the important difference that Kant makes this point with reference to a community constituted through human intercourse, rather than with reference to an abstract moral community constituted by the species membership alone. But since the rights of its members must derive from an original contract, Kant is left with the troubling task of explaining how the idea of a social contract can be made intelligible in this boundless context, without assuming any consent on behalf of its members. Such an assumption, writes Kant, 'would mean that we would first have to prove from history that some nation, whose rights and obligations have been passed down to us, did in fact perform such an act, and handed down some authentic record or legal instrument, orally or in writing, before we could regard ourselves as bound by a pre-existing civil constitution'.[77] Kant hereby puts an end to an old controversy in the contract tradition by regarding the social contract as wholly fictitious, rather than implying that such a contract

---

[75] Kant, 'Metaphysics of Morals', p. 133.
[76] Kant, 'Perpetual Peace', pp. 98–9.
[77] Immanuel Kant, 'On the Common Saying: "This May be True in Theory, but it does not Apply in Practice"', in Reiss, *Kant: Political Writings* (Cambridge: Cambridge University Press, 1991), pp. 61–92, at p. 79.

could indeed have been entered into by men at some point in the distant past. To Kant, the social contract was 'an idea of reason, which nonetheless has undoubted practical reality; for it can oblige every legislator to frame his laws in such a way that they could have been produced by the united will of a whole nation, and to regard each subject, in so far as he can claim citizenship, as if he had consented within the general will'.[78] This implies that those who are supposed to give their consent in order to lend legitimacy to a governing authority must also derive their identity directly from the principle of autonomy, and hence indirectly from their humanity. Since the principle of moral autonomy knows no spatio-temporal restrictions on its applicability, *political community is boundless in principle.* Hence the predominance of bounded communities is the outcome of a series of historical accidents that have confined peoples within distinct territories, rather than of any reasoned consent among the members of mankind to divide themselves into such distinct communities before entering into contractual obligations within each of them.

This way of handling the problem of legitimacy is different from that of Rousseau and Sieyès, who both emphasized the constitutive role of people or nation. While both those authors struggled unsuccessfully to account for the identity of that people in terms that were independent of political authority, Kant accepts that such governing authority might indeed constitute the political community as long as it does so in accordance with the general will. Kant thereby reverses the relationship between the identity of the political community and the legitimacy of political authority, and since the general will is a principle of reason rather than an expression of prior consent, the legitimacy of authority is not subjected to any predetermined restriction on its scope. Kant thereby implies that a mutually constitutive relationship can be created and upheld between political authority and human communities without presupposing the prior existence of a homogeneous people or nation.

In contrast to Diderot, however, Kant uses the concept of a general will to articulate a concept of political right that assumes the reciprocal freedom of agents to be necessary in order to turn this community of all mankind into a *political* one. This makes it possible for Kant to

[78] Kant, 'Theory and Practice', p. 79.

justify those rights which human beings are thought to enjoy within this universal community with reference to their moral autonomy rather than with reference to their sociability. While human sociability harbours those dark passions that will ultimately propel the entire species into a condition of political maturity, they will also eventually compel mankind to regulate the terms of interaction in accordance with the demands of moral autonomy. A universal community of human beings coexisting in conformity with the principle of reciprocal freedom will then gradually expand until its boundaries coincide neatly with the physical limits of the globe: to Dante, the ocean was the limit; to Kant, it is the sky. But if a world community encompassed all existing communities, and if each such community was ideally governed according to the same basic principle of moral autonomy, would not such a world community bring an end to human diversity?

In response to this problem, but in contrast to Kant, Herder took the idea of a world community one step further.[79] Whereas Kant had articulated his vision of community in the context of physical geography, Herder situates his idea of community in a wider cosmological framework. To him, a universal community of all human beings is but one possible community in many possible worlds. As he notes in his *Outlines of a Philosophy of the History of Man* (1784–91), 'the Earth is of itself nothing, but derives its figure and constitution, its faculty of forming organized beings ... from those heavenly powers that pervade the whole universe ... Thus the whole space and sphere of action of my species is precisely determined and prescribed.'[80] Within the universe, our world coexists with a plurality of other worlds which have the sun as their common centre. Since on our planet the greatest variety is always combined with unconstrained uniformity, this applies to the members of the human species as well. As Herder goes on to ask, 'Where is the country of man? Where the central point of the earth? Everywhere, the answer may be.'[81] But the fact that the cultural differences between different groups of men are caused primarily by

---

[79] For this contrast, see John H. Zammito, *Kant, Herder, and the Birth of Anthropology* (Chicago: University of Chicago Press, 2002).
[80] Johann Gottfried Herder, *Outlines of a Philosophy of the History of Man* (London, 1800), pp. 1–3. See also Muthu, *Enlightenment Against Empire*, pp. 210–58.
[81] Herder, *Outlines of a Philosophy of the History of Man*, p. 11.

differences in the natural environment must not lead us to disregard the ethical significance of those differences, since they are what make us human in the fullest possible sense. As Herder goes on to explain, 'the human intellect ... seeks unity in every kind of variety, and the divine mind ... has stamped the most innumerable multiplicity on the earth with unity'.[82] Furthermore, and as we learn from one of his *Letters*, 'Just as each individual human being is guided by the law of nature to humanity ... so it is that the diverse characters and mentalities work for the benefit of the larger whole.'[83] In order for a world community to be both desirable and viable, it must find a balance between the demands for unity and the intrinsic value of human diversity. In order to overcome the apparent tension between these different ends of mankind, a world community must be based on the principles of reason and justice.[84] It must cultivate not only reciprocal freedom among human beings, but also a deep sense of mutual respect between the different peoples of the world. All cultures contain their own moral standards, and cannot therefore be judged from any external viewpoint over and above the resulting plurality. Therefore, each and every human community must 'provide for and facilitate in each individual case the mutually most beneficial impact of one human being upon the other, That, and that alone can be the purpose of all human community'.[85] Thus, and in contrast to Kant, Herder viewed a world community as the outcome of gradual progress to the point of making states and nations *redundant* as the vanguards of cultural diversity. Having outgrown the state and the nation through the painstaking cultivation of reason and justice, the peoples of the world would be free to enter into spontaneous cooperation, unconstrained by any boundaries, as long as this cooperation served the higher ends of a true human community on a global scale.[86]

[82] Herder, *Outlines of a Philosophy of the History of Man*, p. 164.
[83] Johann Gottfried Herder, 'On the Character of Humankind' [1793], in *Johan Gottfried Herder On World History. An Anthology*, ed. Hans Adler and Ernest A. Menze (Armonk, NY: Sharpe, 1997), pp. 99–104, at pp. 103–4.
[84] Herder, *Outlines of a Philosophy of the History of Man*, pp. 452–60.
[85] Herder, 'On the Character of Humankind', p. 100.
[86] Vicki Spencer, 'In Defense of Herder on Cultural Diversity and Interaction', *Review of Politics*, vol. 69, 2007, pp. 79–105.

In this chapter, we have seen how Kant rearticulated the concept of world community found in authors like Diderot and Wolff in historicist terms. Kant supplemented their notions of a united mankind with an account of its historical progress towards political unity. As we have also seen, Kant did so against the backdrop of a series of geographical assumptions, according to which the planetary surface constituted the stage on which human history could play itself out. In his view, such progress towards political unity is both enabled and constrained by the geographical features of the earth, which compel people from different places to enter into interaction with each other, while simultaneously posing obstacles to such interaction which have to be overcome through human ingenuity. While articulating this vision, Kant also sought to reconcile the need for universal rules with the inescapable presence of particular communities. Kant believed that a continuous intercourse would bring both particular communities and individual human beings together into a global community within which all further interaction would eventually be regulated by cosmopolitan laws based on reciprocal freedom. Thus, the same principles of republican liberty which ought to govern political life *within* particular communities should also ideally govern the relations *between* them.

We know well that this cosmopolitan moment was not to last long. Not long after the French Revolution, the particularizing tendencies described in Chapter 4 culminated in the fusion of the nation and the state, a fusion which was to become the predominant solution to the problem of political order for the foreseeable future. When Hegel later tried to make sense of the complex achievements of the French Revolution, it was this remarkable outcome – the fusion of nation and state – that he thought was the ultimate subject of history. In the *Philosophy of Right* (1821), we learn that 'the nation state is the spirit in its substantial rationality and immediate actuality, and is therefore the absolute power on earth; each state is consequently a sovereign and independent entity in relation to others'.[87] To Hegel, the French Revolution was not only a historical event, but was based on a wholesale reconfiguration of past and present that

---

[87] Georg W. F. Hegel, *Elements of the Philosophy of Right* (Cambridge: Cambridge University Press, 1991), §331, p. 366.

necessitated the substitution of the state for the idea of a common humanity.[88] To him, the notion of a world community lacked the kind of actuality he found embodied in the nation-state, and this compelled humanity to adjust itself to a permanent division into particular nation-states rather than seeking to overcome it. This system of states had grown out of a logic of identity that located the sources of human belonging and fulfilment exclusively and firmly within the socio-political domain. According to this logic of sameness and otherness, each particular state is identical with itself by virtue of being different from every other state, and the totality of such states forms an international society to the extent that states are able to mutually recognize each other's claims to sovereignty and individual identity. Within this vision, there is no longer any need for a vantage point over and above that of the particular community in order to make sense of human affairs. Not only is such a vantage point rendered redundant, but so is any connection between conceptions of community and cosmological beliefs about the earth and its place in the universe. The sources of human belonging are now fully anthropocentric and particularized, as the limits of human destiny coincide neatly with national boundaries. Thus, the problem of community had been reformulated in such a way that the aspiration of finding belonging elsewhere became equivalent to the impossible task of transcending the state system altogether.[89] As Hegel tells us, 'The principles of the national spirits in their necessary progression are themselves only moments of the one universal spirit, which ascends to them in the course of history to its consummation in an all-embracing totality.'[90]

---

[88] Robert Wokler, 'Contextualizing Hegel's Phenomenology of the French Revolution and the Terror', *Political Theory*, vol. 26, no. 1, 1998, pp. 33–55.

[89] See Mark Shelton, 'The Morality of Peace: Kant and Hegel on the Grounds for Ethical Ideals', *Review of Metaphysics*, vol. 54, no. 2, 2000, pp. 379–408. For a different interpretation, see Robert Fine, 'Kant's Theory of Cosmopolitanism and Hegel's Critique', *Philosophy and Social Criticism*, vol. 29, no. 6, 2003, pp. 609–30.

[90] Georg W. F. Hegel, *Lectures on the Philosophy of World History* [1837] (Cambridge: Cambridge University Press, 1975), p. 65. See also Friedrich Meinecke, *Cosmopolitanism and the National State* [1907] (Princeton, NJ: Princeton University Press, 1970); Jeanne Morefield, *Covenants*

Globalizing community 169

The emerging academic disciplines of history and political science had then to make empirical sense of what went on within the system of states into which mankind was now about to be trapped. To Ranke, the greatest achievement of the French Revolution and its aftermath was 'the fact that nationalities were rejuvenated, revived, and developed anew. They became part of the state, for it was realized that without them the state could not exist.'[91] Thus, to the extent that Hegel had regarded the nation-state as historically constituted, historians such as Ranke turned the nation-state into the main object of historical inquiry. There was no history – and hence no repository of collective memory – apart from the historiography of particular states and nations and their progressive unfolding in time. The fusion of nation and state brought by the Revolution was supported by new modes of historical writing that could account for this fusion by positing state and nation on converging planes of historicity.[92]

As I have argued elsewhere, the outcome of this transition was that subsequent efforts to understand the political world took place within a *living museum*, containing manifold vibrant customs, institutions, and practices that had now been sealed off in distinct spatio-temporal compartments, as if only awaiting discovery by the historian or the early political scientist. As we have seen, this domain of objectivity had been crafted by the sequential superimposition of memories and identities upon each other, so that by all measures the nation and the state had come to look as indispensable in the present as they seemed to have been from the beginning of historical time.[93] National communities and the differences between them were regarded as manifestations of prior and more profound divisions of humanity into the less malleable categories of race. These new naturalistic and philological grounds of classification not only constituted the start-

Without Swords: Idealist Liberalism and the Spirit of Empire (Princeton, NJ: Princeton University Press, 2005), chs. 1–2.

[91] Leopold von Ranke, *The Great Powers*, in *Leopold Ranke: The Formative Years*, ed. Theodore H. von Laue (Princeton, NJ: Princeton University Press, 1950), pp. 181, 215.

[92] Reinhart Koselleck, 'Historical Criteria of the Modern Concept of Revolution', in *Futures Past: On the Semantics of Historical Time* (Cambridge, MA: MIT Press, 1985), pp. 39–54.

[93] Jens Bartelson, *The Critique of the State* (Cambridge: Cambridge University Press, 2001), ch. 2.

ing point of modern social science, but also provided the commercial empires with one final source of legitimacy. As different races could be arranged on a continuum from the most primitive to the most advanced, claims to colonial dominion could now be backed with reference to the best-established scientific facts of the day.[94] The route from this point to our present difficulties in making coherent sense of the idea of world community is surprisingly short. When mankind had been subdivided along so many dimensions, and when the nation-state had been reified into an inescapable fact of human life, the only remaining way of formulating the problem of world community was in terms of the insurmountable difficulties involved in *transcending* all these divisions simultaneously. What had been an indispensable part of the background understanding of political reflection from the Middle Ages to the Enlightenment had now finally been relegated to the status of an unattainable utopia. And as we saw in Chapter 2, contemporary political theory still largely finds itself in this predicament, wrestling with a nationalized conception of human community without access to any clear alternatives. But have the preceding chapters offered anything more than a diagnosis of this predicament? Have they in any way brought us closer to a solution? These are the questions to be addressed in the next and final chapter of this book.

[94] See Edward Keene, *Beyond the Anarchical Society. Grotius, Colonialism and Order in World Politics* (Cambridge: Cambridge University Press, 2002); Martti Koskenniemi, *The Gentle Civilizer of Nations. The Rise and Fall of International Law 1870–1960* (Cambridge: Cambridge University Press, 2001), pp. 98–178.

7 | *Community unbound?*

WHY does the idea of a world community look so morally compelling yet so politically impossible? I started this book by describing a fundamental paradox that modern theories of world community have had to confront, and which has made them easy to dismiss on grounds of their incoherence and impracticality: while a world community must be based on some set of universal values, every effort to impose such values is likely to be met with resistance on the grounds of its particularity. But rather than trying to solve this paradox, I suggested that we should investigate how it came into being, thereby explaining why universalistic and particularistic conceptions of community have ended up in such rigid opposition within modern political thought. I then suggested that our present difficulties in making coherent sense of the idea of world community are the outcome of a successful nationalization of the concept of community. Consequently, understanding how this nationalization took place can hopefully help us understand how the tension between universalistic and particularistic conceptions of community emerged, and by implication, how it can be overcome. The time has now come to follow up on these suggestions.

I

The first thing to note is that the paradox described above is of fairly recent origin. It would have been hard to formulate this paradox in a more distant past, since the opposition between universalistic and particularistic conceptions of community itself is rather recent. This is because a world community is based upon a social ontology very different from that of particular communities. While the identity of individual communities is widely believed to be based on a dialectic between Same and Other, a world community is based on the idea that mankind as a whole constitutes one single community by virtue of sharing a set of natural capacities and a terrestrial habitat in common. Given this basic commonality, theories of world community further assume that the universal and the particular are *mutually implicating* categories within a larger social whole. From this presupposition several other assumptions follow. First, conceptions of world community are based on the idea that universalistic and particularistic forms of community are *co-constituted* in time, and that they are also *interpenetrating*. In most theories of world community, the assumptions of co-constitution and interpenetration are frequently used to explain the gradual emergence of a sense of community as a result of intercourse between different peoples from different places. Second, theories of world community assume that there is some *isomorphism* between the universal community of all mankind and the individual communities that compose it. This isomorphism derives from the fact that all communities are but instances of human sociability and rationality, and is reflected in the family resemblance of institutions and practices. Consequently, even if the fact of human diversity makes it inconceivable that all human communities should be governed according to the same set of principles, the same minimal rules of intercourse which ought to apply *within* human communities also ought to apply *between* them, such as reciprocal freedom and respect. Third, theories of world community assume that all social relations between individual human beings as well as the relations between the communities they inhabit are essentially *embedded* within a universal community of all mankind. Being essentially embedded within this wider community entails that none of these social relations is either fully intelligible, or possible to judge morally, in isolation from the overarching framework provided by this singular community.

As we have seen in this book, many of those authors who struggled to articulate conceptions of world community did so by emphasizing the co-constitution between human communities of different scope. In this process, new visions of community were created out of old ones, but in order for the former to take hold of human imagination, they had to be rendered intelligible in terms of the latter. Seemingly universalistic conceptions were thus created out of apparently particularistic ones, and vice versa. For example, Dante's vision of a universal human community took the Aristotelian *polis* as its starting point, but was then expanded into an imaginary realm of human associations which it would hardly have been possible to fit into the paradigm of the *polis*. By the same token, Camões and Pinto could capitalize on the universalistic aspirations of both Christians and Romans in their efforts to construct the identity of the Portuguese nation and justify its imperial claims, as could Hakluyt and Davenant when doing *their* king and country the same dubious favours. Also, we have seen how Las Casas, Shaftesbury and Vico were all able to model their respective visions of community on the basis of what had originally had been considerably more narrow conceptions of human community, but whose logical boundaries they transgressed in order to realign them with current cosmological beliefs, thereby making these conceptions more ethically inclusive. This logic was also obvious to some of those who later struggled to nationalize conceptions of community. Many of those who were involved in the task of nationalizing the concept of community during the French Revolution did so in ways that indicate a high degree of awareness of the mechanisms of co-constitution, and many of those who lamented the end result of this endeavour – such as Diderot, Kant and Herder – actively sought to reverse the thrust of the process of nationalization.

Within this tradition of thought, sovereign states are regarded as fundamentally embedded within a wider community. While thinkers within this tradition lamented the accidental division of mankind into separate communities, they also suggested remedies against the undesirable implications of this division, such as warfare and imperialism. This critique took place within a context of cosmological beliefs that emphasized the planetary scope of human affairs, as well as the necessity of viewing the totality of human relations from a vantage point situated *above* rather than within the system of states. Accepting the possibility and legitimacy of such a vantage point also implied that the order of states could hardly be seen as being exhaustive of the ways in which human life could be organized on a planetary scale, but that it represented but one specific and contingent option among an infinite number of possibilities, corresponding to the primordial diversity of human customs and values. The idea that different forms of community are co-constituted was now being rearticulated against the backdrop of a fully inhabitable planet in which human intercourse had taken on a distinctively *global* scope, thanks to the multiple forces of commerce. But in the absence of any effective global authority or any common cultural identity, some of these authors considered reciprocal freedom the only viable principle that could bring an end to both despotism and imperialism. We must therefore conclude that the principles of co-constitution and interpenetration make it hard to distinguish sharply between universalistic and particularistic conceptions of community prior to the nineteenth century without thereby inviting anachronism.

The paradox of world community arises the moment the early social sciences meet and mingle with the conceptions of community bequeathed by revolutionaries and romantics. This also happens at a point in time when the sources of human belonging are conclusively relocated from the realm of nature to the realm of culture, and when it becomes necessary to distinguish the domains of the natural and the social sciences from each other. During the later part of the nineteenth century, when core concepts of Enlightenment political reflection are recycled to fit the increasingly nationalist agenda of early historiography, the nation-state finally becomes *the* paradigmatic form of political community, and the identity of both political science and academic international relations later become premised on the existence of such entities. Assumptions about the bounded character of human communities then found their way into the classics of early sociology, where they set the terms for subsequent attempts to understand and explain the now enigmatic phenomena of human association and belonging. Hence, the modern paradox of world community emerged the moment we started to forget that mankind might be something more than just the sum total of its parts. At that point, the concept of human community is disconnected from the web of cosmological belief, and instead becomes both particularized and anthropocentric. Consequently, if no human community is conceivable beyond that of individual nations, every norm or value aspiring to universality will be particularistic in kind as a consequence of being particularistic in origin.

The success with which the concept of community has been nationalized is hardly more evident than in the attempts to escape its consequences. While the problems of community have been much debated within contemporary political theory, most responses still assume that communities have to be bounded in order to qualify as communities in the first place. Yet, arguably, this kind of ontological nationalism has projected the tensions between universalistic and particularistic conceptions of community into the global realm. Set against the backdrop of such modern understandings of community, visions of world community look like little more than thinly disguised claims to Western dominance. By contrast, many pre-modern and early modern visions of world community were based on the idea that mankind as a whole constitutes one single and universal community, human beings being human by virtue of sharing certain natural capacities in common. Such basic assumptions gave visions of world community enough integrity to provide a real alternative to the *ius naturalist* view of an international society of states stuck in a state of nature. While these visions were articulated within a wide range of cosmological contexts, and hence were based on assumptions about human nature and the nature of the human habitat, their validity rested on their ability to reconcile human differences, by telling us how to make moral sense out of our encounters with other human beings whose basic values might be radically different from our own. While imperial ideologies take the universal validity of certain values for granted and then go on to project them onto the world, visions of world community regard these values and their validity as matters of agreement by the parties involved. While the former assume that these values need to be enforced from above, the latter assume that they have to be created through actual intercourse between human beings of flesh and blood across the very boundaries that keep them apart.

II

So would it be possible to restore these default settings of political thought? I think so. As Judith Butler has argued, if 'standards of universality are historically articulated, then it would seem that exposing the parochial and exclusionary character of a given historical articulation of universality is part of the project of extending and rendering substantive the notion of universality itself'.[1] Much in the same vein, I think it is possible to dissolve the tension between universalistic and particularistic views of human community once we realize why conceptions of world community have been articulated against the backdrop of cosmological beliefs about our common habitat. Visions

---

[1] Judith Butler, 'Universality in Culture', in Joshua Cohen, ed., *For Love of Country? Debating the Limits of Patriotism* (Boston: Beacon Press, 1996), pp. 45–53, at p. 47.

of world community invariably imply cosmological conceptions of the planet that we inhabit, and locate the sources of human belonging and completion within a larger cosmological framework rather than within the individual community. Instead of being based on the idea of mutual recognition between already given groups of people, a world community is based on the common awareness of inhabiting the same planet.

The historical parts of this book focused on how modern visions of world community were articulated in response to the Copernican revolution, and how this new worldview was turned into a *social fact* by those visions. The geographical and cartographical revolutions that took place simultaneously reinforced the conviction that the entire dry surface of the planet was inhabitable, and that human communities had been dispersed across this surface in such a way that they were compelled to enter into intercourse with one another in order to survive and thrive. Later visions of world community specified the conditions of such intercourse in terms of human achievement and progress, and discussed under what conditions different forms of human intercourse would minimize the political importance of boundaries and cultural differences between communities, gradually leading to the realization of human community on a truly global scale. While this prophecy seems to have come true in that part of the world where this idea first emerged, peoples outside Europe, which were in a condition of statelessness back then, today struggle to achieve a future that is rapidly becoming a part of our past.[2]

But these visions of world community were also built upon notions of *mankind* that take the human species to be an agent in its own right by virtue of its shared capacities for meaningful intercourse. Yet since the concept of mankind is devoid of any determinate content, it seems to lack any real normative import: humanity is a fig leaf large enough to conceal the greatest atrocities. But what matters in the present context is not what the concept of humanity ultimately might be taken to mean or what it might refer to, but what has been done by means of this concept within the different visions of world

---

[2] See Stephen D. Krasner, 'Sharing Sovereignty: New Institutions for Collapsed and Failing States', *International Security*, vol. 29, no. 2, 2004, pp. 85–120.

community discussed in this book. If we accept that the meaning of the concept of mankind is nothing but the sum total of its different usages, we can conclude that the only perennial part of its meaning lies in the very *aspiration* to universality embodied in the consistent effort to transcend the particular circumstances of its articulation. At the heart of these attempts we find nothing but circularity: human beings are members of mankind by virtue of being human, and they are human beings by virtue of being members of mankind. Yet it is precisely this circularity that has allowed for a gradual extension of membership in the face of radical otherness and difference, to the point of making diversity a constitutive feature of humanity. It seems as if this concept has been able to gradually universalize its range of reference through the constant contestation of its meaning, thus inviting the equal inclusion of all on the basis of the uniqueness of each.

It is hard to distil any moral precepts from this social ontology of world community, other than in very general terms. But if we accept that the meaning of the concept of mankind has been determined by its usage, and that this usage has been conditioned by a consistent aspiration to universality within the context of changing cosmological beliefs, some implications should become plain. As already stated, the concept of mankind makes it possible to regard all human beings and the communities to which they happen to belong as equally embedded within a larger moral framework. A world community is boundless for the simple reason that it ultimately makes boundaries between individual communities morally irrelevant and ultimately redundant, since the sources of its sameness lie elsewhere. So while Charles Taylor famously argued that all morality presupposes human beings cohabiting within concrete communities, he also conceded that our commitment to our particular communities might come into conflict with certain other goods, 'in particular the demands of universal and equal respect and of our modern self-determining freedom'.[3] To

---

[3] Charles Taylor, *Sources of the Self. The Making of Modern Identity* (Cambridge, MA: Harvard University Press, 1989), p. 101. Compare also Sonya O. Rose, 'Cultural Analysis and Moral Discourses: Episodes, Continuities, and Transformations', in Victoria E. Bonnell and Lynn Hunt, eds., *Beyond the Cultural Turn* (Berkeley: University of California Press, 1999), pp. 217–38.

him, the moral demands put upon us by our particular communities can sometimes override but never preclude the existence of a more encompassing moral framework that includes consideration for all of humanity. But, according to this view, the individual community can only function as an authoritative source of moral values through the mediating experience of people sharing those values in common with other people, since this kind of experience is what turns a mere multitude into a community. When people succeed in rendering this experience meaningful to themselves and others, this provides the raw material necessary for crafting both a moral vocabulary and a sense of belonging.

But if our moral values do not derive from the particular communities we happen to inhabit, but rather from our ability to share meaningful experiences in common with other people, then such values would stand an equal chance of evolving irrespective of the existence of boundaries between the people doing the sharing. So even if we agreed that some sense of community is indeed necessary in order for any morality to evolve, there is no reason to assume that this sense of community requires the prior existence of bounded societies in order to emerge and spread. From this point of view, the seeds of human community are sown the moment human beings enter into intercourse with each other, not the moment they decide to settle down together within the same territory. Rather than being necessary, boundaries are therefore arbitrary restrictions on such intercourse, and on those very practices of sharing that are constitutive of the possibility of human community. To insist that communities have to be bounded in order for morality to be possible is therefore to narrow down the range of possible sources of morality to an unnecessary minimum. Therefore, the only moral precept that follows from the social ontology of world community is the requirement of *mutual respect* in the face of human diversity. What matters from the vantage point of mankind is not the actual content of all those norms and values that aspire to universal validity within a world community, but the very *contest* that inevitably arises as a consequence of these claims. Since this contest cannot be judged with reference to any higher principles, it can only be mitigated by an acceptance that such diversity is an inescapable part of the human condition. The message that transpires from the visions of world community discussed in this book is that the task becomes considerably easier once this diversity is understood against the backdrop of a shared human destiny as a consequence of inhabiting the same planet.

III

This brings us to the question of political authority. Visions of world community challenge the ways in which the relationship between political authority and community has conventionally been conceived. While most modern accounts presuppose that political authority ought to derive from the will of the people in order to be legitimate, efforts to legitimize the presence of global authority in a similar way are bound to fail due to the obvious absence of anything resembling a global *demos*, let alone democratic relations between existing *demoi*. The existence of any political authority over and above sovereign states is therefore hard to justify in terms that are analogous to those once used to legitimize the transfer of sovereignty from kings to people within already bounded societies. By the same token, the strategies once used to nationalize the idea of community seem less viable on a global scale precisely because of their previous success in the domestic context. The true believers in global governance therefore find themselves in a predicament not unlike that of those in the past who wanted to defend imperial authority, but who could no longer point upwards in the search for legitimacy, and were therefore faced with the impossible task of explaining why people should voluntarily subject themselves to a political authority over which they have no real control.

Visions of world community solve this problem by suggesting that authority and community ideally ought to be congruent. While ideologies of empire typically assume that the prior presence of political authority is necessary to constitute a corresponding community, visions of world community regard this relationship as a two-way street, authorities and communities being made interdependent through the actual historical processes of formation. This implies that it would be pointless to speak of political authority over and above that of sovereign states as long as there is no real world community from which this authority could derive its legitimacy, and that it is equally pointless to speak of such a world community without implying that such a global authority is possible, if not desirable. This ideal of congruence was well captured by Dante in poetic terms when he invoked the image of a *humanitas* who 'crowns and mitres' over itself, thus being both ruler ruled simultaneously.[4] Similar images recurred during the Enlightenment. Authors like Turgot and Condorcet took mankind as a whole to be both the ultimate agent and the ultimate object of governmental authority on a global scale, and both Kant and Herder regarded such congruence as the very *telos* of human self-realization. Their respective accounts implied that the final challenge of human reason was to relate political authority and community in such a way that constituting authority and constituted authority eventually become mutually implicating, thereby undoing the need for any founding act of force. Then and only then would the maps of empire become redundant, other than perhaps as shelters for an occasional beast or beggar, or so they believed. Yet these proposals were anthropocentric insofar as they ruled out the possibility that political authority might emanate from other than purely human sources.

All of this might seem like a distant dream today, when both states and empires are competing to maintain their authority over mankind by keeping it divided into distinct peoples and civilizations. Simultaneously, new cosmological beliefs about the essential fragility of the human habitat emphasize the need to overcome these divisions for the sake of sustainable development, while human intercourse on a global scale has never been easier. And whenever there has been a similar mismatch between our beliefs about our physical habitat and prevalent conceptions of community, the latter have usually been aligned to the former. This brings us to the last conclusion concerning the concept of world community: one of the main functions of this concept throughout its history has been to legitimize *resistance* against those forms of political authority that divide human beings from each other. While Augustine defined the idea of a common humanity against the excesses of pagan authority, Dante articulated the concept of a universal humanity in explicit opposition to papal claims to temporal authority. While Cusa struggled to redefine the community of the faithful to accommodate other religions, Las Casas tried to resist the dispossession of the Indians by reconceptualizing

---

[4] See Ernst Kantorowicz, *The King's Two Bodies. A Study in Medieval Political Theology* (Princeton, NJ: Princeton University Press, 1957), pp. 494–5.

the human community in order to accommodate them and their strange customs. While Vico and Shaftesbury revived universalistic conceptions of mankind in order to handle the fallout from secularization, Diderot, Turgot and Raynal translated these conceptions of humanity into a powerful critique of secular statecraft. Finally, while Wolff lamented the division of mankind into particular communities, Kant and Herder sought to mitigate the more undesirable consequences of this division by articulating theories of world community that were critical of the anarchical international system which was then in the process of emerging in Europe. Most modern theories of cosmopolitanism have continued this critical task, but with the important difference that they have been articulated within the same anthropocentric and particularized political universe that they promise to deliver us from. Since the wider universalistic framework within which these theories were once articulated has been marginalized and forgotten, they are perceived to be incoherent and impractical.

But the concept of world community has fulfilled an important critical function within the history of political thought, sometimes to the point of being *a condition of possible resistance*. Whenever modern political institutions and practices are resisted in the name of mankind, this usually implies not only that these institutions and practices go against the best interests of humanity, but also that they help to reproduce those forms of authority that keep mankind divided. But as the historical analysis has hopefully made plain, the concept of world community has been able to function as a source of such resistance only by virtue of having been articulated in the context of cosmological beliefs about the human habitat and the role of mankind within this habitat. As we have seen, visions of world community depend for their coherence and persuasiveness on the existence of a cosmological vantage point situated over and above the plurality of human communities and the multitude of individual human beings. In the absence of such a vantage point, the concept of world community loses its critical edge and the corresponding visions become little more than a weak substitute for the good old nation.

Today this leaves us with the task of reformulating our conceptions of community in the light of our cosmological beliefs about the human habitat, rather than conversely. This is the philosophical import of problems of climate change and sustainability, since these indicate a major change in current cosmological beliefs about the role of mankind in the shaping of our habitat. If mankind is no longer separate from nature, we might as well reunite in the face of the Flood that threatens to diminish the habitability of our planet. But that very Flood is also what now promises to wash the maps of empire away for good.

Bibliography

Aarsleff, Hans. *From Locke to Saussure: Essays on the Study of Language and Intellectual History* (Minneapolis: University of Minnesota Press, 1982).

Agamben, Giorgio. *The Coming Community* (Minneapolis: University of Minnesota Press, 1993).

'Tradition of the Immemorial', in *Potentialities. Collected Essays in Philosophy* (Stanford, CA: Stanford University Press, 1999), pp. 104–115.

Albert, Mathias. '"Globalization Theory": Yesterday's Fad or More Lively than Ever?' *International Political Sociology*, vol. 1, no. 2, 2007, pp. 165–82.

Alighieri, Dante, *Monarchy* (Cambridge: Cambridge University Press, 1996).

A Question of the Water and of the Land, trans. C. H. Bromby (London: David Nutt, 1897).

Alker, Hayward R. 'The Humanities Movement in International Studies: Reflections on Machiavelli and Las Casas', *Alternatives*, vol. 36, no. 4, 1992, pp. 347–71.

Anderson, Benedict. *Imagined Communities: Reflections on the Origin and Spread of Nationalism* (London: Verso, 1991).

Appiah, Kwame Anthony. 'Cosmopolitan Patriots', in Joshua Cohen, ed., *For Love of Country. Debating the Limits of Patriotism* (Boston: Beacon Press, 1996), pp. 21–9.

Aquinas, Thomas. *On There Being Only One Intellect*, in Ralph McInerny, ed., *Aquinas Against the Averroists* (West Lafayette, IN: Purdue University Press, 1993), pp. 17–145.

Archibugi, Daniele. 'Cosmopolitan Democracy and its Critics: A Review', *European Journal of International Relations*, vol. 10, no. 3, 2004, pp. 437–73.

'Demos and Cosmopolis', *New Left Review*, vol. 13, January/February 2002, pp. 24–38.

'Immanuel Kant, Cosmopolitan Law and Peace', *European Journal of International Relations*, vol. 1, no. 4, 1995, pp. 429–56.

'Principles of Cosmopolitan Democracy', in Daniele Archibugi, David Held and Martin Köhler, eds., *Re-Imagining Political Community* (Oxford: Polity Press, 1998), pp. 198–222.

Arendt, Hannah. *The Human Condition* (Chicago: University of Chicago Press, 1958).

Lectures on Kant's Political Philosophy (Chicago: University of Chicago Press, 1982).

Armitage, David. 'Edmund Burke and Reason of State', *Journal of the History of Ideas*, vol. 61, no. 4, 2000, pp. 617–34.

'The Elizabethan Idea of Empire', *Transactions of the Royal Historical Society*, vol. 14, 2004, pp. 269–77.

The Ideological Origins of the British Empire (Cambridge: Cambridge University Press, 2000).

'John Locke, Carolina, and the Two Treatises of Government', *Political Theory*, vol. 32, no. 5, 2004, pp. 602–27.

Armour, Peter. 'Dante and Popular Sovereignty', in John Woodhouse, ed., *Dante and Governance* (Oxford: Clarendon Press, 1997), pp. 27–45.

Arneil, Barbara. *John Locke and America. The Defence of English Colonialism* (Oxford: Clarendon Press, 1996).

'John Locke, Natural Law, and Colonialism', *History of Political Thought*, vol. 13, no. 4, 1992, pp. 587–603.

Arrhenius, Thordis. *The Fragile Monument: On Conservation and Modernity* (Stockholm: Royal Institute of Technology, 2003).

Augustine. *The City of God Against the Pagans* (Cambridge: Cambridge University Press, 1998).

Bachelard, Gaston. *The Poetics of Space* (Boston: Beacon Press, 1994).

Baldry, H.C. *The Unity of Mankind in Greek Thought* (Cambridge: Cambridge University Press, 1965).

Bartelson, Jens. 'The Concept of Sovereignty Revisited', *European Journal of International Law*, vol. 17, no. 2, 2006, pp. 463–74.

The Critique of the State (Cambridge: Cambridge University Press, 2001).

A Genealogy of Sovereignty (Cambridge: Cambridge University Press, 1995).

'Philosophy and History in the Study of Political Thought', *Journal of the Philosophy of History*, vol. 1, no. 1, 2007, pp. 101–24.

'Short Circuits: Society and Tradition in International Relations Theory', *Review of International Studies*, vol. 22, no. 3, 1996, pp. 239–60.

'The Trial of Judgment: A Note on Kant and the Paradoxes of Internationalism', *International Studies Quarterly*, vol. 39, no. 2, 1995, pp. 255–79.

Bauböck, Rainer. 'Political Community Beyond the Sovereign State, Supranational Federalism, and Transnational Minorities', in Steven Vertovec and Robin Cohen, eds., *Conceiving Cosmopolitanism. Theory, Context, Practice* (Oxford: Oxford University Press, 2002), pp. 110–38.

Bauman, Zygmunt. *Community* (Cambridge: Polity Press, 2001).

Globalization. The Human Consequences (Cambridge: Polity Press, 1998).

Baumeister, Andrea T. 'Kant: The Arch-Enlightener', in Norman Geras and Robert Wokler, eds., *Enlightenment and Modernity* (London: Routledge, 2005), pp. 50–65.

Beaulac, Stéphane. *The Power of Language in the Making of International Law* (Leiden: Martinus Nijhoff, 2004).

Beck, Ulrich. 'The Cosmopolitan Perspective: Sociology in the Second Age of Modernity', in Steven Vertovec and Robin Cohen, eds., *Conceiving Cosmopolitanism. Theory, Context, and Practice* (Oxford: Oxford University Press, 2002), pp. 61–85.

Beitz, Charles R. *Political Theory and International Relations* (Princeton, NJ: Princeton University Press, 1979).

Bell, David A. *The Cult of the Nation in France. Inventing Nationalism, 1680–1800* (Cambridge, MA: Harvard University Press, 2001).

Bellamy, Richard and Castiglione, Dario. 'Between Cosmopolis and Community: Three Models of Rights and Democracy within the European Union', in Daniele Archibugi, David Held and Martin Köhler, eds., *Re-Imagining Political Community* (Oxford: Polity Press, 1998), pp. 152–78.

Benedict of St Peters. *The Marvels of Rome* (New York: Italica Press, 1986).

Benhabib, Seyla. *The Claims of Culture. Equality and Diversity in a Global Era* (Princeton, NJ: Princeton University Press, 2002).

The Rights of Others. Aliens, Residents, and Citizens (Cambridge: Cambridge University Press, 2004).

Benot, Yves. 'Diderot, Pechmeja, Raynal et l'anticolonialisme', in Yves Benot, *Les lumières, l'esclavage, la colonisation*, ed. Roland Desné and Marcel Dorigny (Paris: Éditions la Découverte, 2005), pp. 107–23.

'Diderot–Raynal: l'impossible divorce', in Yves Benot, *Les lumières, l'esclavage, la colonisation*, ed. Roland Desné and Marcel Dorigny (Paris: Éditions la Découverte, 2005), pp. 138–53.

Berlin, Isaiah. *Vico and Herder. Two Studies in the History of Ideas* (New York: Vintage, 1976).

Bohman, James. 'The Democratic Minimum: Is Democracy a Means to Global Justice?', *Ethics and International Affairs*, vol. 19, no. 1, 2005, pp. 101–16.
  'From *Demos* to *Demoi*: Democracy across Borders', *Ratio Juris*, vol. 18, no. 3, 2005, pp. 293–314.
  'Republican Cosmopolitanism', *Journal of Political Philosophy*, vol. 12, no. 3, 2004, pp. 336–52.
Boholm, Åsa. 'Reinvented Histories: Medieval Rome as a Memorial Landscape', *Ecumene*, vol. 4, no. 3, 1997, pp. 247–72.
Bossuet, Jacques Bénigne. *Discourse on Universal History* (Chicago: University of Chicago Press, 1976).
Boyarin, Jonathan. 'Space, Time and the Politics of Memory', in Jonathan Boyarin, ed., *Remapping Memory: The Politics of Timespace* (Minneapolis: University of Minnesota Press, 1994), pp. 1–37.
Boyde, Patrick. *Perception and Passion in Dante's Comedy* (Cambridge: Cambridge University Press, 1993).
Bozeman, Adda. 'The International Order in a Multicultural World', in Hedley Bull and Adam Watson, eds., *The Expansion of International Society* (Oxford: Clarendon Press, 1984), pp. 387–406.
Bravo, Michael T. 'Ethnographical Navigation and the Geographical Gift', in David N. Livingstone and Charles W. J. Withers, *Geography and Enlightenment* (Chicago: University of Chicago Press, 1999), pp. 199–235.
Brennan, Timothy. *At Home in the World. Cosmopolitanism Now* (Cambridge, MA: Harvard University Press, 1997).
Brotton, Jerry. *Trading Territories. Mapping the Early Modern World* (London: Reaktion Books, 1997).
Brown, Chris. 'Cultural Diversity and International Political Theory: From the Requirement to "Mutual Respect"', *Review of International Studies*, vol. 26, no. 2, 2000, pp. 199–213.
  International Relations Theory. New Normative Approaches (Hemel Hempstead: Harvester, 1992).
Brown, Garrett Wallace. 'State Sovereignty, Federation and Kantian Cosmopolitanism', *European Journal of International Relations*, vol. 11, no. 4, 2005, pp. 495–522.
Bruner, M. Lane. *Strategies of Remembrance: The Rhetorical Dimensions of National Identity Construction* (Columbia: University of South Carolina Press, 2002).
Buchanan, Allen. 'In the National Interest', in Gillian Brock and Harry Brighouse, eds., *The Political Philosophy of Cosmopolitanism* (Cambridge: Cambridge University Press, 2005), pp. 110–26.

Bull, Hedley. *The Anarchical Society. A Study of Order in World Politics* (London: Macmillan, 1977).
  'Society and Anarchy in International Relations', in Martin Wight and Herbert Butterfield, eds., *Diplomatic Investigations* (London: Allen and Unwin, 1966), pp. 35–50.
Buffon, Georges-Louis Leclerc, comte de. 'The Geographical and Cultural Distribution of Mankind', in Emmanuel Chukwudi Eze, ed., *Race and the Enlightenment. A Reader* (Oxford: Blackwell, 1997), pp. 14–28.
Bunbury, E. H. *A History of Ancient Geography*, vol. II (New York: Dover, 1959).
Burke, Edmund. *Letters on a Regicide Peace II, Genius and Character of the French Revolution*, in *Select Works of Edmund Burke* (Liberty Fund: Indianapolis, 1999).
Butler, Judith. 'Universality in Culture', in Joshua Cohen, ed., *For Love of Country? Debating the Limits of Patriotism* (Boston: Beacon Press, 1996), pp. 45–53.
Buzan, Barry. *From International to World Society? English School Theory and the Structure of Globalization* (Cambridge: Cambridge University Press, 2004).
Calhoun, Craig. 'The Class Consciousness of Frequent Travelers: Toward a Critique of Actually Existing Cosmopolitanism', *South Atlantic Quarterly*, vol. 101, no. 4, 2002, pp. 869–97.
Camões, Luís Vaz de. *The Lusiads* (Harmondsworth: Penguin, 1952).
Campbell, David. 'The Deterritorialization of Responsibility: Levinas, Derrida, and Ethics after the End of Philosophy', in David Campbell and Michael J. Shapiro, eds., *Moral Spaces. Rethinking Ethics and World Politics* (Minneapolis: University of Minnesota Press, 1999), pp. 29–56.
  Writing Security: United States Foreign Policy and the Politics of Identity (Manchester: Manchester University Press, 1992).
Canto, Paul A. 'The Uncanonical Dante: The Divine Comedy and Islamic Philosophy', *Philosophy and Literature*, vol. 20, no. 1, 1996, pp. 138–53.
Carey, Daniel. *Locke, Shaftesbury, and Hutcheson. Contesting Diversity in the Enlightenment and Beyond* (Cambridge: Cambridge University Press, 2006).
Carruthers, Mary. *The Book of Memory: A Study of Memory in Medieval Culture* (Cambridge: Cambridge University Press, 1990).
Cassirer, Ernst. *The Individual and the Cosmos in the Renaissance* (Philadelphia: University of Pennsylvania Press, 1972).
Casson, Lionel. *Travel in the Ancient World* (Baltimore, MD: Johns Hopkins University Press, 1994).

Choay, Françoise. *The Invention of the Historic Monument* (Cambridge: Cambridge University Press, 2001).
Clifford, James. 'On Ethnographic Self-Fashioning: Conrad and Malinowski', in Thomas C. Heller, Morton Sisna and David E. Wellbery, eds., *Reconstructing Individualism. Autonomy, Individuality, and the Self in Western Thought* (Stanford, CA: Stanford University Press, 1986), pp. 140–62.
Cochran, Molly. 'A Democratic Critique of Cosmopolitan Democracy: Pragmatism from the Bottom-Up', *European Journal of International Relations*, vol. 8, no. 4, 2002, pp. 517–48.
  Normative Theory in International Relations. A Pragmatic Approach (Cambridge: Cambridge University Press, 1999).
Coffey, Thomas F., Davidson, Linda Kay and Dunn, Maryjane. *The Miracles of Saint James. Translations from the Liber Sancti Jacobi* (New York: Italica Press, 1996).
Cohen, Jean L. 'Whose Sovereignty? Empire versus International Law', *Ethics and International Affairs*, vol. 18, no. 3, 2004, pp. 1–24.
Coleman, Janet. *Ancient and Medieval Memories* (Cambridge: Cambridge University Press, 1993).
  A History of Political Thought. From the Middle Ages to the Renaissance (Oxford: Blackwell, 2000).
Condorcet, Marie-Jean-Antoine Nicolas de Caritat, marquis de. 'Observations on the Twenty-ninth Book of the *Spirit of the Laws*, by the Late M. Condorcet', in Antoine Louis Claude Destutt de Tracy, *A Commentary and Review of Montesquieu's Spirit of Laws* (Philadelphia, PA: William Duane, 1811), pp. 261–82.
  Sketch for a Historical Picture of the Progress of the Human Mind (London: Weidenfeld and Nicolson, 1955).
Congreve, William. *Love for Love* (London: Macmillan, 1967).
Connolly, William E. 'Cross-State Citizen Networks: A Response to Dallmayr, *Millennium*, vol. 30, no. 2, 2001, pp. 349–55.
  The Ethos of Pluralization (Minneapolis: University of Minnesota Press, 1995).
  Identity\Difference: Democratic Negotiations of Political Paradox (Ithaca, NY: Cornell University Press, 1991).
  Pluralism (Durham, NC: Duke University Press, 2005).
  'Speed, Concentric Culture, and Cosmopolitanism', *Political Theory*, vol. 28, no. 5, 2000, pp. 596–618.
Copernicus, Nicolaus. *On the Revolutions of the Heavenly Spheres*, trans. Edward Rosen (Baltimore, MD: Johns Hopkins University Press, 1991).
Cosgrove, Denis. *Apollo's Eye. A Cartographic Genealogy of the Earth in the Western Imagination* (Baltimore, MD: Johns Hopkins University Press, 2001).

'Globalism and Tolerance in Early Modern Geography', *Annals of the Association of American Geographers*, vol. 93, no. 4, 2003, pp. 852–70.

'Mapping New Worlds: Culture and Cartography in Sixteenth-Century Venice', *Imago Mundi*, vol. 44, 1992, pp. 65–89.

Cruz, Laura. 'The 80 Years' Question: The Dutch Revolt in Historical Perspective', *History Compass*, vol. 5, no. 3, 2007, pp. 914–34.

Dahl, Robert. 'Can International Organizations be Democratic?', in Ian Shapiro and Casiano Hacker-Cordón, *Democracy's Edges* (Cambridge: Cambridge University Press, 1999), pp. 19–36.

'Federalism and the Democratic Process', in J.R. Pennock and John W. Chapman, eds., *Liberal Democracy* (New York: New York University Press, 1983), pp. 95–108.

Dallmayr, Fred. 'Conversations across Boundaries: Political Theory and Global Diversity', *Millennium*, vol. 30, no. 2, 2001, pp. 331–47.

'Cosmopolitanism. Moral and Political', *Political Theory*, vol. 31, no. 3, 2003, pp. 421–42.

Darby, Graham, ed. *The Origins and Development of the Dutch Revolt* (London: Routledge, 2001).

D'Argenson, Marquis. *Considérations sur le gouvernement ancien et présent de la France, comparé avec celui des autres états* [1737], 2nd edn (Liege: Plompteux, 1787).

Darnton, Robert. *The Forbidden Best-Sellers of Pre-Revolutionary France* (New York: Norton, 1995).

Davidson, Herbert A. *Alfarabi, Avicenna, and Averroes on Intellect* (Oxford: Oxford University Press, 1992).

D'Entrèves, A.P. *Dante as a Political Thinker* (Oxford: Clarendon Press, 1952).

Derrida, Jacques. *On Cosmopolitanism and Forgiveness* (London: Routledge, 2001).

De Wulf, Maurice. *Philosophy and Civilization in the Middle Ages* (Princeton, NJ: Princeton University Press, 1922).

Diderot, Denis. *Political Writings*, ed. John Hope Mason and Robert Wokler (Cambridge: Cambridge University Press, 1992).

Dietz, Thomas, Ostrom, Elinor and Stern, Paul C. 'The Struggle to Govern the Commons', *Science*, vol. 302, 2003, pp. 1907–12.

Diez, Thomas and Steans, Jill. 'A Useful Dialogue? Habermas and International Relations', *Review of International Studies*, vol. 31, no. 2, 2005, pp. 127–40.

Donnelly, Jack. 'Twentieth-Century Realism', in Terry Nardin and David R. Mapel, *Traditions of International Ethics* (Cambridge: Cambridge University Press, 1992), 82–111.

Doucet, Marc G. 'The Democratic Paradox and Cosmopolitan Democracy', *Millennium: Journal of International Studies*, vol. 34, no. 1, 2005, pp. 137–55.
Doyle, Michael W. 'Kant, Liberal Legacies, and Foreign Affairs', in Michel E. Brown, Sean M. Lynn-Jones and Steven E. Miller, eds., *Debating the Democratic Peace* (Cambridge, MA: MIT Press, 1996), pp. 3–57.
Dryzek, John. 'Transnational Democracy', *Journal of Political Philosophy*, vol. 7, no. 1, 1999, pp. 30–51.
Dupré, Louis. 'Kant's Theory of History and Progress', *Review of Metaphysics*, vol. 51, no. 4, 1998, pp. 813–28.
Durkheim, Émile. *The Division of Labor in Society* (London: Macmillan, 1964).
Eco, Umberto. *The Search for the Perfect Language* (Oxford: Blackwell, 1995).
Edgerton, Samuel Y. *The Renaissance Discovery of Linear Perspective* (New York: Basic Books, 1975).
Elias, Norbert. *The Society of Individuals* (New York: Continuum, 1991).
Elsner, Jas and Rubiés, Joan-Pau. 'Introduction', in Jas Elsner and Joan-Pau Rubiés, eds., *Voyages and Visions. Towards a Cultural History of Travel* (London: Reaktion Books, 1999), pp. 1–56.
Euben, Peter. 'The Polis, Globalization, and the Politics of Place', in Aryeh Botwinick and William E. Connolly, eds., *Democracy and Vision: Sheldon Wolin and the Vicissitudes of the Political* (Princeton, NJ: Princeton University Press, 2001), pp. 256–89.
Eze, Emmanuel Chukwudi, ed. *Race and the Enlightenment. A Reader* (Oxford: Blackwell, 1997).
Fasolt, Constantin. *The Limits of History* (Chicago: University of Chicago Press, 2003).
Fine, Robert. 'Kant's Theory of Cosmopolitanism and Hegel's Critique', *Philosophy and Social Criticism*, vol. 29, no. 6, 2003, pp. 609–30.
  'Taking the "Ism" out of Cosmopolitanism. An Essay in Reconstruction', *European Journal of Social Theory*, vol. 6, no. 4, 2003, pp. 451–70.
Fine, Robert and Smith, Will. 'Jürgen Habermas's Theory of Cosmopolitanism', *Constellations*, vol. 10, no. 4, 2003, pp. 469–87.
Flint, Valerie I. J. 'Monsters and the Antipodes in the Early Middle Ages and Enlightenment', *Viator*, vol. 15, 1984, pp. 65–80.
Fortin, E. L. *Dissidence et philosophie au moyen âge. Dante et ses antécédents* (Paris: Vrin, 1981).
Foucault, Michel. *The Order of Things. An Archaeology of the Human Sciences* (London: Routledge, 1989).

Franceschet, Antonio. 'Popular Sovereignty or Cosmopolitan Democracy? Liberalism, Kant, and International Reform', *European Journal of International Relations*, vol. 6, no. 2, 2000, pp. 277–302.

'Sovereignty and Freedom: Immanuel Kant's Liberal Internationalist Legacy', *Review of International Studies*, vol. 27, no. 2, 2001, pp. 209–28.

Franke, Mark F. N. *Global Limits. Immanuel Kant, International Relations, and Critique of World Politics* (Albany: State University of New York Press, 2001).

Freccero, John. 'Satan's Fall and the *Quaestio de aqua et terra*', *Italica*, vol. 38, 1961, pp. 99–115.

Friedman, John Block. *The Monstrous Races in Medieval Art and Thought* (Cambridge, MA: Harvard University Press, 1981).

Gadamer, Hans-Georg. *Truth and Method* (New York: Continuum, 1989).

Galston, William A. *Kant and the Problem of History* (Chicago: University of Chicago Press, 1975).

Gelderen, Martin van. *The Political Thought of the Dutch Revolt 1555–1590* (Cambridge: Cambridge University Press, 1992).

Genequand, Charles. *Ibn Rushd's Metaphysics. A Translation with Introduction of Ibn Rushd's Commentary on Aristotle's Metaphysics, Book Lam* (Leiden: E. J. Brill, 1986).

Gibson, Walter S. *Mirror of the Earth. The World Landscape in Sixteenth-Century Flemish Painting* (Princeton, NJ: Princeton University Press, 1989).

Gierke, Otto von. *Community in Historical Perspective* (Cambridge: Cambridge University Press, 1990).

Political Theories of the Middle Age (Cambridge: Cambridge University Press, 1900).

Gilson, Étienne. *Dante et la philosophie* (Paris: Vrin, 1953).

Glacken, Clarence J. *Traces on the Rhodian Shore. Nature and Culture in Western Thought from Ancient Times to the End of the Eighteenth Century* (Berkeley: University of California Press, 1967).

Godinho, Vitorino Magalhães. 'Entre myth et utopie: les grandes découvertes. La construction de l'espace et l'invention de l'humanite aux XVe et XVIe siècles', *Archives Européenes de Sociologie*, vol. 32, 1991, pp. 3–52.

Góis, Damião de. *Lisbon in the Renaissance. A New Translation of the Urbis Olisiponis Descriptio by Jefferey S. Ruth* (New York: Italica Press, 1996).

Goizueta, Roberto S. 'Bartolomé de Las Casas, Modern Critic of Modernity: An Analysis of a Conversion', *Journal of Hispanic/Latino Theology*, vol. 4, no. 4, 1996, pp. 6–19.

Goldmann, Kjell. *The Logic of Internationalism. Coercion and Accommodation* (London: Routledge, 1994).
Transforming the European Nation-State (London: SAGE, 2001).
Goldstein, Thomas. 'Geography in Fifteenth-Century Florence', in John Parker, ed., *Merchants and Scholars. Essays in the History of Exploration and Trade* (Minneapolis: University of Minnesota Press, 1965), pp. 11–32.
'The Renaissance Concept of the Earth in its Influence upon Copernicus', *Terrae Incognitae*, vol. 4, 1972, pp. 19–51.
'The Role of the Italian Merchant Class in Renaissance and Discoveries,' *Terrae Incognitae*, vol. 8, 1976, pp. 19–27.
Grant, Edward. *Planets, Stars, and Orbs. The Medieval Cosmos, 1200–1687* (Cambridge: Cambridge University Press, 1994).
Greenfeld, Liah. *Nationalism: Five Roads to Modernity* (Cambridge, MA: Harvard University Press, 1992).
Grotius, Hugo. *De iure praedae commentarius (de Indis)*, Carnegie Endowment for International Peace (Oxford: Clarendon Press, 1950).
Gueorguieva, Valentina. 'La connaissance de l'indéterminé. Le sens commun dans la théorie de l'action', unpublished dissertation (Université Laval, Quebec: Faculté des Sciences Sociales, 2004).
Hacking, Ian. *Historical Ontology* (Cambridge, MA: Harvard University Press, 2002).
Hakluyt, Richard. *Principal Navigations, Voyages, Traffiques and Discoveries of the English Nation* (London, 1589).
Halbwachs, Maurice. *On Collective Memory* (Chicago: University of Chicago Press, 1992).
Harley, J.B. 'Silences and Secrecy. The Hidden Agenda of Cartography in Early Modern Europe', in Paul Laxton, ed., *The New Nature of Maps. Essays in the History of Cartography* (Baltimore, MD: Johns Hopkins University Press, 2001), pp. 84–107.
Harrison, Peter. *The Bible, Protestantism, and the Rise of Natural Science* (Cambridge: Cambridge University Press, 1998).
Hartshorne, Richard. 'The Concept of Geography as a Science of Space: From Kant and Humboldt to Hettner', *Annals of the Association of American Geographers*, vol. 48, no. 2, 1958, pp. 97–108.
Hazareesingh, Sudhir. *The Saint-Napoleon. Celebrations of Sovereignty in Nineteenth-Century France* (Cambridge, MA: Harvard University Press, 2004).
Headley, John M. 'Geography and Empire in the Late Renaissance: Botero's Assignment, Western Universalism, and the Civilizing Process', *Renaissance Quarterly*, vol. 53, 2000, pp. 1119–55.

'The Sixteenth-Century Venetian Celebration of the Earth's Total Habitability: The Issue of the Fully Habitable World for Renaissance Europe', *Journal of World History*, vol. 8, no. 1, 1997, pp. 1–27.

Tommaso Campanella and the Transformation of the World (Princeton, NJ: Princeton University Press, 1997).

'The Universalizing Principle and Process: On the West's Intrinsic Commitment to a Global Context', *Journal of World History*, vol. 13, no. 2, 2002, pp. 291–321.

Heffernan, Michael. 'On Geography and Progress: Turgot's *Plan d'un ouvrage sur la géographie politique* (1751) and the Origins of Modern Progressive Thought', *Political Geography*, vol. 13, no. 4, 1994, pp. 328–43.

Hegel, Georg W. F. *Elements of the Philosophy of Right* (Cambridge: Cambridge University Press, 1991).

Lectures on the Philosophy of World History (Cambridge: Cambridge University Press, 1975).

Held, David. 'Cosmopolitan Democracy and the Global Order: Reflections on the 200th Anniversary of Kant's "Perpetual Peace"', *Alternatives*, vol. 20, no. 4, 1995, pp. 415–29.

'Cosmopolitanism: Globalisation Tamed?', *Review of International Studies*, vol. 29, no. 4, 2003, pp. 465–80.

'Democracy and Globalization', in Daniele Archibugi, David Held and Martin Köhler, eds., *Re-imagining Political Community. Studies in Cosmopolitan Democracy* (Cambridge: Polity Press, 1998), pp. 11–27.

Democracy and the Global Order (Cambridge: Polity Press, 1995).

'Principles of Cosmopolitan Order', in Gillian Brock and Harry Brighouse, eds., *The Political Philosophy of Cosmopolitanism* (Cambridge: Cambridge University Press, 2005), pp. 10–38.

'The Transformation of Political Community: Rethinking Democracy in the Context of Globalization', in Ian Shapiro and Casiano Hacker-Cordón, *Democracy's Edges* (Cambridge: Cambridge University Press, 1999), pp. 84–111.

Helgerson, Richard. *Forms of Nationhood. The Elizabethan Writing of England* (Chicago: University of Chicago Press, 1992).

Hemleben, Sylvester J. *Plans for Peace Through Six Centuries* (Chicago: University of Chicago Press, 1943).

Herder, Johann Gottfried. 'On the Character of Humankind', in *Johan Gottfried Herder On World History. An Anthology*, ed. Hans Adler and Ernest A. Menze (Armonk, NY: Sharpe, 1997), pp. 99–104.

Outlines of a Philosophy of the History of Man (London, 1800).

Himmelfarb, Gertrude. *The Roads to Modernity. The British, French, and American Enlightenments* (New York: Knopf, 2004).

Hinsley, Francis H. *Power and the Pursuit of Peace. Theory and Practice in the History of Relations between States* (Cambridge: Cambridge University Press, 1963).

Hirsch, Elisabeth Feist. 'The Discoveries and the Humanists', in John Parker, ed., *Merchants and Scholars. Essays in the History of Exploration and Trade* (Minneapolis: University of Minnesota Press, 1965), pp. 33–46.

Hobbes, Thomas. *Leviathan*, ed. Richard Tuck (Cambridge: Cambridge University Press, 1991).

Höffe, Otfried. *Kant's Cosmopolitan Theory of Law and Peace* (Cambridge: Cambridge University Press, 2006).

Hoffmann, Stanley. *Duties Beyond Borders: On the Limits and Possibilities of Ethical International Politics* (Syracuse, NY: Syracuse University Press, 1981).

  The State of War. Essays on the Theory and Practice of International Relations (New York: Praeger, 1965).

Hollis, Martin. 'Of Masks and Men', in Michael Carrithers, Steven Collins and Steven Lukes, eds., *The Category of the Person: Anthropology, Philosophy, History* (Cambridge: Cambridge University Press, 1985), pp. 117–33.

Honig, Bonnie. *Democracy and the Foreigner* (Princeton, NJ: Princeton University Press, 2001).

  'Ruth, the Model Émigré: Mourning and the Symbolic Politics of Immigration', in Pheng Chea and Bruce Robbins, eds., *Cosmopolitics. Thinking and Feeling Beyond the Nation* (Minneapolis: University of Minnesota Press, 1998), pp. 192–215.

Honneth, Axel. *The Struggle for Recognition. The Moral Grammar of Social Conflicts* (Cambridge: Polity Press, 1995).

Hont, Istvan. *Jealousy of Trade. International Competition and the Nation-State in Historical Perspective* (Cambridge, MA: Harvard University Press, 2005).

Hume, David. *An Enquiry Concerning Human Understanding* (Oxford: Oxford University Press, 1902).

  'Of Jealousy of Trade', in David Hume, *Essays, Moral, Political, and Literary*, available at: http://oll.libertyfund.org/title/704/137536 (accessed 21 April 2009).

  A Treatise of Human Nature (London: Longmans, Green and Co., 1874).

Idzerda, Stanley J. 'Iconoclasm during the French Revolution', *American Historical Review*, vol. 60, no. 1, 1954, pp. 13–26.

Inayatullah, Naeem and Blaney, David L. *International Relations and the Problem of Difference* (New York: Routledge, 2004).

Ingram, David. 'The Postmodern Kantianism of Arendt and Lyotard', *Review of Metaphysics*, vol. 42, no. 1, 1988, pp. 51–77.
Jahn, Beate. 'Kant, Mill and Illiberal Legacies in International Affairs', *International Organization*, vol. 59, no. 1, 2005, pp. 177–207.
Jaume, Lucien. 'Citizen and State under the French Revolution', in Bo Stråth and Quentin Skinner, eds., *States and Citizens* (Cambridge: Cambridge University Press, 2003), pp. 131–44.
Johnson, Nuala. 'Cast in Stone: Monuments, Geography, and Nationalism', *Environment and Planning D: Society and Space*, vol. 13, no. 1, 1995, pp. 51–65.
Jones, Charles. *Global Justice. Defending Cosmopolitanism* (Oxford: Oxford University Press, 1999).
Kant, Immanuel. 'Conjectures on the Beginning of Human History', in Hans Reiss, ed., *Kant: Political Writings* (Cambridge: Cambridge University Press, 1991), pp. 221–33.
  'The Contest of the Faculties', in Hans Reiss, ed., *Kant: Political Writings* (Cambridge: Cambridge University Press, 1991), pp. 176–90.
  The Critique of Judgment (New York: Hafner, 1951).
  'Idea for a Universal History with a Cosmopolitan Purpose', in Hans Reiss, ed., *Kant: Political Writings* (Cambridge: Cambridge University Press, 1991), pp. 41–53.
  The Metaphysics of Morals, in Hans Reiss, ed., *Kant: Political Writings* (Cambridge: Cambridge University Press, 1991), pp. 131–75.
  'On the Common Saying: "This May be True in Theory, but it does not Apply in Practice"', in Hans Reiss, ed., *Kant: Political Writings* (Cambridge: Cambridge University Press, 1991), pp. 61–92.
  'Perpetual Peace', in Hans Reiss, ed., *Kant: Political Writings* (Cambridge: Cambridge University Press, 1991), pp. 93–115.
  'Theory and Practice', in Hans Reiss, ed., *Kant: Political Writings* (Cambridge: Cambridge University Press, 1991), pp. 61–92.
Kantorowicz, Ernst. *The King's Two Bodies. A Study in Medieval Political Theology* (Princeton, NJ: Princeton University Press, 1957).
  '*Pro Patria Mori* in Medieval Political Thought', *American Historical Review*, vol. 56, no. 3, 1951, pp. 472–92.
Keen, Benjamin. *Latin American Civilization: History and Society. 1492 to the Present* (Boulder, CO: Westview, 1996).
  'The Legacy of Bartolomé de Las Casas', *Ibero-Americana Pragensia*, vol. 11, 1977, pp. 57–67.
Keene, Edward. *Beyond the Anarchical Society* (Cambridge: Cambridge University Press, 2002).
Kennedy, David. 'Primitive Legal Scholarship', *Harvard International Law Journal*, vol. 27, no. 1, 1986, pp. 1–98.

Kleingeld, Pauline. 'Kant on the Unity of Theoretical and Practical Reason', *Review of Metaphysics*, vol. 52, no. 2, 1998, pp. 311–39.
— 'Six Varieties of Cosmopolitanism in Late-Eighteenth-Century Germany', *Journal of the History of Ideas*, vol. 60, no. 3, 1999, pp. 505–24.
Koselleck, Reinhart. *Critique and Crisis. The Pathogenesis of Modern Society* (Oxford: Berg, 1988).
— 'The Eighteenth Century as the Beginning of Modernity', in Reinhart Koselleck, *The Practice of Conceptual History. Timing History, Spacing Concepts* (Stanford, CA: Stanford University Press, 2002), pp. 154–69.
— 'Historical Criteria of the Modern Concept of Revolution', in Reinhart Koselleck, *Futures Past: On the Semantics of Historical Time* (Cambridge, MA: MIT Press, 1985), pp. 39–54.
— 'Transformations of Experience and Methodological Change: A Historical-Anthropological Essay', in Reinhart Koselleck, *The Practice of Conceptual History. Timing History, Spacing Concepts* (Stanford, CA: Stanford University Press, 2002), pp. 44–83.
— 'The Unknown Future and the Art of Prognosis', in Reinhart Koselleck, *The Practice of Conceptual History. Timing History, Spacing Concepts* (Stanford, CA: Stanford University Press, 2002), pp. 131–53.
Koskenniemi, Martti. *The Gentle Civilizer of Nations. The Rise and Fall of International Law 1870–1960* (Cambridge: Cambridge University Press, 2001).
— 'International Law as Political Theology: How to Read *Nomos der Erde*?', *Constellations*, vol. 11, no. 4, 2004, pp. 492–511.
Krasner, Stephen D. 'Sharing Sovereignty: New Institutions for Collapsed and Failing States', *International Security*, vol. 29, no. 2, 2004, pp. 85–120.
Kristeva, Julia. *Étrangers à nous-mêmes* (Paris: Gallimard, 1988).
Kuhn, Thomas S. *The Copernican Revolution: Planetary Astronomy in the Development of Western Thought* (Cambridge, MA: Harvard University Press, 1957).
Kuper, Andrew. 'Rawlsian Global Justice Beyond *The Law of Peoples* to a Cosmopolitan Law of Persons', *Political Theory*, vol. 28, no. 5, 2000, pp. 640–74.
Kymlicka, Will. *Multicultural Citizenship* (Oxford: Clarendon Press, 1995).
Las Casas, Bartolomé de. *In Defense of the Indians. The Defense of the Most Reverend Lord, Don Fray Bartolomé de Las Casas, of the Order of Preachers, Late Bishop of Chiapa, Against the Persecutors and Slanderers of the Peoples of the New World Discovered Across*

the Seas, trans. Stafford Poole (DeKalb: Northern Illinois University Press, 1992).

Latour, Bruno. 'Whose Cosmos, Which Cosmopolitics: Comments on the Peace Terms of Ulrich Beck', *Common Knowledge*, vol. 10, no. 3, 2004, pp. 450–62.

Layne, Christopher. 'Kant or Cant: The Myth of Democratic Peace', in Michel E. Brown, Sean M. Lynn-Jones and Steven E. Miller, eds., *Debating the Democratic Peace* (Cambridge, MA: MIT Press, 1996), pp. 157–201.

Lebow, Richard Ned. 'Homer, Vergil and Identity in International Relations', in Gideon Baker and Jens Bartelson, eds., *The Future of Political Community* (London: Routledge, 2009), pp. 144–74.

Lecoq, Anne-Marie. 'The Symbolism of the State. The Images of the Monarchy from the Early Valois Kings to Louis XIV', in Pierre Nora, *Rethinking France: Les lieux de mémoire*, vol. I: *The State* (Cambridge, MA: Harvard University Press, 2001), pp. 217–67.

Lestringant, Frank. *Mapping the Renaissance World. The Geographical Imagination in the Age of Discovery* (Cambridge: Polity Press, 1994).

Lindahl, Hans. 'Sovereignty and Representation in the European Union', in Neil Walker, ed., *Sovereignty in Transition* (Oxford: Hart, 2003), pp. 87–114.

Linklater, Andrew. 'Dialogic Politics and the Civilising Process', *Review of International Studies*, vol. 31, no. 2, 2005, pp. 141–54.

Men and Citizens in the Theory of International Relations (London: Macmillan, 1982).

'The Problem of Community in International Relations' *Alternatives*, vol. 15, no. 2, 1990, pp. 135–53.

The Transformation of Political Community. Ethical Foundations of the Post-Westphalian Era (Cambridge: Polity Press, 1998).

Linklater, Andrew and Suganami, Hidemi. *The English School of International Relations: A Contemporary Reassessment* (Cambridge: Cambridge University Press, 2006).

Livingstone, David N. 'Geographical Inquiry, Rational Religion, and Moral Philosophy: Enlightenment Discourses on the Human Condition', in David N. Livingstone and Charles W. J. Withers, *Geography and Enlightenment* (Chicago: University of Chicago Press, 1999), pp. 93–119.

Livingstone, D. N. and Harrison, R. T. 'Immanuel Kant, Subjectivism and Human Geography: A Preliminary Investigation', *Transactions of the Institute of British Geographers*, vol. 6, no. 3, 1981, pp. 359–74.

Livingstone, David N. and Withers, Charles W. J. *Geography and Enlightenment* (Chicago: University of Chicago Press, 1999).

Locke, John. *An Essay Concerning Human Understanding* (London: Dent, 1976).
  Two Treatises of Government, ed. Peter Laslett (Cambridge: Cambridge University Press, 1988).
Lu, Catherine. 'The One and Many Faces of Cosmopolitanism', *Journal of Political Philosophy*, vol. 8, no. 2, 2000, pp. 244–67.
Luhmann, Niklas, 'World Society as a Social System', in Niklas Luhman, *Essays on Self-Reference* (New York: Columbia University Press, 1990), pp. 175–90.
Lyotard, Jean-François. *L'enthousiasme. La critique kantienne de l'histoire* (Paris: Galilée, 1986).
McCarthy, Thomas. 'On Reconciling Cosmopolitan Unity and National Diversity', *Public Culture*, vol. 11, no. 1, 1999, pp. 175–208.
Macedo, Helder. 'The Rhetoric of Prophecy in Portuguese Renaissance Literature', *Portuguese Studies*, vol. 19, no. 1, 2003, pp. 9–18.
MacIntyre, Alasdair. *A Short History of Ethics* (London: Routledge, 1998).
Makkreel, Rudolf A. *Imagination and Interpretation in Kant. The Hermeneutical Import of the Critique of Judgment* (Chicago: University of Chicago Press, 1990).
Mali, Joseph. *The Rehabilitation of Myth. Vico's New Science* (Cambridge: Cambridge University Press, 1992).
Mancusi-Ungaro, Donna. *Dante and the Empire* (New York: Peter Lang, 1987).
Markell, Patchen. *Bound by Recognition* (Princeton, NJ: Princeton University Press, 2003).
Mastnak, Tomaz. 'Abbé Saint-Pierre: European Union and the Turk', *History of Political Thought*, vol. 19, no. 4, 1998, pp. 570–98.
Mead, George H. *Mind, Self, and Society* (Chicago: University of Chicago Press, 1962).
Mehta, Pratap Bhanu. 'Cosmopolitanism and the Circle of Reason', *Political Theory*, vol. 28, no. 5, 2000, pp. 619–39.
Meinecke, Friedrich. *Cosmopolitanism and the National State* (Princeton, NJ: Princeton University Press, 1970).
Melczer, William, ed. *The Pilgrim's Guide to Santiago de Compostela* (New York: Italica Press, 1993).
Mendes Pinto, Fernão. *The Voyages and Adventures of Fernand Mendez Pinto*, trans. H. Cogan (London: Dawsons of Pall Mall, 1969).
Meyer, John W., Boli, John, Thomas, George M. and Ramirez, Francisco O. 'World Society and the Nation-State', *American Journal of Sociology*, vol. 103, no. 1, 1997, pp. 144–81.
Mignolo, Walter D. 'The Many Faces of Cosmo-Polis: Border Thinking and Critical Cosmopolitanism', in Carol A. Breckenridge, Sheldon Pollock,

Homi K. Bhabha and Dipesh Chakrabarty, eds., *Cosmopolitanism* (Durham, NC: Duke University Press, 2002), pp. 157–88.
Morefield, Jeanne. *Covenants Without Swords: Idealist Liberalism and the Spirit of Empire* (Princeton, NJ: Princeton University Press, 2005).
Mota, A. Texeira da. 'Some Notes on the Organization of Hydrographical Services in Portugal before the Beginning of the Nineteenth Century', *Imago Mundi*, vol. 28, 1976, pp. 51–60.
Muldoon, James, *The Americas in the Spanish World Order. The Justification for Conquest in the Seventeenth Century* (Philadelphia: University of Pennsylvania Press, 1994).
Popes, Lawyers, and Infidels. The Church and the Non-Christian World 1250–1550 (Liverpool: Liverpool University Press, 1979).
Solórozano's *De Indiarum Iure*: Applying a Medieval Theory of World Order in the Seventeenth Century', in James Muldoon, *Canon Law, the Expansion of Europe, and World Order* (Aldershot: Variorum, 1998), pp. 29–45.
Muthu, Sankar. *Enlightenment Against Empire* (Princeton, NJ: Princeton University Press, 2003).
Nagel, Thomas. 'The Problem of Global Justice', *Philosophy and Public Affairs*, vol. 33, no. 2, 2005, pp. 113–47.
Nardi, Bruno. *La caduta di Lucifero e L'autenticità della 'Quaestio de aqua et terra'* (Turin: Societá Editrice Internazionale, 1958).
Näsström, Sofia. 'What Globalization Overshadows', *Political Theory*, vol. 31, no. 6, 2003, pp. 808–34.
Nederman, Cary J. 'Empire and the Historiography of European Political Thought: Marsiglio of Padua, Nicholas of Cusa, and the Medieval/Modern Divide', *Journal of the History of Ideas*, vol. 66, no. 1, 2005, pp. 1–15.
Worlds of Difference. European Discourses of Toleration c.1100–c.1550 (University Park: Pennsylvania State University Press, 2000).
Neocleous, Mark. 'Off the Map. On Violence and Cartography', *European Journal of Social Theory*, vol. 6, no. 4, 2003, pp. 409–25.
Nicholas of Cusa. *De coniecturis*, in *Nicholas of Cusa: Metaphysical Speculations*, ed. Jasper Hopkins (Minneapolis, MN: Arthur J. Banning, 2000).
De docta ignorantia, in *The Complete Philosophical and Theological Treatises of Nicholas of Cusa*, ed. Jasper Hopkins, vol. I (Minneapolis, MN: Arthur J. Banning, 2001), pp. 132–3.
De pace fidei, in *Nicholas of Cusa's De pace fidei and Cribratio alkorani*, ed. Jasper Hopkins (Minneapolis, MN: Arthur J. Banning, 1990).
Nietzsche, Friedrich. 'On the Uses and Disadvantages of History for Life', in Friedrich Nietzsche, *Untimely Meditations* (Cambridge: Cambridge University Press, 1983), pp. 57–125.

Nora, Pierre. 'Between Memory and History: *Les lieux de mémoire*', *Representations*, no. 26, 1989, pp. 7–24.
  Rethinking France: Les lieux de mémoire, vol. I: *The State* (Cambridge, MA: Harvard University Press, 2001).
Nussbaum, Martha. 'Beyond the Social Contract: Capabilities and Global Justice', in Gillian Brock and Harry Brighouse, eds., *The Political Philosophy of Cosmopolitanism* (Cambridge: Cambridge University Press, 2005), pp. 196–218.
  'Kant and Stoic Cosmopolitanism', *Journal of Political Philosophy*, vol. 5, no. 1, 1997, pp. 1–25.
  'Patriotism and Cosmopolitanism', in Joshua Cohen, ed., *For Love of Country. Debating the Limits of Patriotism* (Boston: Beacon Press, 1994), 3–17.
Odysseos, Louiza. 'On the Way to Global Ethics?', *European Journal of Political Theory*, vol. 2, no. 2, 2003, pp. 183–208.
Ohler, Norbert. *The Medieval Traveller* (Woodbridge: Boydell Press, 1989).
Olick, Jeffrey K. and Robbins, Joyce. 'Social Memory Studies: From "Collective Memory" to the Historical Sociology of Mnemonic Practices', *Annual Review of Sociology*, vol. 24, pp. 105–40.
O'Neill, Onora. 'Bounded and Cosmopolitan Justice', *Review of International Studies*, vol. 26, no. 1, 2000, pp. 45–60.
Onuf, Nicholas Greenwood. '*Civitas Maxima*: Wolff, Vattel and the Fate of Republicanism', *American Journal of International Law*, vol. 88, no. 2, 1994, pp. 280–303.
  The Republican Legacy in International Thought (Cambridge: Cambridge University Press, 1998).
  World of Our Making. Rules and Rule in Social Theory and International Relations (Columbia: University of South Carolina Press, 1989).
Orr, D. Alan. 'Sovereignty, Supremacy and the Origins of the English Civil War', *History*, vol. 87, no. 288, 2002, pp. 474–90.
Osiander, Andreas. 'Before Sovereignty: Society and Politics in *Ancien Régime* Europe', *Review of International Studies*, vol. 27, special issue, 2001, pp. 119–45.
  'Rereading Early Twentieth-Century IR Theory: Idealism Revisited', *International Studies Quarterly*, vol. 42, 1998, pp. 409–32.
  'Sovereignty, International Relations, and the Westphalian Myth', *International Organization*, vol. 55, no. 2, 2001, pp. 251–87.
Pagden, Anthony. 'Dispossessing the Barbarian: The Language of Spanish Thomism and the Debate over the Property Rights of the American Indians', in Anthony Pagden, ed., *The Languages of Political Theory in Early Modern Europe* (Cambridge: Cambridge University Press, 1987), pp. 79–98.

European Encounters with the New World. From Renaissance to Romanticism (New Haven, CT: Yale University Press, 1993).
  'The Forbidden Food: Francisco de Vitoria and José de Acosta on Cannibalism', *Terrae Incognitae*, vol. 13, 1981, pp. 17–29.
  'Human Rights, Natural Rights, and Europe's Imperial Legacy', *Political Theory*, vol. 31, no. 2, 2003, pp. 171–99.
  'Ius et Factum: Text and Experience in the Writings of Bartolomé de las Casas', *Representations*, vol. 33, 1991, pp. 147–62.
  Lords of all the World. Ideologies of Empire in Spain, Britain and France c.1500–c.1850 (New Haven, CT: Yale University Press, 1995).
  Spanish Imperialism and the Political Imagination. Studies in European and Spanish-American Social and Political Theory (New Haven, CT: Yale University Press, 1990).
  'Stoicism, Cosmopolitanism, and the Legacy of European Imperialism', *Constellations*, vol. 7, no. 1, 2000, pp. 3–22.
Paine, Thomas. 'Letter to the Abbé Raynal', in D. E. Wheeler, ed., *Life and Writings of Thomas Paine*, vol. VIII (New York: Vincent Park, 1908), pp. 180–5.
  The Rights of Man (Ware, Hertfordshire: Wordsworth, 1996).
Pangle, Thomas. 'Justice Among Nations in Platonic and Aristotelian Political Philosophy', *American Journal of Political Science*, vol. 42, no. 2, 1998, pp. 377–97.
Panitch, Leo. 'Globalization and the State', *Socialist Register*, 1994, pp. 60–93.
Panofsky, Erwin. *Perspective as Symbolic Form* (New York: Zone Books, 1995).
  Studies in Iconology. Humanistic Themes in the Art of the Renaissance (New York: Harper and Row, 1962).
Pennington, Kenneth J. 'Bartolomé de las Casas and the Tradition of Medieval Law', *Church History*, vol. 39, 1970, pp. 149–61.
Peterman, Larry. 'Introduction to Dante's *Monarchia*', *Interpretation*, vol. 3, 1973, pp. 174–5.
Petrarca, Francesco. 'Letter to Cola di Rienzo and the Roman People', in Petrarch, *The Revolution of Cola di Rienzo* (New York: Italica Press, 1996), pp. 10–36.
Petterson, Bo. 'Exploring the Common Ground: *Sensus communis*, Humor and the Interpretation of Comic Poetry', *Journal of Literary Semantics*, vol. 33, 2004, pp. 155–67.
Philpott, Daniel. *Revolutions in Sovereignty. How Ideas Shaped Modern International Relations* (Princeton, NJ: Princeton University Press, 2001).
Pico della Mirandola, Giovanni. 'Oration on the Dignity of Man', in Ernst Cassirer, Paul Oskar Kristeller and John H. Randall, eds., *The*

Renaissance Philosophy of Man (Chicago: University of Chicago Press, 1948), pp. 223–54.

Pizzorno, Alessandro. 'On the Individualistic Theory of Social Order', in Pierre Bourdieu and James S. Coleman, eds., *Social Theory for a Changing Society* (Boulder, CO: Westview, 1991), pp. 209–31.

Pocock, John G. A. *Barbarism and Religion*, vol. IV: *Barbarism, Savages and Empires* (Cambridge: Cambridge University Press, 2005).

Pogge, Thomas. 'Cosmopolitanism: A Defence', *Critical Review of International Social and Political Philosophy*, vol. 5, no. 3, 2002, pp. 86–91.

  'Cosmopolitanism and Sovereignty', *Ethics*, vol. 103, 1992, pp. 48–75.

Pollock, Sheldon. 'Cosmopolitan and Vernacular in History', in Carol A. Breckenridge, Sheldon Pollock, Homi K. Bhabha and Dipesh Chakraborty, eds., *Cosmopolitanism* (Durham, NC: Duke University Press, 2002), pp. 15–53.

Porter, Roy. *The Enlightenment* (Houndmills: Palgrave, 2001).

Pratt, Mary Louise. *Imperial Eyes. Travel Writing and Transculturation* (London: Routledge, 1992).

Quint, David. *Epic and Empire. Politics and Generic Form from Virgil to Milton* (Princeton, NJ: Princeton University Press, 1993).

Rae, Heather. *State Identities and the Homogenisation of Peoples* (Cambridge: Cambridge University Press, 2002).

Ranke, Leopold von. *The Great Powers*, in *Leopold Ranke: The Formative Years*, ed. Theodore H. von Laue (Princeton, NJ: Princeton University Press, 1950).

Rasmussen, Mikkel Vedby. *The West, Civil Society and the Construction of Peace* (Houndmills: Palgrave, 2003).

Rawls, John. *The Law of Peoples* (Cambridge, MA: Harvard University Press, 1999).

  A Theory of Justice (Cambridge, MA: Harvard University Press, 1971).

Raynal, Guillaume Thomas, *Histoire philosophique et politique des établissements et du commerce des Européens dans les deux Indes* (The Hague, 1776).

Ree, Jonathan. 'Cosmopolitanism and the Experience of Nationality', in Pheng Chea and Bruce Robbins, eds., *Cosmopolitics. Thinking and Feeling Beyond the Nation* (Minneapolis: University of Minnesota Press, 1998), pp. 77–90.

Reeves, Marjorie. 'Marsiglio of Padua and Dante Alighieri', in Beryl Smalley, ed., *Trends in Medieval Political Thought* (Oxford: Basil Blackwell, 1965), pp. 86–104.

Renan, Ernest. 'What is a Nation?' in Geoff Eley and Ronald Grigor Suny, eds., *Becoming National: A Reader* (Oxford: Oxford University Press, 1996), pp. 41–55.

Reus-Smit, Christian. *The Moral Purpose of the State. Culture, Social Identity, and Institutional Rationality in International Relations* (Princeton, NJ: Princeton University Press, 1999).

Reynolds, Susan. *Kingdoms and Communities in Western Europe 900–1300* (Oxford: Clarendon Press, 1997).

Richards, Paul. 'Kant's Geography and Mental Maps', *Transactions of the Institute of British Geographers*, no. 61, 1974, pp. 1–16.

Ricoeur, Paul. *Memory, History, Forgetting* (Chicago: University of Chicago Press, 2004).

Riley, Patrick. *The General Will before Rousseau* (Princeton, NJ: Princeton University Press, 1986).

  Kant's Political Philosophy (Totowa, NJ: Rowman and Littlefield, 1983).

Ringmar, Erik. *Identity, Interest and Action. A Cultural Explanation of Sweden's Intervention in the Thirty Years War* (Cambridge: Cambridge University Press, 1996).

Risse, Thomas. '"Let's Argue": Communicative Action in World Politics', *International Organization*, vol. 54, no. 1, 2000, pp. 1–39.

Risse, Thomas, Ropp, Stephen C. and Sikkink, Kathryn. *The Power of Human Rights: International Norms and Domestic Change* (Cambridge: Cambridge University Press, 1999).

Robbins, Bruce. 'Actually Existing Cosmopolitanism', in Pheng Chea and Bruce Robbins, eds., *Cosmopolitics. Thinking and Feeling Beyond the Nation* (Minneapolis: University of Minnesota Press, 1998), pp. 1–19.

Romm, James S. *The Edges of the Earth in Ancient Thought. Geography, Exploration, and Fiction* (Princeton, NJ: Princeton University Press, 1992).

Rorty, Richard. *Contingency, Irony, and Solidarity* (Cambridge: Cambridge University Press, 1989).

  'Justice as a Larger Loyalty', in Pheng Chea and Bruce Robbins, eds., *Cosmopolitics. Thinking and Feeling Beyond the Nation* (Minneapolis: University of Minnesota Press, 1998), pp. 45–58.

Rosanvallon, Pierre. *Democracy Past and Future* (New York: Columbia University Press, 2006).

Rosato, Sebastian. 'The Flawed Logic of the Democratic Peace Theory', *American Political Science Review*, vol. 97, no. 4, 2003, pp. 585–602.

Rose, Sonya O. 'Cultural Analysis and Moral Discourses: Episodes, Continuities, and Transformations', in Victoria E. Bonnell and Lynn Hunt, eds., *Beyond the Cultural Turn* (Berkeley: University of California Press, 1999), pp. 217–38.

Rosen, Allen D. *Kant's Theory of Justice* (Ithaca, NY: Cornell University Press, 1996).

Rousseau, Jean-Jacques. 'A Discourse on the Origin of Inequality', in Jean-Jacques Rousseau, *The Social Contract and Discourses* (London: Dent, 1990).
'L'état de guerre', in C.E. Vaughan, ed., *The Political Writings of Jean-Jacques Rousseau*, vol. I (Cambridge: Cambridge University Press, 1915), pp. 297–306.
The Social Contract, in *The Social Contract and Discourses* (London: Dent, 1990).
Rubiés, Joan-Pau. 'Futility in the New World: Narratives of Travel in Sixteenth-Century America', in Jas Elsner and Joan-Pau Rubiés, eds., *Voyages and Visions. Towards a Cultural History of Travel* (London: Reaktion Books, 1999), pp. 74–100.
'Hugo Grotius's Dissertation on the Origin of the American Peoples and the Use of Comparative Methods', *Journal of the History of Ideas*, vol. 52, no. 2, 1991, pp. 221–4.
'The Oriental Voices of Mendes Pinto, or the Traveller as Ethnologist in Portuguese India', *Portuguese Studies*, vol. 10, no. 1, 1994, pp. 24–43.
Rubinstein, Nicolai. 'The Beginnings of Political Thought in Florence. A Study in Medieval Historiography', *Journal of the Warburg and Courtauld Institutes*, vol. 5, 1942, pp. 198–227.
Ruggie, John Gerard. 'Territoriality and Beyond: Problematizing Modernity in International Relations', *International Organization*, vol. 47, no. 1, 1993, pp. 139–74.
Rupp, Teresa. 'Damnation, Individual and Community in Remigio dei Girolami's *De Bono Communi*', *History of Political Thought*, vol. 21, no. 2, 2000, pp. 217–25.
Sandel, Michael. *Liberalism and the Limits of Justice* (Cambridge: Cambridge University Press, 1982).
Sassen, Saskia. *Losing Control? Sovereignty in an Age of Globalization* (New York: Columbia University Press, 1996).
Schaeffer, John D. *Sensus Communis. Vico, Rhetoric, and the Limits of Relativism* (Durham, NC: Duke University Press, 1990).
Schneewind, Jerome B. *The Invention of Autonomy* (Cambridge: Cambridge University Press, 1998).
Schofield, Malcolm. *The Stoic Idea of the City* (Cambridge: Cambridge University Press, 1991).
Scholte, Jan Aart. *Globalization. A Critical Introduction* (London: Macmillan, 2000).
Seglow, Jonathan. 'Universals and Particulars: The Case of Liberal Cultural Nationalism', *Political Studies*, vol. 64, 1998, pp. 963–77.

Seigel, Jerrold. *The Idea of the Self. Thought and Experience in Western Europe since the Seventeenth Century* (Cambridge: Cambridge University Press, 2005).
Sewell, William H. 'The Concept(s) of Culture', in Victoria E. Bonnell and Lynn Hunt, eds., *Beyond the Cultural Turn* (Berkeley: University of California Press, 1999), pp. 35–61.
Shaftesbury, Anthony Ashley Cooper, third earl of. *Characteristics of Men, Manners, Opinions, Times* (Cambridge: Cambridge University Press, 1999).
Shapcott, Richard. 'Cosmopolitan Conversations: Justice Dialogue and the Cosmopolitan Project', *Global Society*, vol. 16, no. 3, 2002, pp. 221–43.
  Justice, Community and Dialogue in International Relations (Cambridge: Cambridge University Press, 2001).
Shaw, Martin. *Theory of the Global State. Globality as an Unfinished Revolution* (Cambridge: Cambridge University Press, 2000).
Shelton, Mark. 'The Morality of Peace: Kant and Hegel on the Grounds for Ethical Ideals', *Review of Metaphysics*, vol. 54, no. 2, 2000, pp. 379–408.
Sieyès, Emmanuel de. *What is the Third Estate?* (London: Pall Mall Press, 1963).
Skinner, Quentin. *Foundations of Modern Political Thought*, vol. I (Cambridge: Cambridge University Press, 1978).
  'Hobbes on Representation', *European Journal of Philosophy*, vol. 13, no. 2, 2005, pp. 155–84.
  'Hobbes's Changing Conception of Civil Science', in Quentin Skinner, *Visions of Politics*, vol. III (Cambridge: Cambridge University Press, 2002), pp. 66–86.
  Visions of Politics, vol. I (Cambridge: Cambridge University Press, 2002).
Smith, Anthony D. *Chosen Peoples. Sacred Sources of National Identity* (Oxford: Oxford University Press, 2003).
  'Towards a Global Culture?' in Mike Featherstone, ed., *Global Culture. Nationalism, Globalization, and Modernity* (London. Sage, 1991), pp. 171–91.
Smith, Rogers M. *Stories of Peoplehood. The Politics and Morals of Political Membership* (Cambridge: Cambridge University Press, 2003).
Spencer, Vicki. 'In Defense of Herder on Cultural Diversity and Interaction', *Review of Politics*, vol. 69, 2007, pp. 79–105.
Sprigge, T. L. S. 'Personal and Impersonal Identity', *Mind*, no. 385, 1988, pp. 29–49.

Springborg, Patricia. 'Global Identity: Cosmopolitan Localism', paper presented at IPSA, Seoul, 17–21 August 1997.
Spruyt, Hendrik. *The Sovereign State and its Competitors* (Princeton, NJ: Princeton University Press, 1994).
Suganami, Hidemi. *On the Causes of War* (Oxford: Oxford University Press, 1996).
Sumien, Norbert. *La correspondence du savant florentin Paolo del Pozzo Toscanelli avec Christophe Colomb* (Paris, 1927).
Sylvest, Casper. 'Continuity and Change in British Liberal Internationalism, c. 1900–1930', *Review of International Studies*, vol. 31, no. 3, 2005, pp. 263–83.
  'Interwar Internationalism, the British Labour Party, and the Historiography of International Relations', *International Studies Quarterly*, vol. 48, no. 4, 2004, pp. 409–32.
Tagore, Rabindranath. *The Home and the World* (Harmondsworth: Penguin, 1985).
Tamir, Yael. 'Who is Afraid of a Global State?', in Kjell Goldmann, Ulf Hannerz and Charles Westin, eds., *Nationalism and Internationalism in the Post-Cold War Era* (London: Routledge, 2000), 244–67.
Tan, Kok-Chor. 'The Demands of Justice and National Allegiances', in Gillian Brock and Harry Brighouse, eds., *The Political Philosophy of Cosmopolitanism* (Cambridge: Cambridge University Press, 2005), pp. 164–79.
  Justice Without Borders. Cosmopolitanism, Nationalism and Patriotism (Cambridge: Cambridge University Press, 2004).
Taylor, Charles. *Human Agency and Language. Philosophical Papers 1* (Cambridge: Cambridge University Press 1985).
  'The Politics of Recognition', in *Philosophical Arguments* (Cambridge, MA: Harvard University Press, 1995), pp. 225–56.
  Sources of the Self. The Making of Modern Identity (Cambridge, MA: Harvard University Press, 1989).
Taylor, Richard C. 'Averroes on Psychology and the Principles of Metaphysics', *Journal of the History of Philosophy*, vol. 36, no. 4, 1998, pp. 507–23.
Theoderich of Würzburg. *Guide to the Holy Land* (New York: Italica Press, 1986).
Thompson, C. R. *The Colloquies of Erasmus* (Chicago: University of Chicago Press, 1965).
Tierney, Brian. *The Idea of Natural Rights. Studies on Natural Rights, Natural Law and Church Law 1150–1625* (Atlanta, GA: Scholars Press, 1997).
Todorov, Tzvetan. *The Conquest of America: The Question of the Other* (New York: Harper and Row, 1992).

On Human Diversity: Nationalism, Racism, and Exoticism in French Thought (Cambridge, MA: Harvard University Press, 1993).

Tönnies, Ferdinand. *Community and Society: Gemeinschaft und Gesellschaft* (Minneapolis: Michigan State University Press, 1957).

Tornay, Stephen Chak. 'Averroes' Doctrine of the Mind', *Philosophical Review*, vol. 52, no. 3, 1943, pp. 270–88.

Tuck, Richard. 'The "Modern" Theory of Natural Law', in Anthony Pagden, ed., *The Languages of Political Theory in Early Modern Europe* (Cambridge: Cambridge University Press, 1987), pp. 99–119.

Philosophy and Government 1572–1651 (Cambridge: Cambridge University Press, 1993).

The Rights of War and Peace. Political Thought and International Order from Grotius to Kant (Oxford: Oxford University Press, 1999).

Tully, James. 'The Kantian Idea of Europe: Critical and Cosmopolitan Perspectives', in Anthony Pagden, ed., *The Idea of Europe: From Antiquity to the European Union* (Cambridge: Cambridge University Press, 2002).

'Rediscovering America: The Two Treatises and Aboriginal Rights', in James Tully, *An Approach to Political Philosophy: Locke in Context* (Cambridge: Cambridge University Press, 1993), pp. 147–76.

'The Unfreedom of the Moderns in Comparison to their Ideals of Constitutional Democracy', *Modern Law Review*, vol. 65, no. 2, 2002, pp. 204–28.

Turnbull, David. 'Cartography and Science in Early Modern Europe: Mapping the Construction of Knowledge Spaces', *Imago Mundi*, vol. 48, 1996, pp. 5–24.

Toulmin, Stephen. *Cosmopolis. The Hidden Agenda of Modernity* (Chicago: University of Chicago Press, 1990).

Tudela, Benjamin of. *The Itinerary of Benjamin de Tudela. Travels in the Middle Ages* (Malibu, CA: Joseph Simon/Pangloss Press, 1983).

Turgot, Anne Robert Jacques. *Œuvres de Turgot et documents le concernant*, ed. Gustave Schelle (Paris: Félix Alcan, 1913).

Ullmann, Walter. 'Dante's "*Monarchia*" as an Illustration of a Politico-Religious "*Renovatio*"', in Walter Ullmann, *Scholarship and Politics in the Middle Ages* (London: Variorum, 1978), pp. 101–13.

A History of Political Thought: The Middle Ages (Harmondsworth: Penguin, 1965).

Medieval Foundations of Renaissance Humanism (London: Paul Elek, 1977).

Principles of Government and Politics in the Middle Ages (London: Methuen, 1974).

Urry, John. *Sociology Beyond Societies. Mobilities for the Twenty-First Century* (London: Routledge, 2000).

Van Roermund, Bert. 'Sovereignty: Unpopular and Popular', in Neil Walker, ed., *Sovereignty in Transition* (Oxford: Hart, 2003), pp. 33–54.
Veyne, Paul. *Did the Greeks Believe in their Myths?* (Chicago: University of Chicago Press, 1988).
Vico, Giambattista. *The New Science* (Ithaca, NY: Cornell University Press, 1976).
Vincent, Andrew. *Nationalism and Particularity* (Cambridge: Cambridge University Press, 2002).
Vincent, R. J. 'The Idea of Rights in International Ethics', in Terry Nardin and David R. Mapel, *Traditions of International Ethics* (Cambridge: Cambridge University Press, 1992), pp. 250–69.
Vogel, Ursula. 'Cosmopolitan Loyalties and Cosmopolitan Citizenship in the Enlightenment', in Michael Waller and Andrew Linklater, eds., *Political Loyalty and the Nation-State* (London: Routledge, 2003), pp. 17–26.
  'The Sceptical Enlightenment: Philosopher Travellers Look Back at Europe', in Norman Geras and Robert Wokler, eds., *Enlightenment and Modernity* (London: Routledge, 2005), pp. 3–24.
Waldron, Jeremy. *God, Locke, and Equality. Christian Foundations in Locke's Political Thought* (Cambridge: Cambridge University Press, 2002).
  'What Is Cosmopolitan?', *Journal of Political Philosophy*, vol. 8, no. 2, 2000, pp. 227–43.
Walker, R. B. J. *Inside/Outside. International Relations as Political Theory* (Cambridge: Cambridge University Press, 1993).
Walker, Thomas C. 'The Forgotten Prophet: Tom Paine's Cosmopolitanism and International Relations', *International Studies Quarterly*, vol. 44, no. 1, 2000, pp. 51–72.
Walzer, Michael, ed. *The Jewish Political Tradition*, vol. II: *Membership* (New Haven, CT: Yale University Press, 2003).
  'Spheres of Affection', in Joshua Cohen, ed., *For Love of Country. Debating the Limits of Patriotism* (Boston: Beacon Press, 1996), 125–7.
  Thick and Thin: Moral Argument at Home and Abroad (Notre Dame, IN: University of Notre Dame Press, 1994).
Waltz, Kenneth N. 'Kant, Liberalism and War', *American Political Science Review*, vol. 56, no. 3, 1962, pp. 331–40.
  Man, the State, and War: A Theoretical Analysis (New York: Columbia University Press, 1959).
Waswo, Richard. 'The Formation of Natural Law to Justify Colonialism, 1539–1689', *Literary History*, vol. 27, no. 4, 1996, pp. 743–59.

Watt, J. A. 'The Theory of Papal Monarchy in the Thirteenth Century: The Contribution of the Canonists', *Traditio*, vol. 20, 1964, pp. 179–318.

Welsh, Jennifer. *Edmund Burke and International Relations* (London: Macmillan, 1995).

Wendt, Alexander. 'A Comment on Held's Cosmopolitanism', in Ian Shapiro and Casiano Hacker-Cordón, eds., *Democracy's Edges* (Cambridge: Cambridge University Press, 1999), pp. 127–33.

Social Theory of International Politics (Cambridge: Cambridge University Press, 1999).

Wendt, Alexander and Duvall, Raymond. 'Sovereignty and the UFO', *Political Theory*, vol. 36, no. 4, 2008, pp. 607–33.

Wight, Martin. *International Theory. The Three Traditions* (Leicester: Leicester University Press, 1991).

Wilks, Michael. *The Problem of Sovereignty in the Later Middle Ages: The Papal Monarchy with Augustinus Triumphus and the Publicists* (Cambridge: Cambridge University Press, 1963).

Williams, Howard. '*Metamorphosis* or *Palingenesis*? Political Change in Kant', *Review of Politics*, vol. 63, no. 4, 2001, pp. 693–722.

Williams, Wes. '"Rubbing up Against Others": Montaigne on Pilgrimage', in Jas Elsner and Joan-Pau Rubiés, *Voyages and Visions. Towards a Cultural History of Travel* (London: Reaktion Books, 1999), pp. 101–23.

Withers, Charles W. J. 'Eighteenth-Century Geography: Texts, Practices, Sites', *Progress in Human Geography*, vol. 30, no. 6, 2006, pp. 711–29.

Withers, Charles W. J. and Livingstone, David N. 'Introduction. On Geography and Enlightenment', in Charles W. J. Withers and David N. Livingstone, *Geography and the Enlightenment* (Chicago: University of Chicago Press, 1999), pp. 1–28.

Wokler, Robert. 'Anthropology and Conjectural History in the Enlightenment', in Christopher Fox, Roy Porter and Robert Wokler, eds., *Inventing Human Science: Eighteenth Century Domains* (Berkeley: University of California Press, 1996), pp. 31–52.

'Contextualizing Hegel's Phenomenology of the French Revolution and the Terror', *Political Theory*, vol. 26, no. 1, 1998, pp. 33–55.

'The Enlightenment and the French Revolutionary Birth Pangs of Modernity', in Johan Heilbron, Lars Magnusson and Björn Wittrock, eds., *The Rise of the Social Sciences and the Formation of Modernity* (Dordrecht: Kluwer, 1998), pp. 22–40.

'The Enlightenment: The Nation-State and the Primal Patricide of Modernity', in Norman Geras and Robert Wokler, eds., *Enlightenment and Modernity* (London: Routledge, 2005), pp. 161–83.

'The Influence of Diderot on the Political Theory of Rousseau: Two Aspects of a Relationship', in Theodore Besterman, ed., *Studies on Voltaire and the Eighteenth Century*, vol. 132, 1975, pp. 55–112.

'Isaiah Berlin's Enlightenment and Counter-Enlightenment', in Mali Joseph and Robert Wokler, eds., 'Isaiah Berlin's Counter-Enlightenment', special issue of *Transactions of the American Philosophical Society*, vol. 93, no. 3.

'Rousseau's Pufendorf: Natural Law and the Foundations of Commercial Society', *History of Political Thought*, vol. 15, no. 3, 1994, pp. 373–402.

Wolff, Christian. *Jus gentium methodo scientifica pertractatum* (Oxford: Clarendon Press, 1934).

Yack, Bernard. 'The Myth of the Civic Nation', in Ron Beiner, ed., *Theorizing Nationalism* (Albany: State University of New York Press, 1998), pp. 103–18.

'Popular Sovereignty and Nationalism', in *Political Theory*, vol. 29, no. 4, 2001, pp. 517–36.

Yar, Majid. 'From Nature to History, and Back Again: Blumenberg, Strauss and the Hobbesian Community', *History of the Human Sciences*, vol. 15, no. 3, 2002, pp. 53–73.

Yates, Frances A. *The Art of Memory* (Chicago: University of Chicago Press, 1966).

Astraea. The Imperial Theme in the Sixteenth Century (London: Routledge, 1975).

Giordani Bruno and the Hermetic Tradition (London: Routledge, 1964).

Yovel, Yirmiyahu. *Kant and the Philosophy of History* (Princeton, NJ: Princeton University Press, 1980).

'Kant's Practical Reason as Will: Interests, Recognition, Judgment, Choice', *Review of Metaphysics*, vol. 52, no. 2, 1998, pp. 267–94.

Zammito, John H. *Kant, Herder, and the Birth of Anthropology* (Chicago: University of Chicago Press, 2002).

Zedler, Beatrice H. 'Introduction', in Thomas Aquinas, *On the Unity of the Intellect Against the Averroists*, ed. Beatrice H. Zedler (Milwaukee, WI: Marquette University Press, 1968), pp. 1–19.

Zuckerman, Charles. 'The Relationship Between Theories of Universals to Theories of Church Government in the Middle Ages: A Critique of Previous Views', *Journal of the History of Ideas*, vol. 36, no. 4, 1975, pp. 579–94.

Index

Agamben, Giorgio 8, 55
anarchy
   international 20, 29, 115, 122
anthropocentrism 144, 168, 174, 180, 181
Appiah, Anthony Kwame 33
Aquinas, Thomas 57, 80
Arendt, Hannah 131
Aristotle 51, 80
   on actuality and potentiality 59–63
   on cosmology 68, 69
   on the human intellect 56
   on the soul 57
Arrhenius, Thordis 110–2
Augustine
   on human discord 50–1
   on pilgrimage 63
   on the Roman Empire 52
authority 22, 24, 27, 49, 52–4, 179–81
   Enlightenment theories of 119, 130
   global 21–2, 25, 29
   imperial 49
   medieval conceptions of 50
autonomy
   of individuals 145–6, 157, 160, 163, 164, 165
   of states 22–3
Averroës
   on the possible intellect 57–9

balance of power 134–5
Benhabib, Seyla 3, 37, 38, 39
Benjamin de Tudela 66
boundedness, of communities 8–9, 19, 178
Bossuet, Jacques Bénigne 121
   on universal history 121
Buffon, comte de 118–29
Bull, Hedley 1, 4

Butler, Judith 175

Calixtus 65
Camões, Luiz Vaz de 96–9, 103, 104, 128, 173
Campanella, Tommaso 94
Campbell, David 77
cartography
   early modern 97, 100, 107
   medieval 72–4
Chak Tornay, Stephen 59
Choay, Francois 110
city-states 95
civil war, English 108
civitas maxima, 143
Clifford, James 89
Cochran, Molly 26
co-constitution of communities 11, 172–3
Codex Calixtinus, 63, 64–5
commerce 137–8, 151, 155–6, 173
community
   ambiguity of 10
   Christian 48
   concept of 7–8
   and language 14–15, 50–1
   medieval 46
Condorcet, Marie-Jean-Antoine Nicolas de Caritat, marquis de 139, 159, 180
Connolly, William 40, 41
Constantine, donation of 53
context, cosmological 12–14
Copernicus, Nicolaus 71–2, 73, 94, 97
Cosgrove, Denis 62
cosmology 12–13, 44–5, 107, 117, 130–1, 141, 143–67, 168, 173, 176, 181–2
   medieval, 46–7, 61

211

cosmopolitanism 19
  and democracy 20, 23–8, 153–4
Cusa, Nicholas of 69–70, 72, 180

Da Gama, Vasco 96, 98, 99
Dallmayr, Fred 38
Dante Alighieri 49–61, 76, 84–5, 128, 165, 172, 180
  on community 54–6
  on cosmology 68
  on empire 49–50, 52–4
  on the human intellect 56–7
  on human potential 51–2
  on truth 51
Davenant, William 105–6, 112, 173
De Wulf, Maurice 46
democratic peace, theories of 152–3
despotism, critique of 133–7, 174
Diderot, Denis 133, 134, 135, 139, 140, 163, 164, 167, 173, 181
  on the discoveries 132
  on the general will 135–7
  on national character 134
  on sociability 135
dignity, human 26
diplomacy 20
discourse ethics 36–7
diversity
  Enlightenment conceptions of 120, 133, 165
  medieval conceptions of 67, 77, 78, 82
  problem of 36, 39, 40, 41–2, 174, 177, 178
domestic analogies 28, 42
Drayton, Michael 105–6
Dryzek, John 27
Dutch Revolt 108

embeddedness 11, 44, 163, 172, 173–4
empire 52–5, 77, 93, 115, 170
  critique of 115, 119–20, 133–40, 141, 174
  ideology of 2, 17, 96–108, 115, 175, 179
  Roman 48, 52
  Spanish 94
  universal 115
Erasmus, Desiderius 102
equality 26, 37, 78

Fasolt, Constantin 47
Fernandes, Valentim 100
French Revolution 88, 108–14, 120, 167, 169, 173

Gadamer, Hans-Georg 127
general will 135–7
geography
  and astronomy 68–9, 70–1
  and community 12–13
  Enlightenment 133
  medieval 61–3
Gierke, Otto von 48
global justice 29–35
globalization 22–3
Góis, Damião de 100, 103
Goncalves, Lopo 72
Grotius, Hugo 87–8, 119, 126, 139, 156

habitability of the earth 72–4, 76, 130–1, 155, 173, 176, 182
Hacking, Ian 15
Hakluyt, Richard 105, 173
Halbwachs, Maurice 92
Harrison, Peter 76
Headley, John 67, 74, 76
Hegel, Georg Wilhelm Friedrich 5, 167–8, 169
  on the modern state 167
Held, David 22, 24, 25
Herder, Johann Gottfried 173, 180, 181
  on cosmology 165
  on diversity 166
  on world community 165–6
hermeneutics 37–9
Hobbes, Thomas 119, 122, 139
Honig, Bonnie 40
Hume, David
  on memory 91, 113
  on the uniformity of mankind 121

identity 23, 35–42
  and community 9
  construction of 89
  logic of 1–5, 11–12, 20, 43, 168, 171–2
immortality 56–7
impartiality 26

Index

Indians
  American 78–83
  barbarism of 78–81
Innocent IV 78
institutions, supranational 8, 22
international law 20, 162
  early modern 91–2
international society 86, 114, 137–8, 154, 158–60
internationalism 20
interpenetration of communities 11, 172
isomorphism of communities 11, 172

Jones, Charles 31

Kant, Immanuel 4, 173, 180, 181
  on civilization 156–7
  on commerce 155–6
  on the division of mankind 146–7, 151
  on Eurocentrism 158
  on federalism 159–60
  on freedom 145–7
  on geography 143–4, 154–5
  on habitability 154
  on hospitality 157
  on human reason 145–6
  on intercourse 155–6
  on international anarchy 158–9
  on judgement 149–50
  on legitimacy 164
  on popular sovereignty 160
  on sociability 147–8, 165
  on the social contract 163–4
  on world community 142, 143–67
Kantorowicz, Ernst 54
Kleingeld, Pauline 150
Koselleck, Reinhart 139
Kristeva, Julia 40
Kuper, Andrew 31

Lactantius 63
Las Casas, Bartolomeo de 77–85, 173, 180
legitimacy 8, 31, 164
  democratic 9, 25–7
  of empire 55
  of global institutions 22, 29, 179–80
  of revolution 108–10
Lenoir, Alexandre 111
Libellus de locis sanctis, 63
Linklater, Andrew 36, 38
Locke, John 15, 122, 139, 156
  on the division of mankind 120
  on memory 87–8, 90

Mali, Joseph 128
Mancusi-Ungaro, Donna 59
mankind 11–13, 51, 52, 67, 75–6, 77, 84, 87, 91, 116–19, 141–2, 144, 146–8, 151, 176–7
  division of 47, 83–5, 87–8, 115–16, 122–3, 143
Martins, Fernão 72
memory
  ancient accounts of 92–3
  collective 91–2
  and identity 110–93
  and space 88–93
Metha, Pratap Bhanu 37
Mirabilia urbis Romae, 63
monopsychism, doctrine of 57
monsters 62
monuments and memory 90, 110–2, 113
museums and identity 111–12
multiculturalism 7
Muthu, Sankar 130, 148
myth, foundational 86, 90, 93–9, 118–29

Näsström, Sofia 25
nationalism 19, 34, 174
  early modern 96–106
  in political theory 31
  in social theory 5
nationalization
  of concepts 4, 5–6, 17–18, 88–9, 120, 171, 173
  of community 96, 113–14
nationhood
  English 105–6
  Portuguese 96–9
nations, early modern 96–9
nation-states 169–70
natural history 117, 131
navigability of oceans 72–4, 130–1, 155

nominalism 14
  dynamic 15
Nussbaum, Martha 33, 148

Ortelius, Abraham 74

Pagden, Anthony 1, 132
Paine, Thomas 151
particularism
  and community 1–3, 5, 7, 8, 9, 14–16, 17
  and cosmopolitanism 28, 32–5, 41–2, 42–3
  early modern 88
  medieval 85
  modern 171–5
patria, 96
Petrarch 96
pilgrimage
  early modern 102
  medieval 63–7
Pinto, Fernão Mendes 99–104, 173
Plato 57
pluralism 1–3, 40–2
Pogge, Thomas 31
potentiality 51–2, 55–6, 59–60
progress, concept of 139, 141
providence 121
Pufendorf, Samuel von 126

race, conceptions of 118, 140
Ranke, Leopold von 169
Ramusio, Giovanni Battista 73
Raynal, Guillaume Thomas 133–40, 181
  on balance of power 134–5
  on commerce 137–8
  on the discoveries 132
  on the general will 136–7
  on global society 134–5
Rawls, John 30
recognition 39–40, 43
  mutual 5, 168, 176
Renan, Ernst 113
republicanism 160, 167
resistance 180, 181
Reynolds, Susan 48, 64
Rienzo, Cola di 96
Robespierre 109

Rousseau, Jean-Jacques 109, 115–16, 164
  on the general will 136–40
  Same and Other 5, 40

Saint Giles 64
Saint James 65–6
Schmitt, Carl 5
Selden, John 106
Seneca 16
sensus communis, 124, 129–30, 149–50
Sepúlveda, Juan Gínes 78–81
Shaftesbury, earl of 121–4, 173, 181
  on mankind 129–30, 139
  on sociability 122–4, 129
Shapcott, Richard 38, 39
Sieyès, Joseph Emmanuel de 109–10, 112, 164
Smith, Rogers 7
sociability 139
social ontology 10, 12, 20, 28, 42, 45, 75, 171, 177, 178
society, global 20–2
sovereignty 1, 29, 30, 49, 59, 87, 105–6, 108, 121, 141
  popular 152, 153
stoicism 16, 75, 82, 83, 123
Strabo 100
sustainability 8, 182
symbols and identity 93–5

Tagore, Rabindranath 33, 34
Taylor, Charles 7, 37, 177
Tocco, William of 56
Todorov, Tzvetan 77, 82, 83
Tönnies, Ferdinand 6
Toscanelli, Paolo dal Pozzi 72
travelogue 18
  early modern 96–106
  medieval 63–7
Tully, James 158
Turgot, Anne Robert Jacques 131–2, 139, 180, 181
  on universal history 132

universalism
  and community 1–3, 5, 7, 9, 10–12, 14–16, 17

Index

and cosmopolitanism 20, 28, 32–5, 36, 37, 41
early modern 86, 88
Enlightenment 117–18, 141
medieval 75–6
problem of 171–5, 175–9

Veneranda dies, 65
Vico, Giambattista 99, 121–2, 139, 173, 181
  on providence 125–6
  on sociability 124–6, 129
  on universal history 126–7
Virgil 52, 129
Vives, Juan 72

Wendt, Alexander 25
Westphalia, myth of 86, 114

Wokler, Robert 139
Wolff, Christian 142–3, 162, 167, 181
  on international anarchy 142
  on international society 143
world community
  concept of 13
  medieval conception of 75–6
  paradox of 1–3, 19, 171, 174
  problem of 3–4, 16
  secular conceptions of 118, 119–20
world government 20

Yates, Frances 94
Yovel, Yirmiyahu 145

Zacuto, Abraham 100